D0458867

ABOUT ISLAND PRESS

Island Press, a nonprofit organization, publishes, markets, and distributes the most advanced thinking on the conservation of our natural resources—books about soil, land, water, forests, wildlife, and hazardous and toxic wastes. These books are practical tools used by public officials, business and industry leaders, natural resource managers, and concerned citizens working to solve both local and global resource problems.

Founded in 1978, Island Press reorganized in 1984 to meet the increasing demand for substantive books on all resource-related issues. Island Press publishes and distributes under its own imprint and offers these services to other nonprofit organizations.

Support for Island Press is provided by The Geraldine R. Dodge Foundation, The Energy Foundation, The Charles Engelhard Foundation, The Ford Foundation, Glen Eagles Foundation, The George Gund Foundation, William and Flora Hewlett Foundation, The John D. and Catherine T. MacArthur Foundation, The Andrew W. Mellon Foundation, The Joyce Mertz-Gilmore Foundation, The NewLand Foundation, The J. N. Pew, Jr. Charitable Trust, Alida Rockefeller, The Rockefeller Brothers Fund, The Rockefeller Foundation, The Tides Foundation, and individual donors.

VISIONS
UPON THE LAND

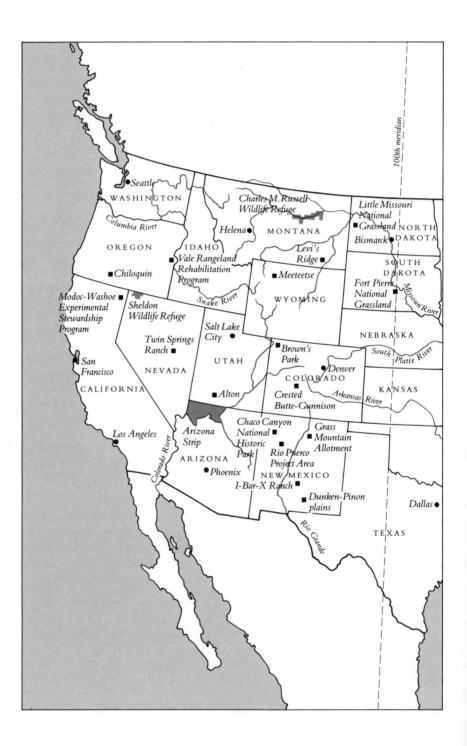

Seattle

WASHINGTON

Columbia River

OREGON

Chiloquin

Modoc-Washoe
Experimental
Stewardship
Program

San
Francisco

CALIFORNIA

Los Angeles

IDAHO
Vale Rangeland
Rehabilitation
Program

Sheldon
Wildlife Refuge

Twin Springs
Ranch

NEVADA

Arizona
Strip

ARIZONA

Phoenix

Colorado River

Helena

Charles M. Russell
Wildlife Refuge

MONTANA

Levi's
Ridge

Meeteetse

WYOMING

Snake River

Salt Lake
City

UTAH

Alton

Brown's
Park

COLORADO

Crested
Butte-Gunnison

Denver

Chaco Canyon
National
Historic
Park

Rio Puerco
Project Area

I-Bar-X Ranch

NEW MEXICO

Dunken-Pinon
plains

Grass
Mountain
Allotment

Little Missouri
National
Grassland NORTH
Bismarck DAKOTA

SOUTH
DAKOTA

Fort Pierre
National
Grassland

Missouri River

NEBRASKA

South Platte River

KANSAS

Arkansas River

TEXAS

Rio Grande

Dallas

100th meridian

VISIONS UPON THE LAND

Man and Nature on the Western Range

Karl Hess, Jr.
The Cato Institute

Foreword by John A. Baden

ISLAND PRESS

Washington, D.C. □ *Covelo, California*

Library of Congress Cataloging-in-Publication Data

Visions upon the land : man and nature on the western range/ Karl Hess, Jr.; foreword by John Baden.
    p.   cm.
  Includes bibliographical references and index.
  ISBN 1-55963-183-X
  1. Environmental policy—West (U.S.)   2. Land use—
  Environmental aspects—West (U.S.)   I. Hess, Karl, 1947- .
HC107.A17V57   1992   92-14446
333.7'0978—dc20   CIP

Printed on recycled, acid-free paper

♻

Manufactured in the United States of America

10 9 8 7 6 5 4 3 2 1

Contents

Foreword *by John A. Baden*   xi
Preface   xv
Acknowledgments   xix

Introduction: Levi's Ridge   1

PART I: THE WESTERN RANGE

Chapter 1: Window to the Western Range   9
   The Public Grazing Lands   10
   A Land Despoiled   14
   The Common Denominator   18

Chapter 2: Like a City upon a Hill   24
   Visions   25
   Of Soul and Soil   30
   Choice and Consequence   33

Chapter 3: Visions upon the Land   36
   The Natural Link   38
   Ecology of Visions   44
   Landscape Visions on the Western Range   50

PART II: THE LANDSCAPE VISIONS

Chapter 4: Jefferson's Legacy   55
   Chaos on the Open Range   56
   A Question of the Commons   61
   Origins of the Agrarian Vision   64

Contents

Vision, Policy, and Environmental Harm   66
Beyond the Tragedy of the Commons   69

Chapter 5: Progressivism's Response   73
Coping with the Open Range:
    An Overview, 1891–1934   75
The Progressive Vision   76
Essentials of Visionary Reform   78
Redefining Democracy   79

Chapter 6: The Grassland Experiment   82
Boom and Bust on the Great Plains   84
New Deal Directions   86
National Grasslands in Transition   89
A Different Path: The Nebraska Sandhills   93

Chapter 7: Technocracy and Empire   97
The Bureaucratic Imperative for Control   99
Building a Grazing Bureaucracy: The BLM   104
Building a Grazing Bureaucracy:
    The Forest Service   108
Testaments to Technocracy   114

Chapter 8: The Visionary Harvest   121
Forging a New Commons   124
Owning Numbers, Not Land   125
What the Range Can Bear   129
Divvying Up the Western Range   132
The Commons in Place   139

Chapter 9: Demise of Stewardship   140
Layers of Disincentives   142
Mandate for Grazing Management   143
Vanishing Roles and Incentives:
    The Plight of Caring   150
Reflections of the Failed Commons   155
Rise of the Welfare Rancher and the
    Triumph of Mediocrity   163

Chapter 10: Cleansing the Land   171
Rumblings of Dissent   173

Breaking New Ground   176
Prophets of Purification   182
Closing Eden's Door   188
Coming Full Circle   194

PART III: THE PROMISE OF MANY VISIONS

Chapter 11: Limits of the Visionary State   199
   The Environmental Welfare State   201
   Using and Abusing the Land   206
   Man and Nature on the Western Range   210

Chapter 12: A Market of Landscape Visions   215
   Ecology, Markets, and Landscape Visions   217
   Diversity, Process, and Environmental Gain   223
   Democratization of the Western Range   231

Conclusion: The Ecology of Freedom   242

Notes   249
Index   273

Foreword

*"Conflicts of interests dominate the short run
but conflict of visions dominate history."*
Thomas Sowell, *A Conflict of Visions*

Karl Hess may be the last sane optimist who deals with America's federal lands. He brings intelligence, goodwill, and empathy to this analysis. His ethical and logical consistency is impressive. After completing this book, the reader will be in a better position to gauge rangeland policy and practice.

Among informed observers, there is a "sense of the meeting" that throughout the West, governments have operated as engines of plunder as well as arbiters of justice. For more than a century, there was a coherent direction to culture, economics, and politics. This paradigm favored development and the institutional arrangements that fostered it. Exploitation and centralized management of the West's resources dominated federal policy. Even nonexploitive ideals such as national parks, wilderness areas, and wildlife refuges were under politically dominated scientific management.

The Bureau of Reclamation, the Forest Service, and the Bureau of Land Management have exemplified this perspective and attempted to manage via centralized command and control. Throughout the West, the results have been much the same as in Eastern Europe—tragedies of ecological, ethical, and economic erosion at the end of the vision. Even legislative mandates requiring multiple use considerations have not altered the outcomes.

In the West, as elsewhere in the United States, the rubric of "free enterprise" was and is opportunistically used to camouflage subsidies and justify environmentally costly behavior. Authority to act, often with others' money, was granted through politics. Through politics, institutions were created that insulated actors from the consequences of actions. Hence, on the federal lands we see the subsidized "chaining" of millions of acres of piñon and juniper and the subsidized clear-cutting of national forests. Subsidized dams provide subsidized water to produce subsidized crops stored through subsidized fees. These distortions of the market process have predictable and grotesque environmental and economic consequences. *Visions upon the Land: Man and Nature on the Western Range* explains how such actions result in devastation to the rangelands and communities of the West.

Throughout history, most people who depend on land and natural resources have learned how to avoid the tragedy of the commons. However, when politics insulates actions from the reality checks of nature—a political perversion Hess discovers throughout the West—the tragedy of the commons becomes institutionalized. Today, several groups (for example, welfare ranchers and sylvan socialists) have become dependent upon the continuation of the tragedy. If we are to see our way to a new vision of and for our West, a new approach recognizing the needs and capability of the land and its people is needed.

The policy questions of the western range *are* scientifically complex. These questions also carry heavy ethical and economic baggage. Few people can unpack these bags and not be affected by their personal evaluations of the contents. Today, traditional institutions and practices of the West are challenged by an increasingly strong coalition of disparate interests and philosophies. The reformers include fiscal conservatives who oppose subsidies to the wealthy, classic liberals who believe that good intentions exercised through government power too often lead to corruption and waste, and environmentalists who are offended by the land management of the iron triangle: bureaucrats, favored interests, and elected politicians. These reformers hold the logical, empirical, and moral high ground against the old-time exploiters of an increasingly precious set of ecological and social values.

In *Visions upon the Land*, Hess challenges the exploitation of the West with a strong blend of Thomas Jefferson's political economy and Aldo Leopold's ecology. He thoughtfully explains how the West's political institutions erode environmental quality. He begins impartially to unpack the baggage and help us understand that because of inappropriate bureaucracies and opportunistic politics, the people of the West have not found a sustainable harmony with their land.

Hess explains the implications of different institutional arrangements. From *Visions upon the Land* we learn how to identify those arrangements that encourage people to adapt their individual behavior, culture, and local institutions to the realities of their environment. Hess believes that these institutional arrangements which harmonize liberty and ecology should replace those based upon political plunder and predation.

In exposing the hypocrisies of special interests hiding behind myths, *Visions upon the Land* makes naked their shortsighted self-interest. It helps us see that there is an even greater distance between Ed Abbey's and Jim Watt's visions of the West than their positions in the alphabet. Honest people have a hard time with these differences, for there are no knockdown arguments to resolve policy questions based upon competing but compelling ethical systems.

Hess gives us stories, experience, and logic to help us resolve policy questions. By creating land communities and disposing of the institutions that impose and engender elitist visions, these philosophical, ethical, and political divides can be closed. Each vision can thrive and coexist with others within the land community. Only the parasitic need be excluded.

Visions upon the Land will not be without its initial critics and skeptics. Individuals put at risk by Karl's data and compelling logic, bureaucratic managers, commodity groups, and environmental crisis entrepreneurs will quickly surface. But this book will be immensely helpful to intelligent and sincere reformers who value and respect the classic liberal values of Jefferson and the ecological ideals of Leopold. And over time, *Visions upon the Land* will develop a steadfast group of supporters, for as Garrett Hardin has often told me, "important ideas have long gestations."

Karl Hess's are such ideas. *Visions upon the Land* is an exceptional field guide to the great remaining mystery of the West–how to preserve the freedom and potential for independence of that region's people while preserving an ecology of which mankind is an integral part.

> John A. Baden
> President
> Foundation for Research on Economics
> and the Environment

Preface

Five years ago, I sat down to outline a book on the western range. I began with the assumption that livestock grazing on public lands was a proper starting point. It was a subject I knew well and one for which I had strong feelings. Starting there, I fleshed out my outline with what I believed to be new and important ideas. Two years and many outlines later, my confidence in those ideas had waned. Only my initial assumption seemed solid and reasonable. I was stuck.

Two events moved me off center. The first was a conference on the land ethic in Big Sky, Montana. There, I learned a lesson in tolerance. My assumptions of what constituted ecological right and wrong, of good and bad, were not universally shared. Others saw the natural world differently from the way I did, arriving at contrasting conclusions of ecological good and bad. A land ethic did not mean the same to each person. This ethical relativism troubled me. It forced me to rethink the meaning and place of a land ethic in a world lacking consensus on a topic I believed to be so vital. I left the conference puzzled, wondering how best to reconcile my strong commitment to a personal land ethic with the demands and constraints of tolerance.

The second event came a year later, at an Earth First! gathering in the Kettle River Mountains of northeastern Washington. I went as an observer, hoping to learn more of how that group envisioned the meaning and purpose of western public lands. It quickly became apparent that livestock grazing had no place in their agenda. They were committed with religious fervor to a vision of a western landscape exorcised of livestock. That vision had taken hold of their lives and was funneling their energies toward a single objective.

Preface

The lessons of visions and tolerance played in my mind as I thought of the book that had eluded me so far. As I reviewed and rethought former outlines and notes, it became clear to me why I was stuck. I had spent three years looking in the wrong places for the handle I needed to bring a fresh perspective to the story of the western range. My attention had been so focused on judging public-land ranchers and the federal agencies that regulated them that I had missed the obvious. Ranchers with their livestock and federal agencies with their public-land policies had shaped and transformed the western landscape. Yet their effects upon the western range had been symptomatic of something more fundamental.

Thinking back once again to the lessons of visions and tolerance, I understood what was fundamental to the history of the western range. The key to its understanding was to be found in the landscape visions that people had brought to the western range and in the degree of tolerance people had exercised while pursuing them. Those visions embodied what people expected from the land. They also fueled people's ambitions to realize those expectations. And their effect on the land was as lasting and real as the farmer's plow upon a virgin field.

Today, I realize that my first conscious encounter with landscape visions came at that Earth First! gathering. The vision of a West freed of ranchers and cattle, however, would be only one of many landscape visions I would encounter as I reexamined the western range. In that process, I would discover that visions of the western landscape had motivated men and women long before the arrival of Earth First!. Such visions had sparked the ambitions of the first settlers and become an enduring part of the West. They thrive and continue today.

The history of the western range is, in part, the story of people's visions of what was and is right for the landscape of America's public lands. It tells of the conflict between those visions and the land and people of the western range. It speaks to the limits of human tolerance in the struggle to effect ecological good. Most of all, the story of the western range is a modern paradox. In a society so conscious of diversity, the western range stands out as a land deprived of diversity in a most crucial sense.

America's public lands are celebrated for a richness of life and a variety of landscapes unmatched elsewhere. Yet beneath the veneer of diversity lies another reality. The dreams and aspirations that have fixed the course of the western range have imposed three singular visions upon the land. Those visions have triumphed at the cost of human diversity. Their intol-

xvi

erance has deprived the land of the promise of what a variety of landscape visions could bring.

This book is about the environmental and ecological consequences of those singular visions and their profound influence on the western range of past and present. Those visions have attended to what people and nature *ought to be,* not to what they *could be* in an environment of freedom and diversity. Those visions have heralded environmental decline on public grazing lands. They have pitted men and women against nature and against their own self-interest. They have weakened our faith in the ability of people to live responsibly and in harmony with the land of the western range. They have brought into being agencies to regulate people in their dealings with nature and then later to exclude them from the natural world. They have diminished the ecological potential of human diversity.

It is to the diminishment of human diversity, to the lost faith in people living with nature, to the intolerance of unchallenged visions, and to the ecological and environmental consequences of all three that I direct my book. Whether public-land grazing should or should not exist is less important than the fact that it does exist. From that vantage, a new vista opens to the history of the western range and to the place of men and women in the natural and social community. Visions on the land lead us beyond the mythology of cows and cowboys to the high drama of man and nature on the western range.

In writing of that drama, I have selected a variety of personal accounts from the many men and women I visited while researching this book. Those accounts appear as narratives before each chapter. They are spoken through my voice and relate the stories of exceptional ranchers—unrepresentative ranchers, perhaps, but ranchers who do exist and have excelled. They are people who have tried to come to terms with the western range peacefully and with respect. Their examples, however, do more than illustrate the personal trials and tribulations of a select group of caring ranchers. They also address the environmental concerns of all caring people. They speak of hope and promise for a land that has seen too little peace and has been shown far too little respect. They point in the same direction this book is intended to lead—toward a western range where people can and will choose to live responsibly and in harmony with the land.

Karl Hess, Jr.
Las Cruces, New Mexico

Acknowledgments

Many individuals have contributed to the making of this book. I thank each and every one of them. Particular thanks are due to John Baden and the Foundation for Research on Economics and the Environment (FREE). Without his encouragement and help, and the resources of FREE, my ideas would have remained silent. I owe a considerable debt to the Redd Foundation and the Cato Institute for their faith in my work and their generous financial support.

I also offer my thanks to the many men and women who shared their time and stories with me as I traveled throughout the West. Some are mentioned by name in the pages that follow. Many are represented in the ideas and examples that give life to my manuscript. All have deeply influenced me. This book is a tribute to their caring and perseverance.

I wish to offer special thanks to Therese Hess for editing what at first was a very rough manuscript and to Marianne Keddington for editing redundancy from the manuscript and polishing and refining the final product. To my wife, Joanne, I offer love and thanks for bearing with me during a very difficult period. I hope the product of three years of work will make our personal sacrifices not in vain.

Finally, I thank my father for instilling in me a profound respect for human creativity and freedom; for providing insight into thought and nature as processes; for encouraging my celebration of diversity in all forms; for teaching me an abiding tolerance for those who, in Thoreau's words, follow a different drummer; and for being my friend.

. . . it is the continuing policy of the Federal Government . . . to create and maintain conditions under which man and nature can exist in productive harmony . . .

The National Environmental Policy Act of 1969

Levi's Ridge

We stopped on a high ridge overlooking a mosaic of mountains and valleys, forests, and open grasslands. Ashland, Montana, was the closest town. The nearest settlements were hidden in the next valley. Along the banks of Otter Creek, homesteads dating back one hundred years dotted the rural landscape. Yet from our perspective, the wildlands of the Custer National Forest stretched unbroken to the horizon.

The sun was close to setting. Shadows stretched across the landscape like so many groping fingers pulling the land into darkness. Marc Stevens, his son Bill, and I stood where three earlier generations of the Stevens family had stood and watched the same shadows elongate imperceptibly into the eastern horizon.

On the rolling terrain below, and among the adjacent hills lay much of the public grazing land leased to Marc by the USDA Forest Service. Broad fescue grasslands and rocky islands of ponderosa pine stood out in sharp contrast against the clear, blue evening sky. Beyond, hidden in the next valley, were the private lands homesteaded a century earlier by Marc's family. Together, those lands made up the Circle Bar Ranch.

Marc's grandfather, Levi Howes, first came to this scenic ridge as a child in the 1880s. Over the years, it became a special place for him, as it now was for Marc. Standing where we stood, Levi had been able to survey the best of his summer grazing range. Until his death in 1967, he had returned again and again to this special spot at this special time of day.

The lay of the land, the broad valley meadows dissected by rocky wooded ridges, was much the same after a hundred years. But some changes had occurred across the generations. Cattle grazed where elk and bison once roamed. Ponderosa pine, protected from fire by the Forest Service, was invading open grasslands. Yet the grass and soil were healthier on balance than they had been in the days of the open range, when the land had been stocked far beyond its capacity. But it was the changes we could *not* see that Levi Howes would have been most aware of. Beneath the evening sky, gazing over the summer range, Marc and his son and I talked about those unseen changes.

Being a rancher was different for Marc from what it had been for Levi. Running the Circle Bar was no longer a matter of simply stewarding the land and raising livestock for distant markets. The Forest Service and vocal outside interests, Marc believed, were driving a wedge between his family and the land that had nurtured five generations. Barriers were mounting between Marc's private bottomlands and the uplands he leased from the Forest Service. The ties that had bound Levi to the private and public lands of the Circle Bar had begun to unravel for Marc. A different world was in the making, and Marc felt increasingly displaced from the public lands he had learned to value and treat as though they were his own.

Not long ago, Marc had changed grazing management to improve a stretch of public land adjacent to one of the few streams crossing his ranch. He had done it because he wanted to, not because he had been told to. We had stopped by the stream a few hours earlier. The banks were healthy with vegetation, the water clear and flowing despite drought conditions. Beyond the stream, the grasses and wildflowers were diverse and profuse.

Following in Levi's footsteps, Marc had helped the land in other ways. He grazed only 80 percent of the cattle allowed by the Forest Service. The Forest Service called Marc's practice "range protection," but Marc considered the agency's terminology an insult. He called what he was doing "range conservation." The range did not need protection from him or his family.

But the Forest Service did not seem to appreciate his caring. Marc sensed the agency's disapproval of his deep historical and familial attachment to the public lands of the Custer National Forest. It did not make sense. After all, it had been Levi who had helped persuade Congress to keep the Custer National Forest intact in 1914. But a lot had changed since then. A quiet indignation, held in check by a generous nature, was apparent in Marc's demeanor as the sun fell below the horizon.

Marc spoke of Forest Service attitudes toward himself and kindred ranchers. To the agency, he was just another rancher, unschooled in the science of land management. His studies in agriculture at Colorado State University counted for little. The Forest Service staff believed that they, not he, best understood the needs of the land.

Several years earlier, the local Forest Service range conservationist had visited the Stevens's allotment and agreed with Marc's prescription for the public lands of the Circle Bar. The two went to the forest supervisor's office in Billings to persuade the supervisor's staff of the advantages of their management scheme. The young range conservationist assured Marc that he would set the record straight on the grazing allotment. The land looked good, the management was sound, and certainly his Forest Service employers would listen to him. After all, Marc knew the land better than they.

Marc waited while the range conservationist met privately with Forest Service staff. Soon, Marc was called into the room, where he was told that his management was not sound and his grazing lands needed a different prescription. The young range conservationist remained silent. On the return trip to Ashland, Marc and the range conservationist said little. The professionals had prevailed again.

To Marc, the issue was a simple matter of control. His ability to continue a family tradition of stewarding the land was threatened because the agency insisted that it, not he, make the decisions. Control, not the health of the range, lay at the heart of the changing world Marc had inherited from Levi.

One symbol of that change was the sharp-tailed grouse, which had been part of Marc's life since childhood. Through dry years and wet years, his family, the cattle, and the sharptails had shared the public and private lands of the Circle Bar Ranch. Marc could not remember a time when the grouse had not been abundant.

3

In 1986, the Forest Service completed the Custer National Forest Plan, which established special management zones for sharp-tailed grouse. This did not mean that sharp-tailed grouse were threatened on the Circle Bar or that their population or habitat was declining. The zones meant only that wildlife in general, and the grouse in particular, would now be formally recognized in the new management plan of the Custer National Forest.

Under the plan, grouse strutting grounds were to be identified and grazing within a one-mile radius of each such area was to be "managed" to maintain a minimum grass height of twelve inches. Besides the fact that in some years the grass did not grow to twelve inches, the regulation would severely restrict and possibly eliminate livestock grazing on portions of the Circle Bar.

Much the same had already happened two-hundred miles north, on the Charles M. Russell National Wildlife Refuge (CMR). Following a belabored process of environmental analysis, the U.S. Fish and Wildlife Service had decided to reduce livestock numbers on the CMR to accommodate the sharp-tailed grouse. Even before that decision was made, however, private and BLM lands on the periphery of the CMR had been grazed at twice the intensity of the lightly grazed refuge. And the density of sharp-tailed grouse they supported was far greater than on the refuge. The grouse were doing best on lands grazed by cattle, not on lands protected from them.[1]

What had happened to the ranchers using the CMR was now happening to Marc. The sharp-tailed grouse had become a threat to the livelihood of the Circle Bar. With each new Forest Service plan, operating the Circle Bar became more difficult and the possibility of the ranch supporting Marc's children became more unlikely. What angered him the most, though, was that the new plan was not needed; the sharp-tailed grouse were thriving without it.

Marc steered his truck down the rough dirt road toward the headquarters of the Circle Bar. As he drove, he wondered aloud whether his grandchildren would have a place on the Circle Bar. He had heard people warn that public-land ranching was headed toward extinction. Some pointed to higher grazing fees as the certain cause. Others warned of legislation eliminating grazing on public lands. But neither was of concern to Marc. He knew that if ranching on the Circle Bar ended, it would not be the result of higher fees or a new law. If grazing stopped on the Circle Bar—and his voice betrayed a sense of inevitability—it would come from the cumulative burden of regulation and control. Public-land grazing would end not with a bang but with a whimper.

There would come a time, he knew, when choices would have to be made. Historical and familial loyalties to Levi's leased public lands, ties already weakened by decades of control and regulation, would be cast aside. The family would retreat to its considerable private holdings in the bottomlands that dissected the Custer National Forest. They would survive. But Marc wondered who would be responsible for the public land. Who would care for it as he and Levi had done for over a century?

Several miles from the ridge top, a large pond, almost emptied of water and choked with algae, was visible in the fading twilight. A dark brown wooden sign announced a thirty-eight-acre complex that included picnicking and camping facilities. It read "Cow Creek Campground." We had stopped there earlier in the day, before reaching Levi's high ridge. A barbed wire fence constructed by the Forest Service protected the area from Marc's cattle. The stream feeding the pond was the same stream that fed the riparian area that Marc managed. Marc's part of the stream was healthy and productive, but the stream through Cow Creek Campground had an aura of decay. The once grass-covered hillsides surrounding the pond were under assault from advancing brush. The picnic area was empty. A sense of desolation had settled upon the enclosed land.

At the center of decay and desolation was the pond. A joint project of the Forest Service and the Montana Game and Fish Department, the pond had provided one of the few fishing spots in that part of the Custer National Forest. Montana Game and Fish had stocked the pond, and the Forest Service had maintained the recreation complex. But things changed when the Forest Service became dissatisfied with the quality of drinking water at one of its field offices a short distance downstream. The pond was tapped, and water was diverted to the office. Consumptive demand combined with drought drained the pond beyond its ability to support fish. Montana Game and Fish stopped stocking the pond, and campers and picnickers went elsewhere. The once prized recreational complex fell into disuse.

Marc and his son and I paused briefly at the dying pond and abandoned campground. A few hunters had used the facilities last fall, but Marc had seen no other people there since then. It seemed inexplicable to Marc and his son that the Forest Service intended to build new recreation sites in the

Custer National Forest. It made no sense, not when Marc thought of the dying pond. But many things had seemed inexplicable or made little sense in the years since Levi's passing. Marc turned on the headlights and drove down the hill, past the Forest Service field office and toward home.

Ahead were the lights of Marc's ranch-style house. Below the house were his son's trailer and the young granddaughter who represented the sixth generation on the Circle Bar. The Forest Service pond and Levi's ridge were behind us, yet the land of the Circle Bar had told a story of the western range—a story of people coping with extraordinary changes on an unparalleled landscape.

The changes here, seen and unseen, were the changes that would greet me as I traveled through the western United States. From the ridge top I had seen more than the face of Levi's landscape. I had discovered the vista from which to view the western range anew and to rethink the turbulent history of man and nature on the western range.

1

The Western Range

CHAPTER ONE

Window to the Western Range

*L*ooking down from the mountains of the Custer National Forest, the hill between Marc Stevens's home and his son's trailer appears as a minor intrusion among the hay fields, houses, and barns of the Circle Bar headquarters. Seen from below, however, the hill is more imposing. Rising more than a hundred feet above the valley floor, it offers an unobstructed view of the surrounding countryside. At its crest are the remains of a rock building.

Built in 1896 by Levi Howes, the small structure was to serve as a fort for defense against Indian attacks. Months earlier, reservation Indians had raided Ashland, prompting fear that a similar attack might be made on the settlements along Otter Creek. But neither the fort nor the residents of Otter Creek ever saw action. Fort Howes, as Levi's structure and the surrounding settlements have come to be called, is a relic of a western range long since transformed.

The irony of Fort Howes is that it was built twenty years too late. In 1876, four years before Levi and his family arrived in southeastern Montana, Custer and the Seventh Cavalry fell at the Little Bighorn—only fifty miles west of Ashland. By the time Levi's family settled on Otter Creek in 1883, the Crow, Sioux, and Cheyenne had been subdued by federal forces.

The hill in 1876 stood sentinel over a western range that was far different from the one that would be seen in 1896 from the narrow gun holes of Fort Howes.

During the first years of settlement, Levi recorded in his diary that elk, antelope, and grizzlies were abundant and bison grazed the open rangelands.[1] The howl of the gray wolf stirred the fears of sheepmen and haunted the imaginations of children. But settlers changed the face of the land. They looked to wildlife for food, saving their livestock for hungry eastern markets. As early as 1885, Levi noted that the country was fully stocked with cattle. Everywhere, he observed, there were cattle and cattle ranches. Livestock grazing had pushed wildlife to the extremities of the landscape and cleared the land of verdant cover.

The winter of 1886–1887 put a chill on the livestock industry but did not return the land to its earlier state. Seen from the hill, the changes were marked and irreversible. The landscape had succumbed to the visions of a new age. Neutral eyes peering through the crumbling gun holes of Fort Howes would acknowledge the overwhelming human presence. Less objective eyes would celebrate or mourn that presence. All would agree that the public grazing lands of Otter Creek were no longer the wildlands of Levi's childhood.

THE PUBLIC GRAZING LANDS

Three hundred miles east of the Circle Bar Ranch is the 100th meridian, marking the eastern boundary of the western range. The line divides the Dakotas and Nebraska at their approximate geographic centers and passes southward through the western thirds of Kansas, Oklahoma, and Texas. The importance of the 100th meridian came about as the result of a federally financed scientific expedition launched in 1868. John Wesley Powell, leader of the expedition, observed dramatic changes as his expedition moved west toward and across the 100th meridian. The changes in climate, vegetation, and soils came gradually, but they were sufficiently pronounced to make the century line of longitude a meaningful transition between the humid East and the arid West. Powell's 1878 *Report on the Lands of the Arid Region of the United States* announced his findings and brought to the public's eye the world of the western range.

Exclusive of Alaska, the western range encompasses almost a billion acres of mountains, prairies, and deserts stretching westward from the Great Plains to the Pacific Coast. Two-fifths of the nation's land mass lies within this vast region. Seventeen western states can be identified within its boundaries, though only the westernmost eleven fall completely within its borders.

Not surprisingly, the western range stirs romantic images. To most people, the western range is synonymous with the West of sculptured canyons, towering mountain peaks, and sagebrush basins. The states of Arizona, Colorado, and Nevada epitomize the romance and exotic quality of a landscape entrenched in American mythology. Yet the idea of the western range would be incomplete without the rolling mixed-grass prairies of western North Dakota south to the shortgrass plains of western Texas. These lands share the history and environment of their more storied neighbors.

Two features of the western range are most striking. The first is the aridity of the landscape. Beyond the 100th meridian, water is scarce. Except in the higher mountains and along the northwestern coast, rain and snow are scant and infrequent. Searing winds and extreme temperature fluctuations intensify the effects of dryness. The dramatic landscape of the western range has its origin in the harshness of its climate.

The second feature follows from the first. The western range is sparsely settled. A harsh climate and the burden of ill-conceived homestead laws guided and restricted human settlement to lands where water was available and soils were suitable for cultivation. Large blocks of federal land were set aside for uses other than settlement, and over half of the region was never claimed. Those lands remain in public ownership.

Publicly owned lands—which include federal lands, state lands, and Indian trust lands—form what amounts to a half-billion-acre backbone of the western range. National parks and wildlife refuges, centerpieces of the federal land system and objects of national pride, account for less than 5 percent of the publicly owned western range. A slightly greater percentage is represented when Indian reservations, military reservations, and state trust lands are included. But the bulk of the public's western range lies elsewhere.

The heart of the western range is the 315 million acres managed by the Bureau of Land Management (BLM) and the Forest Service. Those acres comprise one-third of the entire western range and make up almost two-thirds of the public's share. Put into a different perspective, BLM and Forest Service lands on the western range encompass an area one and one-half times larger than the original thirteen colonies. Texas, twice over, could be placed within its boundaries, and 466 Rhode Islands could be stashed away.

BLM and Forest Service lands are the primary source of public grazing lands on the western range, and nearly every acre is used for livestock forage. Approximately twenty-seven thousand families make their living grazing seven million cattle, sheep, and horses on 307 million acres of the public's western range.[2] Each of the twenty-seven thousand families holds one or more grazing permits, which authorize public-land ranchers, or permittees, to graze fixed numbers of livestock for specified periods of time. Modest grazing fees are assessed on the basis of those fixed numbers. The units of federal land tied to grazing permits are called grazing allotments.

But ranchers are not the only users of federal property. Workers in traditional industries, like mining and timber, still make up the economic backbone of many western communities—communities whose residents in general share economic dependence on public lands. Life on the western range is in flux, however. Increasingly, recreation is encroaching on the preeminence of traditional industries, changing the western range in unexpected ways. Yet the changes brought by new economic patterns neither alter the problems rooted in the past nor change the ecological realities of the present.

It is true that public-land grazing is gradually fading from the landscape of the western range. Each year, fewer ranchers and less livestock return to the public lands, victims of political, economic, and cultural change. Over the past fifty years, stocking on public lands has fallen by more than 50 percent.[3] But the passing of the livestock industry cannot easily erase its mark upon the land.

Present and past on the western range are linked by the legacy of more than a century of livestock grazing. Miners and loggers have come and gone from western public lands, their cumulative effects limited in time and space. Recreation enthusiasts offer a new vision of the West, but the effects of their vision on the land have not yet been felt. Only ranchers have doggedly persisted, clinging tenaciously to the land long after others have forsaken it. Only ranchers' livestock has touched and transformed the most remote reaches of the public's western range. In every sense, grazing on the public land has colored the history of the larger western range.

Public-land ranching extends economically and culturally beyond BLM and Forest Service boundaries. Historically, public-land grazing has been at the center of the West's rural economy. Even today, the bulk of western livestock grazes public grass at some point in its life cycle. Three-quarters of the domestic stock raised in Idaho, Wyoming, Nevada, and Arizona takes sustenance from public lands.[4] At the same time, almost every rural family and community in the West has felt the influence of public-land ranching through networks of kinship, friendship, and religion. Livestock has shaped more than the land; it has also left an indelible mark on the people.

Eclipsing economics and culture is the ecological reality of public-land ranching. BLM and Forest Service lands do not exist in isolation. They extend ecologically beyond the artificial boundaries of Forest Service national forests and BLM resource areas and districts. They are intimately connected to the greater western range by virtue of the intermingling and interdependence of western lands. An artifact of federal land disposal, the political face of the western range is woven of disparate pieces, a quilted landscape of private and public parts. Within the boundaries of BLM and Forest Service public domain and national forest lands, 40 percent of the enclosed lands are privately owned and 17 percent are owned by states.[5]

Public-land ranching depends on those inholdings just as it relies on surrounding federal lands and private lands lying beyond federal boundaries. Phillip Foss, writing on the history of public-land grazing, recognized that for many western ranchers,

> the federal range is an integral part of their ranching operations. Their private holdings may be of little value without continued access to the range. The range is not usually an extra or bonus piece of pasturage; it is more likely to be a necessary part of the ranching unit.[6]

Private and public lands form workable economic units that signify a profound environmental relationship, an ecological whole. The residents of the western range—the people, the wildlife, and the vegetation—live and thrive on the land not because of artificial private and public divisions in property but despite them.

To secure the needed land base to support a viable ranch, ranchers must often integrate private and public lands. Their cattle and sheep may graze the high country grass of a national forest in summer, but winter's snow and cold force the animals to lower elevations, onto private lands and leased BLM allotments.

Wildlife also depends on the intermingled lands that comprise the western range. Meadows in national forest uplands may provide grass for foraging elk during summer, but the elk must look elsewhere for food when the first snows come. They move to the lowlands, to the sagebrush basins managed by the BLM and to the hay fields and meadows of private winter ranges. Their migration underlies a relationship to the western range that is profoundly ecological—a relationship to the land that transcends political divisions.

Ranchers share a similar relationship to the land, one bound by necessity to the land's biological and physical limits. Economic motives aside, their movement of livestock across the western range constitutes an ecological relationship as profound as the natural migrations of elk. And it is the relationship of ranchers to their environment that has, in recent times, most influenced the natural history of the western range. For better or worse, that relationship has dominated almost every facet of the western landscape.

Vital relationships, such as those between elk or ranchers on one hand and the land on the other, remind us of the ecological truism that all things are connected. From atop Levi's hill, those relationships and that truism are starkly apparent. First sight of valley meadows, grazing cattle, ranch buildings, and browsing deer in the morning twilight nudges us toward greater understanding. The sun rises, the vision clears, outlines of the western range emerge.

A LAND DESPOILED

George Marsh, writing at the dawn of the western livestock era, delivered one of the first environmental polemics against mankind's disregard for nature. His 1874 essay, *The Earth as Modified by Human Action*, warned, "Man has too long forgotten that the earth was given to him for usufruct alone, not for consumption, still less for profligate waste."[7] A century later, the truth of Marsh's prophecy could be seen west of the 100th meridian. Writers spoke of ravaged land and a destroyed western range. Eden had been sullied, its virgin land sacrificed to the plow and hoof. They mourned the loss and looked for someone to blame. "What can be said truly," declared William Wyant, "is that much of the pristine quality of what was once an immense and beautiful land is now gone and that although some attrition was inevitable as the nation filled out, there has been disgraceful waste."[8]

Michael Frome, in his popular history of the Forest Service, shared those sentiments and stated them even more strongly. "The rangelands of today," he wrote,

> are the grasslands of history, a part of inner America richly endowed by nature but undone by Western man through stormy generations until now they are caught in the process of desertification. The course of history, as written in lands bordering the Mediterranean and in Africa, has arrived to make the New World old.[9]

Writers also turned to diaries and journals of early pioneers to verify the losses they knew to be true. Bernard Shanks summarized those accounts for the high plains. "Pioneers," he claimed, "described Great Plains grass and hills as a sea with gentle waters. From the Gulf of Mexico, an ocean of grass reached north to the spruce forests of Canada."[10]

These accounts and many others express the beliefs and observations of Americans who are most knowledgeable of the lands west of the 100th meridian. The western range has been transformed. At the very least, it has lost the pristine beauty and complexity that greeted the first non-Indian settlers. At most, it has become a biological desert. Everyone agrees that the land has been changed. Only the degree of change is disputed.

Some changes are obvious. Mine shafts with barren trails of tailings scar once pristine mountainsides. Huge pit mines surrounded by artificial mountains of discarded rock and soil disrupt the continuity of the landscape. Mountain peaks are less majestic, victims of the mechanized search for minerals and wealth. Stumps, the clear-cut remnants of forests past, dot landscapes lifetimes from recovery.

Wildlife has been lost. Free-ranging bison, which numbered in the tens of millions before 1870, numbered only eighty-five in 1889. From 1868 to 1881, more than thirty-one million bison were harvested from the southern herd. The northern herd, estimated at almost six million in 1870, vanished by 1883. Today, free-ranging bison, like those in the Henry Mountains of Utah, are the exception.

Pronghorn antelope, as numerous as bison in the nineteenth century, fell to only a fraction of their estimated forty million population by the twentieth century. During the same time period, ten million elk, representing six subspecies, declined to fewer than fifty thousand individuals of two subspecies. Both elk and antelope still inhabit the public lands, but not in numbers approaching their nineteenth-century populations.[11]

Biological diversity was lost on the western range for many reasons. Settlers relied on wild game for food, saving their domestic stock for cash sale. Sportsmen coveted animal trophies. Commercial agents sought the meat and hides of bison, elk, and pronghorn for lucrative eastern markets. All of these activities drastically reduced, and in some cases eliminated, entire populations of native wildlife.

Livestock quickly filled the biological vacuum created by dwindling numbers of big game species. Where tens of millions of bison, pronghorn, and elk once roamed the western range, tens of millions of cattle, sheep, and horses replaced them. On national forest lands, estimates of forage use in 1920 indicated that more than 95 percent of grazed plants went to domestic livestock. Not until 1960 did the ratio shift back in favor of big game.[12]

Grazed-out riparian areas, gullied hillsides, denuded landscapes, and loss of biological diversity are enduring reminders of the historical presence of domestic stock on the western range.[13] By almost every measure, ecological conditions on western public lands are unsatisfactory. Less than half of all Forest Service lands (46 percent) and only one-third of BLM lands (34 percent) are estimated to be in good or excellent condition. In the arid Southwest, a mere 10 percent of Forest Service lands have high ratings.[14]

It is true that ecological conditions on Forest Service and BLM rangelands have stabilized and, in some cases, improved significantly over the past century.[15] But improvement on arid rangelands is painfully slow and, at current rates, unacceptable to a growing number of Americans. Many believe that the ecological solution is the removal of domestic stock, a first step in the greening of the western range. They see livestock grazing as the environmental culprit. "Like beetles on a carcass," notes one modern observer, "a mere two percent of the nation's cattle are consuming the western public lands that belong to all Americans."[16] The hope is to witness once again an abundance of wildlife, at home on a sea of arid grasslands.

But the dilemma rests with the land. We do not know enough about the land's biological and ecological capacity to justify perceptions and expectations. Literary references may suggest the degree to which the western range has changed. Hope and desire may point to an alluring standard by which to gauge our return to Eden. But the scientific knowledge for judging perceptions and basing expectations is far from conclusive.

BLM and Forest Service measurements of land conditions are imprecise and dated. In 1988, the U.S. General Accounting Office chastised both agencies for their incomplete and unreliable measurements of the health of the public's western range.[17] "Our Ailing Public Rangelands," a two-part report published by the National Wildlife Federation and the Natural Resources Defense Council in 1985 and 1989 fares no better. It speaks more to the inequity of current federal grazing fees than to the physical state of the western range. Scientists and land managers are also unable to gauge the recovery potential of the range.

Despite the dearth of scientific evidence, the conclusion is unavoidable: Western public lands have suffered from overgrazing. BLM lands show most clearly the evidence of livestock damage, though Forest Service lands also bear unhealed scars. In fairness, differences between the two speak more to the environmental resilience of higher elevation Forest Service lands than to management ability. In any case, the lands of both agencies no longer resemble the pristine landscapes that greeted John Wesley Powell as he crossed the 100th meridian.

Although it is important to recognize our inability to quantify the environmental decline of the western range, that is not the most important issue here. The immediate problem is the discrepancy between perceptions of the western range and the changing values and expectations of an affluent society. The changes that have occurred under a land regime dominated by domestic livestock now conflict with the values of an emerging majority of public-land users. Streams desired for fishing, subalpine meadows valued for visual relief, rugged mountains sought for wilderness, and wildlands treasured for wildlife have been trampled and grazed for a century. Today, those areas are a major focus of public-land concern. Their conditions have not markedly changed as many claim, but our expectations for what they can offer us have soared. As unique landscapes, they offer us more than feed and water for domestic livestock: They offer us the peace and solace of wild and open spaces.

Looking down from Levi's fortress, it is clear that peace and solace—however tenuous their grasp may be—are still part of the Circle Bar Ranch. But changes are evident across the landscape. The wildness is gone, the mountains are tamed, and the vitality of nature is somehow altered. If the valley of Otter Creek is less healthy than it once was, and many say it is, who or what is to blame? As answers to this question are debated with moral certainty, cattle graze silently on the distant horizon, biological mowers harvesting another year's crops.

THE COMMON DENOMINATOR

Two approaches have been taken in assigning responsibility for the fate of the western range. The first approach, focused on the role of the individual, defines the problem in ethical terms, suggesting that western environmental problems have their origin in the behavioral aberrations of public-land ranchers. Simply stated, this approach asserts that either a land ethic has not evolved on public grazing lands or it has succumbed to the historical events that transformed the West. The second approach eschews ethics and blames the institutions that supposedly shape human behavior. Specifically, it explains overgrazing and poor land stewardship as functions of bad institutions. Public-land ranchers behave as they do not for want of a land ethic but because of perverse incentives.

The ethical argument is the most common. Long before livestock transformed the landscape of the western range, George Marsh had warned of the dangers of unrestrained human action. "Purely untutored humanity, it is true," he wrote, "interferes comparatively little with the arrangements of nature, and the destructive agency of man becomes more and more energetic and unsparing as he advances in civilization." [18] But it was not Marsh who brought environmental ethics into the argument. That responsibility rested with Aldo Leopold.

In his 1949 essay "The Land Ethic," Leopold concluded that "there is as yet no ethic dealing with man's relation to land and to the animals and plants which grow upon it." [19] Economic self-interest alone, he believed, was determining man's relationship to the land and its creatures. The result, he lamented, was the elimination of "many elements in the land community that lack commercial value." [20] Leopold's solution was a land ethic to transform "the role of Homo sapiens from conqueror of the land-community to plain member and citizen of it." [21]

For Leopold, a land ethic would imply the existence of an ecological conscience and a conviction of individual responsibility for the health of the land. The lack of a land ethic, in Leopold's mind, was a major cause of conservation being delegated to government. "A thing is right," Leopold wrote, "when it tends to preserve the integrity, stability, and beauty of the biotic community. It is wrong when it tends otherwise."[22] If followed, Leopold believed, this simple rule would revolutionize people's relationship to and role in the land community.

As applied to the western range, the land ethic leaves no room for doubt. Dismal federal land conditions, as explained in a multitude of environmental writings, are the result of public-land ranchers pursuing their own short-run self-interest. William Voigt, Jr., in *Public Grazing Lands,* suggests that a land ethic was incompatible with the economic incentives of the Old West. The West, he writes, had no organizations devoted to the land and its stewardship. The organizations that did exist were ranchers' associations, and "these seldom concerned themselves with resource conservation."[23]

The land ethic puts responsibility for the western range squarely on the shoulders of public-land ranchers. It explains in ethical terms what writers like Bernard De Voto summed up in the creed of the nineteenth-century cattle kingdom. Greed and power—not concern for the environment, culture, and history—motivated the cattlemen who settled and dominated the western range. "The Cattle Kingdom overgrazed the range so drastically," De Voto observed, "that the processes of nature were disrupted. Since those high and far-off days the [public] range has never been capable of supporting anything like the number of cattle it could have supported if the cattle barons had not maimed it."[24]

The ethical themes of the past have continued to the present. Books ranging from *Sacred Cows at the Public Trough* to *Free Our Public Lands!* tell of the environmental wrongdoing of public-land ranchers.[25] None says it better than Edward Abbey's colorful essay "Even the Bad Guys Wear White Hats." The ruin of the West, Abbey declares, is the product of greed and environmental ignorance of cowboys and ranchers. Their ethic, or lack thereof, has reduced the public's western range to a "cow-burnt wasteland." "Hordes" of cattle are a pest and a plague, polluting streams and infesting "our canyons, valleys, meadows, and forests." "The whole American West," he declares, "stinks of cattle" and should be freed of their presence.[26]

Abbey reaffirms the ethical pronouncement of his spiritual mentor, John Muir: "Only what belongs to all alike is [protected], and every acre that is left should be held together under the federal government as a basis for a general policy of administration for the public good."[27] The state, and more specifically the Forest Service and the BLM, are seen in the ethical argument as the only defense the public and the grazing lands have against the degradations of uncaring public-land ranchers. Federal control is desired either as a substitute for a personal land ethic or as a necessary evil pending its emergence. Underlying this argument is the assumption of guilt, the certain and singular complicity of western stockmen in the demise of the western range.

The institutional argument arrives at a much different conclusion and follows an altogether different route. This argument denies traditional distinctions between private and public behavior. Individuals and institutions follow similar rules of conduct, each pursuing a course of action beneficial to its well-being. Forest Service and BLM personnel may be devoted to public service and motivated by the purest idealism, yet their organizations must attend to the same worldly matters that, from the ethical point of view, have corrupted the environmental sensibilities of public-land ranchers. Public-land agencies are no less dependent than western stockmen on earning a living.

Crucial to the institutional argument is the manner in which agencies like the Forest Service and the BLM earn their living. Their primary income is not derived from the natural resources they manage. It comes from a political process that has tenuous ties to the welfare of the land. The self-interest of the Forest Service and the BLM is served by maximizing annual budgets through political lobbying. Good resource management may help this effort, but the important point is that good resource management is not necessary. Agency budgets are predicated more on political maneuvering than on the proven track records of specific organizations.

The institutional argument is unequivocal in its assignment of environmental blame. Land management agencies have failed to protect the natural resources on the public land. Policies pursued by the Forest Service and the BLM have responded more to the fiscal needs of their bureaucracies than to the ecological needs of the land and the resource demands of the public. Moreover, political processes have insulated land agencies from accountability for the condition of the land. It makes little difference to the budgets of the Forest Service and the BLM whether their lands are improving or degrading. Lands in better condition provide administrators with a solid argument to continue or expand successful programs. Lands in declining condition allow administrators to plead for additional funding to prevent environmental ruin.

But public-land ranchers do not escape unscathed in the institutional argument either. Stockmen, like other special interest groups, use the political process to pressure land agencies to comply with their wishes. In exchange, they lend political support to Forest Service and BLM requests for new programs and expanded budgets. In this argument, historical overgrazing, far from being the result of ethical failure, is the political outcome of pragmatic alliances among ranchers, agencies, and politicians.

The new resource economics (NRE), a free-market environmentalism developed from the writings of John Baden, Richard Stroup, and Terry Anderson, embodies the institutional argument.[28] It sees the problem of the western range in institutional, not ethical, terms. NRE analysts conclude that free-market processes, predicated on private ownership, are superior to political means in the conservation and protection of natural resources. Those processes ensure accountability for management decisions, and they optimize information that is vital to good land management. Further, waste associated with special interest politics is avoided when decisions are left to the impartial market. Most important, market processes are more responsive to the needs of the land and to the resource demands of the public.

Neither argument is completely wrong, but neither is entirely correct. Certainly, the ethical argument is most clear-cut and simple: There are good people and there are bad people. Responsibility and accountability are placed where they belong. Expose the bad guys and a just solution is at hand. Western stockmen wear black hats; Forest Service and BLM employees play heroic roles. The facts are clear. Livestock overgrazed public rangelands and damaged the western range. Ranchers overgrazed their land by choice, pursuing the ethic of profit, not the ethic of responsibility for what Leopold termed the land community. Their failure was the failing of a personal land ethic.

Persuasive as the ethical argument appears, its foundations are shaky. It assumes that public-land ranchers arrived at choices without coercion or undue influence. It ignores the environment in which public-land ranchers made their choices—an environment of institutional constraints and persuasive political pressures. It overlooks the role of public-land law and federal agencies in shaping the choices made by public-land ranchers. There is even the hint that the central ethical issue is not so much the environmental culpability of ranchers as the propriety of their grazing livestock at all on public lands.

The ethical argument concludes that ranchers overgrazed the public's land because they equated profit with poundage of steers produced, not with the ecological health of the range. Economic gain was unquestionably a goal of western stockmen, but it was not achieved through livestock production. Historically, nominal rates of return on livestock investments have averaged less than 2 percent. The long-term profits made by western ranchers have come from the appreciation (10 to 15 percent annually) of their owned and leased lands.[29] Their economic well-being has been and continues to be tied to the well-being of the land. To whatever extent they have overgrazed the range, the assumption of a narrow pursuit of economic gain fails to explain their behavior.

Understanding the choices and actions of public-land ranchers is part of understanding the story of the western range. Ethical stereotypes do not clarify why ranchers' choices and actions went environmentally astray. Suppose, for a moment, that we could begin anew the history of public-land grazing with the assurance that each rancher were instilled with a land ethic of Leopoldian dimensions. Would good intentions be sufficient to reverse the course of the western range? It is doubtful. Good intentions are useful, but they are rarely instructive. Animal husbandry on arid lands was a new experience for people whose knowledge was limited to regions of high rainfall, rich soils, and abundant grass. Good intentions harnessed to bad information and inadequate knowledge would have laid waste to the western range as surely as narrow economic self-interest.

Institutional arguments also have their limitations. Bureaucracies do attend to interests other than fiscal survival, and shared ideological commitment in an agency can be as powerful an incentive as the material concerns of budget expansion. The Forest Service is a case in point. The idealism and sense of mission instilled in the Forest Service by its first chief, Gifford Pinchot, cannot be overlooked in understanding the agency's lasting impact on the western range. Moreover, the presence of motivated and talented individuals has often lifted bureaucracies from mediocrity to excellence. Their willingness to push the bureaucracy to its limits may explain the ability of agencies like the Forest Service and the BLM to perform as well as they have.

Occasional brilliance and concern do not rescue the Forest Service and the BLM from the flaws perceived in the institutional argument. But where NRE and its institutional model fail most is in the manner and scope of analysis. Agencies do not exist and function in a vacuum, and neither do public-land ranchers. Both choose and act in response to an outside world. Both are ecological creatures that can be understood only in the context of their broader environments.

Narrow institutional critiques omit the ecological dimension of land management institutions—the connections between such institutions, their constituents, and the larger social environment. They brush aside questions of ethics and values. They forget that the moral assumptions behind those ethics and values are as critical to the understanding of natural resource agencies and policies as they are to the story of the western range. Their failure lies in not going far enough, in not perceiving the singular theme underlying both the ethical and the institutional arguments of environmental blame. Proponents of both positions overlook the common denominator of visions—the perceptions and beliefs held by people of how the western range should look and be and the laws and public policies that have given some of those perceptions and beliefs disproportionate political and ecological clout.

This book is about that common denominator. The story of the western range cannot be told without consideration of individual ethics and institutional workings. Yet the ethical shortcomings of ranchers and the institutional weaknesses of agencies—even the environmental state of the western range—are fragments of a larger picture. They are the symptoms as well as the mechanics of the workings of visions on the land. Understanding those visions is the first step toward exposing misconceptions and half-truths. By understanding them, we will gain insight not only into the issue of environmental blame but also into the critical relationship between the people and the lands of the western range.

CHAPTER TWO

Like a City upon a Hill

*L*evi Howes was born in 1872 in Cape Cod, Massachusetts, not *far from where his ancestors landed and settled after sailing from England in 1637. Like generations of Howeses before him, his first memories were of the sea. His father, Calvin, captain of his own vessel, had gone to sea at the age of thirteen. Levi started even younger, spending the first years of his life on board his father's ship. Were it not for Montana, Levi would have followed in his father's footsteps, viewing the world from the bridge of a ship and never knowing of the rolling sea of grasslands stretching from horizon to horizon.*

The winter of 1879–1880 was a turning point for Levi and his family. News from the Montana Territory sparked his father's sense of adventure and stirred a vision of opportunity that overcame his need for place, security, and family roots. In 1880, that vision and a railroad took the Howes family to Bismarck, and from there by wagon to a temporary home along the Tongue River near Ashland. Three years later, the Circle Bar Ranch began operating on Otter Creek.

Levi never doubted that his father's vision would become his own. By the time he took over the Circle Bar in 1896, his loyalty lay with the land, not with the sea his father had left. Levi was a stockman now, and the ranch was thriving. Over two thousand head of cattle grazed the hay fields and grass-lands that bordered Otter Creek.

Sometimes Levi climbed to the high ridge top overlooking his summer range. He was proud of the vision he and his father had brought to the land. They had carved a home in the Montana wildlands and buried roots deep in the southeastern Montana soil. Their cattle and the generations of their family would be the legacy of that vision.

Two and a half centuries and the span of a continent now separated Levi from his Puritan ancestors who had settled in Cape Cod. They, like Levi and his family, had left their homes to pursue a vision. Theirs was a godly vision. Cape Cod gave them the chance to pursue their calling, to build good ships and saintly communities. Levi's father sought a secular vision and found his calling in a mountain valley. Yet both generations had built a way of life from the raw elements of the American wilderness. They had molded a landscape to match their visions.

Levi, from atop his ridge, saw what his ancestors had seen as they looked from their ships toward the coast of Cape Cod. Both saw a vast and empty land, void of any meaning other than what their visions would offer. It was a land beckoning them westward, offering its forests and plains as fodder for their visions.

John Winthrop, governor of the Massachusetts Bay Colony when the first Howes arrived at Cape Cod, had understood the power of visions. The colony he governed would, he hoped, shine forth like a godly beacon from the shores of the new world. Its landscape, shaped by a Puritan vision, would inspire those who dwelled within it and transform the world that viewed it from afar. Seen from Levi's ridge top or from the captain's bridge of the first Howes ship, the Montana and New England skylines were, in Winthrop's words, "as a Citty upon a Hill, [where] the eies of all people are upon us."[1]

VISIONS

Pioneers in the mold of Levi and his father brought more than a physical presence to the West. They came with a purpose in mind. They looked to the American wilderness and imagined a world beyond the virgin forests and rolling prairies. They envisioned new landscapes to meet the designs of their personal dreams and ambitions. As Alexis de Tocqueville observed in *Democracy in America*, pioneers were "insensible to the wonders of in-animate nature and they may be said not to perceive the mighty forests that surround them till they fall beneath the hatchet." Their minds were set, he continued, to marching "across these wilds, draining swamps, turning the course of rivers, peopling solitudes, and subduing nature."[2] They were the vanguard of yeoman farmers, the heart and soul of the virtuous republic envisioned by Thomas Jefferson.

The visions that strove to tame the American wilderness did not go unchallenged. Long before Levi and his family applied their utilitarian vision to the rangelands of Otter Creek, competing visions had brought new meanings and significance to the unsettled lands of the West. Romanticists in the early nineteenth century celebrated the primitive and sought the sublime in unconquered nature. Wilderness, they insisted, was to be worshipped, not subdued. Henry David Thoreau, part of the romantic tradition, found higher truths in the ordinary objects and lessons of nature. In the seclusion of Walden Pond, Thoreau envisioned a transcendent world reflected in the minute details of a diverse nature. He celebrated life in the woods and strengthened his conviction that "in Wildness is the preservation of the World."[3]

Visions of a nature either cultivated or sublime lost meaning and relevance in the wake of the Civil War. The ideals those visions represented had been well suited to an era of self-reliance and fierce independence, but after four years of armed struggle and profligate waste of lives and resources they seemed strangely inappropriate. Jefferson's noble farmer and the ramblings of Thoreau were out of place, relics of a more innocent and undisciplined age. A new vision, one attuned to the regimentation of postwar, industrial America, was needed. By the time Levi Howes assumed control of the Circle Bar Ranch, that vision had taken hold of America's remaining wildlands.

The western range became the storage shed of America's natural resource wealth. Its strategic importance to the nation's well-being called for management based on the principles of efficiency and sustained production. Public lands would be run as businesses, headed by dedicated and selfless public servants. Their uses would be carefully planned and executed to serve the material needs of an expanding industrial society.

By 1970, cracks had appeared in the vision. That year, Earth Day and a burgeoning environmental movement made clear the outlines of a vision more suggestive of the yearnings of antebellum America. The western range was to be the domain of all the people, not the kingdom of special interests. The importance of the public land exceeded the market price of its resources. It was the depository of civic, national, and spiritual values, uplifting Americans and uniting them in a common heritage. As such, the preservation of wildness was not debatable. It was at the center of a new landscape vision.

Landscape visions are crucial to understanding the lands and people of the western range. In the broadest sense, they shape and direct the attitudes and actions of people toward their environments. They are the rose-colored glasses through which nature is viewed. They summarize individual and social expectations, biases, and ambitions. As such, landscape visions are burdened by values, too often bearing only an incidental relation to nature as it exists apart from humanity. These visions are also the vehicles of their own fulfillment. They inspire and compel human action to the purpose of changing the land.

Cultures have molded and reshaped their environments to the dictates of landscape visions—for reasons ranging from basic survival to material, aesthetic, and spiritual enrichment. Those landscape visions and the galaxy of reasons behind them tell much about the solitary dreams of individuals and the sweeping ambitions of societies. The rugged cliffs of Mesa Verde National Park evolved into sophisticated cliff dwellings because of the will of the Anasazi Indians. And the public lands of the western range continue to evolve because of changing landscape visions. But visions are not all alike. On the western range, only a handful of visions have left lasting impressions on the land. As elsewhere, visions on the western range have differed in their effects by virtue of how they are realized. In other words, it is the means by which landscape visions are implemented, not the visions themselves, that makes the crucial difference.

In his book *A Conflict of Visions*, Thomas Sowell examines social visions—visions of human nature—and separates them into two basic types: constrained and unconstrained.[4] Constrained visions are cautious. They are forever suspicious of the motives and capabilities of people and their institutions to achieve social good. Humans are neither so moral nor so endowed with reason that they can be trusted with unlimited power. Accordingly, governments must be restrained in accordance with the natural limitations of men and women. Unconstrained visions are those that deny natural limits to the ability of people to better themselves and their societies. Humans have the capacity to exercise reason and power benignly and successfully. Their governments, when ruled by good men and women, can and do achieve social and economic justice. The potential for human beneficence is seen as unlimited.

Sowell leans heavily on the distinction between constrained and unconstrained visions to explain what he terms the "ideological origins of political struggles." Without stating as much, his "conflict of visions" mimics the historical clash between classic conservatism and modern liberalism. In his view, it is the content of the two social visions or philosophies, not the means people use to realize them, that counts most in political history. His argument is weakened, however, by his choice of Adam Smith and William Godwin to represent the ideals of constrained and unconstrained visions. In many ways, the two historical figures correspond remarkably well to Sowell's model. Yet the differences between the conservative thinking of Smith and the radical philosophy of Godwin mask a striking similarity. Both men explicitly eschew the state as a proper means of achieving social goals. In contrast, there are authoritarian political regimes whose policies call for strict social control and whose leaders and ideologies span the spectrum of Sowell's types. If social visions are seminal to political struggle, it is because of the means of their implementation, not the contents of their ideologies.

Applied to landscape visions, the argument is just as valid. Environmental visions can be fitted to Sowell's types, but their ecological significance has little bearing on whether they are classified as constrained or unconstrained. For example, Henry David Thoreau and John Muir, both celebrated naturalists, shared an intellectual tradition aligned with the unconstrained view. Both men felt deeply about the natural world and wrote prolifically in support of its value and preservation. Yet despite their commitment to a common ecological vision, they differed on the means to achieve it.

Thoreau was thoroughly a product of the antebellum period, his death coming in the second year of the Civil War. In "Civil Disobedience," Thoreau concluded that ultimate sovereignty lay with the individual, not the state. The complicity of the federal government in the enforcement of slave laws had made him distrustful of any authority other than his own conscience. Yet convictions of right and wrong were never so certain in his own mind as to justify imposing his will—or his visions—on other people.

The moral humility Thoreau preached and practiced was intolerant only of those who would use coercion in behalf of their ideas.[5] Even in matters as important as the natural world, moral humility ruled his temperament, making visions of nature the affairs of individual conscience. John Muir, in contrast, grew up in the aftermath of the Civil War. The turbulent years of the late 1800s and the righteousness of his convictions persuaded him that coercive means were proper tools for environmental protection. Forest preservation, Muir believed, would be best achieved by "one soldier in the woods, armed with authority and a gun." The environmental waste of the past, he wrote, called for the government "to begin rational administration of its forests."[6] Unlike Thoreau, Muir did not doubt the moral certainty of his position, nor did he question the propriety of using government authority in the pursuit of his vision.

Tolerance and intolerance of mind, not the substance of visions, distinguish Thoreau from Muir. Tolerance is the quality that persuaded Thoreau to leave visions to the dictates of individual conscience. Intolerance is the quality that persuaded Muir to leave visions to the rule of government. Those qualities, in turn, are crucial to distinguishing among landscape visions on the western range and to explaining the fleeting environmental effects of the tolerant vision and the lasting imprints of the intolerant vision.

There is a compelling reason why tolerant and intolerant visions have had such disparate ecological consequences on the western range. Tolerant landscape visions are constrained, though not in the sense intended by Sowell. They are the stuff of individual dreams and aspirations. They come into being by virtue of the spiritual and material resources people can muster alone or in voluntary association. As such, tolerant visions have limited control—not because they share the moral humility of Thoreau but because they lack the power to extend themselves in an imperial sense. They are tolerant by necessity, not because of choice. Even if Thoreau had wanted to apply his vision of Walden Pond to the surrounding countryside, his meager resources and his distaste for coercion would have prevented him. Most landscape visions fall within this category. Their ambitions may be global in scope, but their effects are inescapably local.

In contrast, intolerant visions are aggressively unconstrained. This is not to suggest that intolerant visions are expressed any more fervently or pursued with any greater idealism than their tolerant cousins. "Unconstrained" has a much simpler meaning here. It stresses the extraordinary means people are willing to use to achieve their environmental goals. Those whose landscape visions are unconstrained seek control in the broadest sense. Their visions are imperial, meant to control landscapes beyond the meager means of individuals and voluntary associations. Coercive means to achieve control and to exercise power are deemed necessary and proper. There is no moral humility to check the unlimited aspirations of unconstrained landscape visions. There is no moral hesitancy to harness the state to the cause of righteous landscape visions. The global ambitions of intolerant visions necessarily assume more than local significance.

The intolerance of visions comes from a basic mistrust in human nature, not from a desire or striving for human perfectibility. Muir's advocacy of soldiers "armed with authority and a gun" to protect national forests was intended to curb "the invading horde of destroyers called settlers."[7] It had nothing to do with moving men and women toward a more harmonious relation with nature. The quality of intolerance that fired Muir's energies to the protection of western forestlands also animated the landscape visions that would change the face of the western range. Intolerant visions, so out of place in a tolerant society, found fertile soil in the prairies, deserts, and mountains west of the 100th meridian.

OF SOUL AND SOIL

Intolerant visions in a tolerant society are one of many anomalies that underscore the social and political complexity of American culture. Tolerance, of course, is basic to the culture's belief system. And despite recurrent fits and spasms of intolerance, the United States has been and continues to be a tolerant society in matters that touch religion, life-style, and political expression.

An intellectual tradition of tolerance has lineage in Thomas Jefferson's "Virginia Statute of Religious Liberty" and in the Declaration of Independence. The first document establishes the sanctity of an individual's belief; the second affirms the inalienable right of all citizens to the pursuit of happiness. Together, they convey the message that freedom of visions is no less important than freedom of religion. After all, visions are the fountainhead of happiness and tolerance the condition for its pursuit. Tolerant visions, whether religious or secular, are deeply imbedded in the fabric of American history.

But tolerance came slowly to American society. It proceeded by a process of evolution that was largely unaffected by legislative decree. Religious freedom, in particular, arrived in the measured steps of gradual change as spiritual conformity yielded to the diversifying spirit of protestant religion. By the time Thomas Jefferson penned his famous act "for establishing Religious Freedom" in Virginia, tolerance in matters of religion had become the standard rather than the exception throughout the new nation. The reality of many beliefs, not the idealism of Jefferson, made religion a matter of conscience rather than of state policy.

Tolerance in matters of the soul did not carry over fully to matters of the soil. From the nation's birth, the founding fathers perceived land and religion differently. Religion was deemed beyond the pale of civil government; land was not. This difference flowed naturally from Enlightenment thought. John Locke, in his *Second Treatise of Government,* made clear the relation of man and state to the land. "As much land as a man tills, plants, improves, cultivates, and can use the product of," he wrote, "so much is his property. He by his labour does, as it were, enclose it from the common." The right to private property, Locke emphasized, was anterior to the state. It was a right founded on the law of nature and subject to only two limitations. Labor could claim land for itself only "where there is enough, and as good left in common for others" and only "as much as any one can make use of to any advantage of life before it spoils. . . . "8

Locke's first constraint on land ownership was of no immediate concern to the founding fathers. For all practical purposes, the new nation was blessed with unlimited territory. Its lands, although inhabited by aborigines, were common property. Only with the mixture of human labor would those lands shift from the state of nature to the state of civil authority. For the founding fathers, civil government was obliged to open the nation's common property to its citizens and to allow for its private ownership. With this objective in mind, the Declaration of Independence denounced the British king for preventing the settlement of western colonial lands.

But the proper role of government did not end with the responsibility of settlement. Locke's second constraint on property ownership implied an even more active role for government in the distribution of America's landed wealth. His prescription evoked the element of equity, the rule that no person could rightfully claim as property more than could be used without waste. The duty of the state, from Locke's perspective, was to limit the exercise of the right of property in the interests of society as a whole. That view, when restated in the agrarian philosophy that flourished in the period between the American Revolution and the Civil War, had far-reaching implications for the future of the western range.

The particulars of that philosophy are dealt with in chapter 4. Here, we need to recognize only its essence—specifically the equation between agrarian values and the land and the yeoman farmer. In his book *Virgin Land*, Henry Nash Smith notes the salient features of agrarianism as envisioned by J. Hector St. John de Crèvecoeur and Thomas Jefferson. Their philosophy dictated, he writes,

> that every man has a natural right to land; that labor expended in cultivating the earth confers a valid title to it; that the ownership of land, by making the farmer independent, gives him social status and dignity, while constant contact with nature in the course of his labors makes him virtuous and happy; . . . and that *government should be dedicated to the interests of the freehold farmer* [emphasis mine].[9]

For Jefferson, the architect of western land policy, these principles held special significance. If the new republic was to thrive and flourish, it would be as an agrarian society in which *all* citizens enjoyed the blessings of property ownership. Small, self-sufficient farmers—in Jefferson's words, "the chosen people of God"[10]—would provide the moral backbone of the nation. These virtuous yeomen would be the bulwark against tyranny and the seeds of future prosperity.

Land lay at the heart of Jefferson's envisioned republic. His landscape vision depended on the unlimited expanse of the American wilderness and the will of a people to subdue it for settlement and cultivation. Even more so, it depended on the wisdom of government to make and apply public-land policies fairly and justly. There was no doubt in his mind that "the proportion which the aggregate of the other classes of [nonfarming] citizens bears in any State to that of its husbandmen, is the proportion of its unsound to its healthy parts."[11] Government, the very institution that Jefferson had sought to free from religious domination, was harnessed with moral fervor to the rising star of a virtuous agrarian republic. Religion, after all, was a matter of personal conscience. Land was the clay from which a free society would be molded and preserved.

The landscape vision of a democratic farmers' republic provided, in a very real sense, what religion had failed to provide since the Reformation. It gave society cohesion and served as the fountainhead of basic values. Land was the icon of a secular religion, one that would rule uncontested until the cataclysm of the Civil War. Significantly, the pluralism that made tolerance a necessity in religious affairs simply was not evident in the nation's attitudes toward land. But that mattered little. Tolerance for landscape visions did not concern a nation united behind westward expansion and committed to federal involvement.

The effects of such consensus were felt immediately. From the first moments of independence, the federal government assumed an active role in the disposal of western lands. At first, the role was constrained to selling lands and securing newly formed property rights. With the onset of the Civil War, that activism expanded into partisan support for a single landscape vision—the agrarianism of Crèvecoeur and Jefferson. The change was innocent enough, fueled by the youthful idealism and naïveté of a people too occupied with the present to appreciate the future. Their intentions, like those of their spokesmen, were admirable and appropriate for free people in a free land. But they set a precedent that would continue and escalate into the twentieth century.

Government, in the brief span between independence and civil war, had changed directions. It would no longer restrict itself to securing private property rights to western lands. This meant a narrowing, if not a corruption, of the hallowed phrase "pursuit of happiness." Those words as applied to western lands would no longer signify the tolerance accorded religion. They would reflect instead the intolerance that had driven immigrants from Europe and moved Jefferson to declare interminable warfare on the tyranny of superstition. The state, not its citizens, would dictate the landscape visions appropriate for the lands west of the 100th meridian. Government would be the final arbiter in matters of the soil.

CHOICE AND CONSEQUENCE

Today's western range is the product of yesterday's choices. Choices made among landscape visions and the ways to attain them clarify and explain the environmental consequences that now enrage environmentalists and haunt public-land ranchers. Ethical and institutional arguments that assign blame to ranchers or agencies miss the salient point of landscape visions. The way in which people actively envision their landscapes influences much more than the land and its natural features. It shapes the social and political institutions that evolve to arbitrate and care for their collective environments. Those responses, in turn, entail values and ethics that are revealing of people's actual and perceived relations to the natural world.

Landscape visions are unequal, and only a few have altered the face of western lands with lasting effects. But those few have touched the western range as certainly as have the forces of nature. Their power to transform the land—to direct human energy and will to their goals—arises from the control they exercise over the minds of men and women. Such visions forsook the tolerance and moral humility of Thoreau for the righteousness and certitude of Muir. They enlisted the power of the state in their drive for control.

It is one of the ironies of history that a defender of tolerance in one sphere of human activity would open the door for intolerance in another. Thomas Jefferson, of all the founding fathers, was most hesitant to grant extensive powers to a central government. Yet the powers he allowed, and those he exercised as president, were precisely the ones that set in motion the precedent of state control of both the land and the visions that would fashion the western landscape. Reinforced by the arguments of the Enlightenment, Jefferson unwittingly sowed the seeds of a centralized hegemony that would emerge later, decades after his death.

But Jefferson cannot be blamed for what neither he nor his countrymen understood or expected. Who could have foreseen that the agrarian decentralism that Jefferson envisioned for the lands of the Louisiana Purchase would evolve into bureaucratic centralism by the twentieth century? And who could have anticipated the subtle shift in government's role from neutral referee to partisan of landscape visions?

The many meanings that his era gave to land may account for Jefferson's willingness to surrender matters of the soil to government control. Land as a property right implied a legal relationship between man and nature that could be formalized and secured only by the police powers of the state. This meaning was most consonant with the rational Enlightenment mind. Land was also the centerpiece of the young nation's self-image. As the foundation for a prosperous republic of yeoman farmers, it was the key to the agrarian vision that most Americans shared. Jefferson understood, in a reasoned sense, the importance of land to the making of America, but he was too immersed in the Enlightenment and intellectually too distant from the romantic revolt against reason to appreciate the emotional content of land and the religious strivings of landscape visions.

Without appreciating the primal quality of land and landscape visions, Jefferson had no way of understanding the power they could exercise over people's minds—nor the influence they could exert on state policies. Even further from his understanding were the environmental effects that landscape visions could, and would, bring to the western range. Limitless lands and so few people, buttressed by an unshakable optimism, made worries about the environment seem inconsequential and even more difficult to entertain.

Reason and education, Jefferson believed, would be sufficient to bring agricultural practices into harmony with cultivated nature. What Jefferson did not realize was that landscape visions rely little on education and even less on reason. Tolerant and intolerant visions alike come into being despite reason and often in the absence of good information. The only difference between the two is that intolerant visions are able to persist longer in ignorance. They alone enjoy the coercive powers and the massive resources to flaunt reason and information without paying the immediate price of environmental failure.

Intolerant visions on the western range, however, have done more than promote environmental ruin and subvert Jefferson's democratic aspirations. They have altered people's relation to nature in ways that would never have been imagined by Jefferson or condoned by the likes of Henry David Thoreau. Landscape visions have built obstacles barring an ecologically sound relationship between people and their environment. They have prevented men and women from adapting to and learning about an environment that was inscrutable from the start and has become even more so in the shadows of intolerant visions.

The challenge is to understand the ecology of landscape visions and their place within the natural and social history of the western range. Landscape visions are not merely the catalysts of human action; they are the mental constructs through which people have encountered and reacted with the natural world. As such, they are ecological factors that must be reckoned with. They cannot be dismissed when judging the actions of public-land ranchers and the successes and failures of land management agencies. Above all, landscape visions provide an ecological perspective— an ecosystem snapshot of western public lands—that ethical and institutional arguments do not. By making the argument ecological, a clearer picture emerges of people and nature on the western range. We begin to understand the consequences of choices made long ago.

CHAPTER THREE

Visions upon the Land

*S*ettlement along the valley of Otter Creek quickened during the decade following Levi Howes's arrival. By 1890, the year the superintendent of the census announced the passing of the American frontier, Otter Creek was populated from Ashland south to Levi's Circle Bar.

The newcomers were strangers to one another and to the lands they homesteaded. But somewhere between the piercing cold of a winter's blue norther and the crackling dry heat of a summer's drought, the people and the land changed. Immigrants, with little in common except hope and daring, coalesced into a community of Montana ranchers, and the lands they had once envisioned as objects of economic opportunity became the fertile fields of family and home. Their ties to one another and to the valley and mountains of Otter Creek gave new permanence and stability to their lives.

Nearly a hundred years later, when Marc Stevens took over the Circle Bar from his grandfather, most of the original families were still on Otter Creek. Individuals had come and gone, but with each passing generation, the legacy of family and land had strengthened the ties between people and place. Ranching as a way of life persisted along the banks of Otter Creek.

The families that remained had become residents of the land, members of a community extending beyond the limited society their ancestors had forged from the wilderness. A hundred years and the passage of generations had earned them a niche in the valleys and hills of southeastern Montana. For Marc and his neighbors, home was along Otter Creek and in the pine forests and fescue grasslands of the Custer National Forest.

The private bottomlands and the public forests formed a vibrant, complex landscape where land, people, and creatures were woven indivisibly into an ecological whole. Marc and his neighbors lived by the natural rhythms that dictated all life on Otter Creek. In summer, they moved their cattle to the greening grass of forested rangelands. In winter, they brought them down to valley meadows and cropped hay fields. The seasons set the ecological balance.

In the late 1970s, that balance changed for Marc and his neighbors. The Forest Service shortened the period of time when livestock could graze on the forest uplands. A new policy dictated that movement of stock from private meadows and hay fields to the forest would begin on May 1, not April 1, and continue to the end of November. To compensate for the shortened period, the Forest Service increased the number of livestock some ranchers could graze. For Marc, this meant an increase from 700 to 800 head.

Marc understood that mathematically, 800 head for seven months was the same as 700 head for eight months, but he also knew that ecologically, it would never work. His private lands, only a fraction of the size of the forest uplands, would have to support more cattle than before for an even longer period. Those lands were already close to capacity. To increase stocking further would erase the margin of safety needed to ensure the well-being of the land, the people, and the creatures. Marc could not understand, nor would he accept, the indifference of the Forest Service toward the valley bottom. It was as much a part of the Otter Creek ecosystem as the public lands above.

In 1987, the problem worsened when the Forest Service shortened the grazing period further by advancing to May 15 the date that stock could go onto the forest. Marc was angry. On his own initiative, he had already delayed stocking one pasture until June 1. Now the Forest Service was asking him to delay stocking his other pastures—not because the conditions of those pastures warranted it but because the new forest policy would not allow exceptions. Marc knew that not all grazing allotments on the Custer were in as good shape as his, and he recognized that some might benefit from two weeks' additional rest. But he felt that the rule was inflexible and potentially harmful to the rich bottomlands of Otter Creek.

Two more weeks of grazing on the valley bottom, Marc feared, might set back the health of the grass. If it did, the next winter's forage might not be enough to *feed his livestock. Worse yet, the condition of his valley meadows would worsen with each year that too many cattle tried to subsist on too little forage. The ecological balance would be upset.*

Marc knew that the balance had to be restored. Ten years earlier, he had asked permission to establish spring pastures at low elevations in the Custer National Forest to ease the transition of livestock from winter to summer range. His request had been denied without explanation. He asked again, and this time the Forest Service agreed. A researcher from Montana State University was called in to evaluate the use of spring pastures on a trial basis. Experimental pastures would be grazed for two weeks and then rested for the remainder of the year.

From the beginning, however, the Forest Service was hesitant in its support of the experiment and restricted the grazing trials to marginal or inferior lands. The researcher protested. Later, when the researcher criticized the Forest Service's grazing plan for a burned area in the Custer, the agency attempted to have him dismissed.

Marc was not surprised by what was happening. He knew that the Forest Service thought the spring pastures were more trouble than they were worth. After all, a two-tiered grazing regime would be much harder to administer than a shortened grazing period. Marc also knew that the spring pastures would work, as test results would later confirm in the summer of 1989. But he was not sure that the workability of the scheme was enough. Administrative obstacles would still have to be overcome and the antagonism of the Forest Service softened.

The greater community of Otter Creek was losing ecological coherence, and control over its fate no longer lay in the hands of local residents. For Marc, this foretold of personal changes as sweeping as the erosion of community power. His place on Otter Creek was being challenged by forces beyond his control. A way of life that he cherished was becoming less tenable. And the ecological rhythms of the past were fading. The visions that had given solace to Levi's generation now threatened Marc and his neighbors.

THE NATURAL LINK

Making ecological sense of landscape visions is possible only when one recognizes that people and their visions have been and continue to be pervasive and unavoidable features of the natural world. Once that mental leap is made, the ecological building blocks of landscape visions—information, resilience, and diversity—fit smoothly into place. Before any such leap is attempted, though, a basic foundation must be laid. Ecology itself must be brought down to earth, to the valleys and hills of the many Otter Creeks that dot the western landscape.

As seen from the banks of Otter Creek, ecology is immediate and tangible. It concerns the web of relationships that define life in the settled bottomlands and the public uplands of southeastern Montana. In a more general sense, it focuses on the infinite and varied links that exist among and unite all living things and their environments. Whether on Otter Creek or on some more distant landscape, people, animals, plants, and the land are vital testaments to a complex and enduring interdependence.

Ecology on Otter Creek and elsewhere is also a perspective, a way of thinking about and viewing the course of natural and social events. It entails seeing the world in terms of multiple processes and patterns of relationships. It means that living creatures are more than isolated organisms whose functions and behaviors are reducible to physiology and genetics. They are the vital parts of living systems, and their ties to one another and to their physical surroundings establish the processes and the relationships that make life possible. The roles they play within their respective environments sustain those processes and perpetuate life's dynamic patterns.

By the same token, the environment is more than a neutral stage upon which living organisms act out their existence. It influences and, in turn, is influenced by the mosaic of life springing from its air, water, and earth. It provides shelter and sustenance for animals and plants. And those animals and plants reduce its barren rock to life-giving soil and enhance the vital properties of its air and water. Organisms and their environments are dynamically related. They form the living matrix that nurtures life and from which the cues that regulate life spring forth. It is impossible to appreciate or understand one without consideration of the other. This is the essence of the ecological perspective.

Applied to the western range and a century of livestock grazing, the ecological perspective allows us to evaluate the environmental consequences of public-land grazing from the standpoint of processes and relationships rather than of ethics or institutions. Public-land ranchers and agency managers can be viewed in the context of their shared environments rather than in the isolation of their stereotyped roles. Seen this way, the motives that have driven them to act become more understandable.

The land and a historical procession of laws and policies are the environmental setting for the story of the western range, and the interplay between that environment and the people who manage and use it is the story's substance. Interpreting the story is another matter, however. Merely identifying the environment and the human actors omits the strategic role of landscape visions in the ecology of the western range.

Landscape visions are the natural link between people and their environments. They are what people see, and wish for, in their surroundings. They may be images of fields planted in wheat or corn, well-planned urban parks populated with playing children, vast western landscapes dotted with cattle or antelope, or even wilderness areas where the human imprint is undetectable. Whatever their particulars, they are the environmental goals toward which people strive.

On the western range, these visions have given form to people's aspirations and forged the laws and institutions determining the place of men and women in nature. They have been the spectacles through which people have viewed the land and the causes that have moved them to action. Landscape visions, by virtue of these roles, are uniquely ecological in their implications. They are, above all else, vital to a proper understanding of how and why the western range has evolved as it has.

The ecology of landscape visions recognizes that people are a part of the natural world. A solitary individual or a congregation of people has no less a place in the scheme of things than a single flower or a grassy meadow. Both contribute to the making of a larger community, to an ecosystem built of people, creatures, and land. As small as a farmer's field or as encompassing as the living planet James Lovelock calls Gaia, ecosystems are the living expressions of earthly landscapes.

But ecosystems, however defined, are still fuzzy concepts, lacking discrete boundaries that otherwise might allow separation of smaller from larger units. The greater Yellowstone ecosystem, for example, is composed of Yellowstone Park and a number of other private and public lands that are themselves ecological units. Their individual boundaries are as artificial as the single boundary that unites them. As conventions of human thought, though, ecosystems do express a basic ecological truth. People, animals, plants, and physical environments combine into living wholes, greater than their individual parts and distinctive in the attributes that characterize them. Whatever their size, however they are delineated, ecosystems are the living space of land, water, and atmosphere where creatures are born, flourish, and die.

The public grazing lands of the western range are an ecosystem—or, put another way, a complex of ecosystems with a shared history of livestock grazing. The debate surrounding those lands invariably turns on the question of naturalness—of the place of humans in the natural scheme of things. A popular line of thought holds that people, at least modern, civilized people, have abdicated their naturalness in the quest of spiritual and secular religions.

Writers in the tradition of David Ehrenfield (*The Arrogance of Humanism*), Theodore Roszak (*Where the Wasteland Ends*), and Lynn White (*The Historical Roots of Our Ecological Crisis*) ascribe our modern alienation from nature to causes ranging from humanism to capitalism to Christianity. Driven by these arrogant "religions," they claim, people have pitted themselves against nature. They have ignored the interests of the world about them in pursuit of narrow self-interests. Their acts of rebellion have severed their ties to the natural world and exiled them from their proper place in nature. From Otter Creek to the most distant lands beyond its borders, humans are intruders to be feared, regulated, and held at bay for the sake of preserving the naturalness that remains.

In conventional wisdom, the capacity for self-interest accounts for most of humankind's divergence from the ways of nature. It persuades people to act for short-term personal enrichment, ignoring whatever long-term environmental costs their actions may incur. The argument has considerable merit, but its application solely to humans is unwarranted. All species are motivated by self-interest. Left to their own devices, without the normal checks and balances provided by nature (such as predation, disease, and limited food), most species would overpopulate and destroy their environments. The introduction of rabbits to Australia is a case in point. An explosion of rabbits, without any natural predator to control their numbers, played ecological havoc with the native plants and animals of that island continent. In nature, narrowly conceived self-interest is the rule, not the exception.

People, of course, pursue a deliberate self-interest rather than the involuntary self-interest of most other species. Stating the debate in these terms, the feature that isolates and distinguishes humans most from the natural world is the power to reason. Fortunately, the question of human reason and its relation to naturalness has more religious significance than it does ecological import. By whatever light one views the naturalness of humankind, the environmental record is unequivocal. For better or worse, natural or not, people have been an ecological force to be reckoned with since their appearance on earth. They have been and remain part of the natural world by virtue of their lasting imprint on the land. On Otter Creek and throughout the western range, that imprint is pervasive and undeniable.

Mankind's environmental presence predates by millennia the settlement of the western range. The wilderness Levi faced as his family traveled westward from Cape Cod was in many ways more tame than wild because of the activities of native people—activities that had dramatically changed the face of the North American continent. In the present-day lower Little Tennessee River valley, 10,000-year-old Indian settlements had tamed the wilderness, and their cultivation practices had displaced native species and made new habitat for plants and animals that could adapt to human disturbance.[1] In the Southwest, fuelwood gathering by local tribes had gradually depleted the woodlands of Chaco Canyon in present-day northern New Mexico. Topsoil erosion accelerated and water tables lowered, destroying the agricultural foundation upon which the tribes' civilization was based.[2]

Modern man has been no less a factor in the making of his environment. But the dramatic impact of today's people on nature should not be seen as an indictment of modernity nor as an absolution of early native societies. The differences between the two, the magnitude of ecological force that each has wielded in the shaping of its landscape, is accounted for by changing numbers of people and types of tools, not by contrasting attitudes regarding nature. And when the factors of culture, time, and opportunity are properly weighed, the environmental effects of early and modern people stand out in marked similarity. Both have profoundly and lastingly altered the land and the life it supports.

Clearly, if one could extrapolate the environmental effects of humans in the brief span they have dwelled on earth to geological time, the degree of their influence would certainly approach that of the geomorphic processes that have sculpted the earth's surface. Nature and the meaning of naturalness have evolved in conjunction with civilization. What is now defined as "nature" and "natural" bears the indelible mark of human culture. People and their landscape visions are inescapably part of the natural world and the processes and relationships that underlie its ecology.

The Sheldon National Wildlife Refuge in northwestern Nevada is a case in point. It was established early in the century, at a time when antelope were endangered and livestock dominated the western landscape. The purpose of the refuge was to re-create an island of naturalness, insulated from man's influence and set aside for the protection and enhancement of the last great herds of antelope. Domestic livestock grazing was excluded from much of the refuge by the late 1920s, and after 1976, when the U.S. Fish and Wildlife Service assumed control of the refuge, it was methodically phased out.

Today, antelope are common throughout the western United States, thriving in numbers far beyond the population of the Sheldon refuge. The refuge still exists, but it is no longer a credible monument to nature. Decades of continuous grazing by large herds of antelope have diminished the plant diversity, weakening the health of the herds and reducing the number of young born. Outside the refuge, where both cattle and antelope graze the same rangelands, plant diversity is measurably greater and antelope herds are healthier.[3]

The reason for the contrast is simple. Cattle and antelope graze different plants. Antelope prefer the broad-leaved plants, called forbs, which benefit from cattle selectively grazing grass. And the grass that the cattle graze is benefited by antelope eating other species. Eliminate cattle, and the landscape will shift from a mixture of grass and broad-leaved plants to a grassy monoculture. Remove antelope, and the opposite occurs.

If there is a moral to the story of the Sheldon refuge, it is this: Visions that would re-create nature and naturalness all too often create only what people *believe* naturalness to be. The Sheldon refuge, for all the good intentions that went into its making, was and remains an artificial environment, arbitrarily set off from the greater landscape that once supported historic antelope herds.[4] The vision of "naturalness" simply failed to achieve what it intended. Today, the spirit of the Sheldon refuge dwells on the lands outside the refuge, where people, the environment, and the antelope thrive.

The lesson of the Sheldon refuge is unmistakenly written on the landscapes of the Old World. In Europe, Africa, and Asia, the pervasive presence of people in nature has spurred the ecological perspective, driven the development of a landscape ecology. That ecology now focuses on the dynamic interplay between humans and their environment. It recognizes that people and nature do not exist apart and that environmental well-being is as much a factor of culture as it is of biology. Mankind and nature are accepted as inseparably entwined in the myriad processes and relationships that sustain life.

Only in the New World is the relation of people to nature viewed dif-

43

ferently—obscured by the appearance of remnant islands mistakenly believed to be natural, wild, and free of the effects of people. Only in the New World is the ecological import of humans ignored or combatted. And on the western range, those mistaken perspectives have elevated the debate of nature and naturalness to an unnatural level.

For too long, the issue of the western range has turned on the false question of naturalness. Countless articles and books have been written on the unnatural effects of livestock grazing on western public lands and on the decline of the western range from some preconceived natural state. But what matters most is understanding the conditions under which human action has sustained or destroyed the ecosystems people depend on for survival. To deal with this question, one must return to basics—to landscape visions, the natural link between people and their environment.

ECOLOGY OF VISIONS

Information, resilience, and diversity are the principles, as well as the features, that determine the viability of ecological systems. The interplay between these principles and landscape visions is the ecological key to the western range. It explains the essential difference between visions of tolerance and visions of intolerance. And it answers the most pressing ecological question of all: What is the quality of landscape visions that promotes or diminishes the capacity and willingness of people to act in harmony with nature?

A proper start to clarifying the ecology of visions begins with two basic observations. First, landscape visions are simply one part of the world of nature and people. They neither dominate nor are dominated by the other elements of ecological systems. And though visions are matters of human hope, desire, and belief, they cannot escape for long the limitations and consequences of nature. They are as dependent on the processes and relationships of ecological systems as is any other part of a living landscape. Second, the world of nature and people has survival as its primary goal—survival not only of the many creatures that live within that world but also of the relationships and processes that enliven it. Landscape visions are one of the factors that affect survival and influence the quality and quantity of life.

Put into the context of Otter Creek, visions can aspire only to what the environmental potential of the land will allow. Ranching was one of the few practical alternatives available to settlers in 1890. And the world of Otter Creek, both before and after the opening of the Circle Bar, followed a narrow course attuned to the biological urge for survival. The land and the people, buffeted by continuous change, adapted as well as they could. Yet in the brief span of a hundred years, the quality and quantity of life on Otter Creek suffered, as they did elsewhere on the western range. Landscape visions bear much of the responsibility.

Seen from the microcosm of Otter Creek, visions appear more concrete and the ecological principles behind them become more clear. People and their visions, the land, and wild and domestic creatures are inescapably linked to basic ecological processes—processes without which there would be no life. On Otter Creek, those processes commence with the first light of day. Sunlight is the energy source, the lifeblood, of all earthly ecosystems. Although 99 percent of sunlight reaching the earth goes unused, the 1 percent that is absorbed by plants initiates and sustains the amazing process called life. From plants to grazing animals to meat-eaters, the energy of the sun moves by a circuitous route through the food chain. At each step it animates matter, though at the cost of its own dissipation. Eighty to 95 percent is lost, dispersed into space in the unusable form of heat, contributing, however minutely, to the entropy of the universe.

Entropy is the cost that ecological systems—or, more correctly, the creatures residing within them—pay to maintain themselves and their environments. They consume the neatly packaged energy of light and food and degrade it in the process of life to the random and inaccessible energy of heat. Energy flows down a one-way path, becoming less usable at each step of the way. Yet with every rising of the morning sun, new energy is added and absorbed to replace the energy lost to entropy. Only in this way is the tendency of living systems toward disorder forestalled and the triumph of maximum entropy—death—averted.

On Otter Creek, as elsewhere, life persists at the expense of energy and at the cost of entropy. Each living link in the food chain relies on the links below and above for sustenance and regulation. A wet year brings a good crop of plants to the valley and uplands. Ample food fortifies the health of a mule deer herd. Fertility increases, more fawns are born, and the herd expands. Not all years are wet, however. A stretch of dry years quickly exhausts the soil's moisture and diminishes the productivity of the land. An expanded deer herd, the legacy of more bountiful years, then faces the harsh reality of a dwindling food supply. The landscape bears the full brunt of the consequences that follow, as its plants are devastated by over-grazing and the herd it once sustained is catapulted into mass starvation.

Fortunately, boom and bust is the exception, not the rule, for the deer on Otter Creek. An expanding population of deer in good times elicits forces that constrain the growth of the herd and diminish the cataclysmic prospects of drought. More deer means more opportunities for coyotes and hunters to hold the deer population in check and to maintain its balance with the land during years of abundance and scarcity. Energy is expended and entropy increased, of course, but life on Otter Creek marches onward with barely the loss of a stride and hardly a sign of change.

Yet break any link of the chain, and the flow of energy would be disrupted, altering the relationship between the deer, the land, and other creatures. The energy that informs and instructs the herd, that nurtures it and maintains its balance within the context of its environment, would dissipate to entropy long before its cues could affect the herd's behavior. The ecological health of Otter Creek would weaken and its chances of survival diminish.

Energy—whether in the form of sunlight, plants, animal flesh, or genetic material—is nothing more than information. At each link in the food chain, energy becomes living matter, and living matter becomes the physical cue that orchestrates the processes of life. Organisms, and the ecological systems that support them, succeed and thrive to the degree that they can acquire energy and use the information it embodies efficiently, with minimum loss to entropy. Abundant information, unfettered in its flow between organisms and their environment, is crucial to life and essential to the functioning of ecological systems.

Adding people and their visions to the picture changes nothing. A healthy and sustainable landscape is still one where all living members best use the energy of the sun—or, for that matter, the energy and information that come in the cycling of nutrients, the falling of rain, the texture of soil, and the lessons of the land. Landscape visions that promote and enhance the transfer of information between people and their environments are ecologically beneficial. Those that do not are ecologically harmful, contributing not to the efficient use of energy and information but to entropy.

The ranchers along Otter Creek who have prospered are those whose visions have made them most receptive to the lessons of the land. They have used the landscape wisely and stewarded its resources with the greatest economy. They have listened to the messages of dry years and parched rangelands, removed their stock from the stressed grass, and shielded their soil from abuse. During more normal years, they have attended to the growth of their grass, monitored its use, and provided sufficient rest for its recovery from grazing. And always, prudent ranchers have watched the health of their stock, maintaining sufficient flexibility to alter their grazing regime to ensure the well-being of domestic animals. At every point, prosperous ranchers are attuned to the information that flows from the soil, grass, and creatures of Otter Creek.

Energy as information is indispensable. From the minuscule world of genetics and gene flows to the endless variety of animal and plant life, its message ensures the continuity of life. It is also the distinguishing mark of civilization. Solar energy, refined, concentrated, and transformed by the human mind into art, culture, science, and technology, is a source of information as vital to the ecology of nature as it is to the economy of human societies. Information, in whatever form it assumes, is the primary tool by which ecological systems self-regulate, adapt, and survive.

The links that bind the people, creatures, and land of Otter Creek into a coherent ecological community are the arteries of communication. A year's growth of grass, the numbers of animals grazing the grass, and the human technology affecting both are among the innumerable bits of information that flow along the links and enable the residents of Otter Creek to survive. They provide, in part, the checks and balances that maintain order and stability in nature and society. Without adequate information and the control it brings, the biological and social world of Otter Creek would shatter. Landscape visions would aspire to goals beyond nature's constraints, asking of the environment more than it could give. And the wild and domestic animals of Otter Creek would increase unchecked, the fescue grasslands would be overgrazed, and the soil would wash or blow away.

Information allows for the long-term stability and continuity of Otter Creek and the ecosystems that span the western range. It offers resilience—the ability of living systems to weather the flux and evolution of their environments without suffering irreparable harm or undergoing some catastrophic change. Seen from the banks of Otter Creek, resilience is the quality that empowers the communities of a landscape to maintain themselves and their environment in relative harmony and constancy.

Resilience is nothing more than responsiveness to new information. It is the trait that allows ecological systems and their living members to adapt to new conditions and to maintain a proper balance between the demands of life and the constraints of the land. It is the exercise of flexibility in the face of an ever-changing environment—a purposeful shifting of direction and behavior in accordance with the cues of the outside world.

The more resilient or flexible an ecological system becomes, the greater is the probability of its sustained survival. When people and their institutions are considered, resilience and flexibility become even more critical. The human element can facilitate or complicate the processes of nature. Landscape visions that allow and encourage people to react wisely and promptly to the demands of their environment contribute to survival. Visions that do otherwise impede the well-being of ecological systems. Survival, in turn, is the benchmark for gauging the durability of any system and assessing its integrity as a self-correcting, living unit.

The informational properties of resilience and flexibility are enhanced by diversity: the numbers of species, their genetic variability, and the distribution of the landscapes they occupy. Diversity on Otter Creek and throughout the western range can be envisioned as an insurance policy of sorts. A wide variety of edible plants, for example, insulates grazing animals from the potential catastrophe that might occur if a single, dominant forage species were lost to climatic stress or disease. Numerous predators, one of which is humans, can also enhance the stability of a landscape by providing multiple assurances that numbers of grazing animals are kept in balance with what the land can grow. Genetic diversity in both plants and animals is an additional factor reducing the risks that attend life. Subtle variations in gene pools may well determine whether a species will thrive or perish in the face of an ever-changing environment. And diversity of landscapes ensures adequate living space for wildlife should fire or human settlement change the face of the land.[5]

No less important to ecosystems on the western range is the diversity that exists among people. A wide variety of management approaches makes it more likely that superior land practices will be discovered and put into operation. Many landscape visions, all different and independent of one another, encourages the proliferation of such management options. Such diversity promotes the ecological health of the land. The spring pastures pushed by Marc Stevens and his neighbors are elements of management diversity that, if they work as envisioned, will benefit the ecosystem of Otter Creek. Conversely, diverse grazing strategies also help ensure that inferior management practices will be limited in environmental effect and will be relatively short-lived. Bad land management is simply unsustainable—at least without the benefit of outside subsidies or interventions.

Applied to other arenas of nature and human society, the benefits of preserving or promoting diversity are even more pronounced. Life for its own sake is honored. The global environment is protected. Climate is stabilized, and evolutionary processes are left unimpeded. From the perspective of mankind, culture is enhanced, standards of living are augmented, and choices and opportunities for individuals are broadened. Unfortunately, diversity is too often taken to be the sacred symbol of life's intended purpose. Freed of that mystique, diversity is but the steward of energy and the handmaiden of information. It is neither magical nor mystical; it is merely a means by which life attains its ultimate goal: survival.

Landscape visions have the potential to enhance diversity or to diminish it through the unfortunate propensity of laws and institutions to simplify that which is inherently complex. On the western range, diversity has been crucial to the health of the land. On the Kaibab Plateau in northern Arizona, for example, deer populations had been historically regulated by wolves, coyotes, and cougars. Federal and state trappers—responding to the wishes (and visions) of hunters and ranchers—eliminated those predators in the early twentieth century, grossly simplifying the landscape and allowing deer to overpopulate the area. The problem was worsened by the removal of cattle and sheep, the only species that seriously competed with deer for forage and browse. The deer rapidly outgrew the food supply of the plateau. Denuded hillsides and starving does and fawns became common sights in an ecosystem destabilized by an imprudent assault on its biological diversity.[6]

Changes in diversity on the western range have also come about by more indirect routes. For nearly fifty years, the Forest Service religiously pursued a policy of fire suppression in the West. During those years, agency employees, backed by considerable in-house research, strove to change the Forest Service's entrenched fear of fire. Despite vigorous opposition from within the agency and scientific evidence that supported the role of fire, the Forest Service stuck to its official position. It dismissed all dissent and covered up scientific information that would have contradicted—and corrected—its official policy. It spent enormous sums of money pursuing and publicly supporting a fire doctrine that many of its administrators knew to be false. Over a period of five decades, the Forest Service elevated fire protection from a national policy to a public symbol devoid of all content except emotion.[7]

The biological effects of half a century of fire control are now all too apparent. National forestlands have been simplified. Their diversity has diminished as trees have encroached upon and filled in former savannah-like rangelands. Wildlife habitat has been lost, and a multitude of plant species has been displaced. Wilderness areas have suffered biological deterioration and diminishing diversity. The policy of fire suppression, of course, was not intended to reduce biological diversity. That came as an unexpected consequence of an inflexible and nonresponsive command structure. For Ashley Schiff, author of *Fire and Water: Scientific Heresy in the Forest Service*, the Forest Service's rigidity left no doubt that the agency was monolithic in ideology if not always in operational structure.[8] Indeed, the success of the Forest Service in quelling discourse among its scientists and suppressing information within its ranks foreshadowed the circumstances and events that would narrow and diminish diversity on the grazing lands committed to its stewardship.

LANDSCAPE VISIONS ON THE WESTERN RANGE

From the Kaibab Plateau to fire-free forests to public grazing lands, landscape visions have left their mark on the western range. In truth, only a handful of the many visions that Americans have entertained have been of environmental consequence in the ecology of western landscapes. They are the visions that have informed and set the public-land policies of the United States since the opening of the western frontier. They are the intolerant visions—intolerant not because they lacked a democratic base but because they set the course of a landed empire. In so doing, they precluded the environmental possibility and the ecological potential of visions.

Intolerant visions have worked their ecological power through the actions of individuals and the force of human law and institutions. They have set the constraints that have channeled and directed the activities of ranchers and land managers. Those constraints have defined the relation of people to grazing lands and determined the ways in which information, resilience, and diversity have been expressed in the ecosystems of the western range. The successes and failures that have accompanied more than a century of public-land grazing are attributable to the ecological workings of landscape visions.

Looking down from the lofty perch of generalities to the valley and hills of Otter Creek, the lessons of that small community echo across the western range, testimony to the pervasiveness of landscape visions. The well-intentioned visions that law and policy have brought to the public rangelands stand out in sharp relief against the arid landscape. Their consequences, so distinct from the hopes and aspirations of those who envisioned them, dominate the deserts, plains, and mountains.

Over the span of more than a century, three visions—the agrarian vision, the progressive vision, and the environmental vision—brought a degree of uniformity to the diverse landscapes of the western range. The spontaneity and economy by which nature had ordered herself was lost. Information was squandered and compromised by administrators who plan and direct the patterns of life according to a unified ideology. The resilience and flexibility of the land were at the mercy of organizations whose boundaries exceed those of the ecosystems they regulate. And diversity gave way to the political reality of a uniform vision.

We need to know how those three landscape visions influenced people's behavior toward the western environment and how institutions encouraged or discouraged that behavior. Once the answers to those questions are known, a more coherent analysis of the western range will be possible. And from that analysis will emerge the first glimmerings of a new vision for the western range—one attuned to the needs and requirements of landscapes where men and women dwell alongside, not apart from, the land and its many living parts.

II

The Landscape Visions

CHAPTER FOUR

Jefferson's Legacy

*T*he train ride from Montana to Washington, DC, offered Levi Howes a study in contrasts.[1] The year was 1916, and he was forty-four years old. Looking through the train window, Levi remembered the long journey from Cape Cod to Ashland and his first years in Montana. He had been so much younger then, full of expectations for what a new land might offer. His optimism and exuberance had made the journey exciting and adventuresome and the early Montana years carefree. But Levi had matured quickly. The demands and duties of frontier ranching left precious little time for the usual activities of boyhood.

Thirty-six years of Montana blizzards and droughts had tried and tested Levi and found him loyal to the land. His trip to Washington was a tribute to that loyalty. News had reached Otter Creek that the government was considering abandoning the Custer National Forest and reopening it to homesteading. Levi had no objections to homesteaders; he and his family were among their ranks. But to reopen the land to settlers now would be devastating to the valley ranchers and folly for new homesteaders, who would find nothing except disappointment in the hills above Otter Creek. Already, the rangelands were filled to capacity with cattle. There was simply no place for new residents to settle, set up operations, and graze cattle—at least not without harming the land.

Just after the turn of the century, large outfits, like the Spear, Three Circle, and OW cattle companies, had tried to take over the public rangelands of Otter Creek. Their strategy, Levi later wrote, was "to monopolize the ranges, and, by overcrowding, to starve out the small holders and not to recognize the rights of these small cattlemen."² But not all of the problems had come from powerful stockmen. Settlers had poured into the valleys and hills near Otter Creek and the Tongue River. Demands on the public range grew beyond the capacity of the land to give, and conflicts escalated between established ranching families and new settlers.

Levi was determined that the lands of the Circle Bar would not fall victim to the open range. He knew that if his leased forestlands were opened to settlers, the Circle Bar would perish. Blocked by law from homesteading any more lands himself, his fate would be to watch helplessly as his grazing lands were subdivided into 640-acre parcels—far too small to support a family in the arid environment of southeastern Montana.

In earlier years, the ranchers of Ashland and Otter Creek had dealt with the open range on their own terms. An August 23, 1884, a notice in the Yellowstone Journal, *signed by Levi's father and a dozen other ranchers, gave warning that the ranges surrounding Otter Creek were "stocked with all the cattle that such ranges will possibly bear" and that potential intruders should look elsewhere for grazing lands.³ Later, Levi and several neighbors fenced off portions of the public range to protect pastures from overgrazing. But fencing was illegal, and Levi and his friends were forced to take their fences down.*

Now Levi could do little but argue the merits of his case. Thirty-six years of Montana ranching had convinced him that the problems of the public range went much further than occasional skirmishes over grazing rights. The roots of the problems were anchored deep in the Montana soil, hopelessly enmeshed in the politics of control. The question he would have to address in Washington was the same one he and his father had struggled to answer since their first days at Otter Creek: Who would control the land? If the virtues of caring and tenacity meant anything, he was certain of the answer.

CHAOS ON THE OPEN RANGE

Russell B. Harrison, secretary of the Montana Stockgrowers Association and son of president-to-be Benjamin Harrison, had the unpleasant task of reporting the state of the livestock industry to his fellow ranchers in 1888. First, he noted, unprecedented drought in the spring and summer of 1887 had "caused a great shortness of food and [made] the cattle poor in flesh for the market and the winter." Second, "the low price of beef that ruled in Chicago during the fall, [shrunk] our receipts materially." Third, "the very severe winter which has just passed, [brought] general loss, more or less severe, depending on circumstances, to every member of the association and, in fact, to every stockman in the northwest." Harrison reflected, in conclusion, that "a drouth without parallel, a market without a bottom, and a winter, the severest ever known in Montana, formed a combination, testing the usefulness of our association on proving its solidity."[4]

Harrison's matter-of-fact report was one of many early warning signs that something was wrong on the western range. A landscape vision, anchored in Jeffersonian agrarianism and built on a firm democratic foundation, was not creating a virtuous republic of sturdy, self-sufficient yeoman farmers. In place of the arcadian bliss promised by abundant western lands, the simultaneous scourges of economic depression, massive starvation of livestock, and crumbling cattle empires were taking their toll on the newly settled western range.

Two record-breaking cold and snowy winters bracketed by spring and summer seasons of extreme drought ensured that the years 1885–1887 would be unforgettable in the history of the western range. Those years revealed what John Wesley Powell had discovered in his scientific expedition to the arid West. They confirmed the severity and harshness of an unforgiving climate. And they foreshadowed what would become increasingly apparent as the century approached its end. The western range, a wilderness only a quarter-century earlier, was grossly overstocked with cattle, sheep, and horses.

Among the factors accounting for the overstocking of the western range, one stands out: The end of the Civil War—the event that heralded the opening of western lands and beef-hungry eastern markets—stirred the imaginations of American and English entrepreneurs. Men like John S. Chisum of New Mexico and cow outfits like the Swan Land and Cattle Company of Wyoming populated the arid West with enormous herds of cattle. They understood the economic bonanza that could be reaped from the abundant grass of the open western range. In 1860, for example, no cattle were recorded in the territories of Colorado, Wyoming, or Montana. Twenty years later, the U.S. census listed 1.8 million head of cattle in those same territories.[5] As one newspaper editor wrote, "Cotton was once crowned king, but grass is now."[6]

When the blizzards and drought came in 1885, the western range was stocked beyond capacity. One ranch in Idaho supported more than one hundred seventy-five thousand cattle and branded more than thirty-eight thousand calves in the spring of 1885. In 1891, the same ranch branded only sixty calves on a range that was "seared to the ground."[7] In Arizona, one rancher reported that "west of Camp Verde one could always see dead cattle and the range was bare as slide rock."[8] Even the most substantial operations were not immune. The impressive Niobrara Cattle Company of Nebraska lost more than 75 percent of its livestock by 1887 and plummeted into debt and bankruptcy. Among smaller outfits, the effects of blizzards and drought were often as severe. As Levi Howes recorded in his diary, the winters of 1886 and 1887 reduced most herds along Otter Creek and the Tongue River by 70 percent or more.

Nature had delivered the verdict on the overstocking of the western range. The cattle empire of quick profits and expansive holdings was gone forever. Yet some good came from the experience. The cattlemen who had weathered the blizzards and drought learned that the health of the grass, the vagaries of the seasons, and the harsh reality of an arid landscape would have to be reckoned with in making future decisions. Presumably that would be easier, now that the numbers of livestock and ranches were more in keeping with the carrying capacity of the land. And prospects for outfits like Levi Howes's Circle Bar would be more promising than ever, now that the western range had been cleansed of opportunistic and short-sighted livestock ventures.

For the stockmen who remained, judicious grazing of the land would have maintained the range through good and bad years had it not been for two factors beyond their control: the infusion of massive sheep herds onto already stocked rangelands and the arrival of more homesteaders. From 1880 to 1900, the states and territories of Oregon, Idaho, Montana, Wyoming, and Colorado experienced a virtual explosion in the sheep population. Figures for 1884, for example, indicate that Wyoming had relatively few sheep. Yet by 1891, the numbers of sheep had grown to over one million, and by 1900, more than five million sheep were grazing the Wyoming range.[9] Similar trends took place in other western states once dominated by cattle. Montana's sheep population went from an estimated two hundred sixty thousand in 1881 to over six million in 1900.[10]

During the same period, settlers arrived in ever-increasing numbers to homestead productive bottomlands where water was available for crop production. But the climate and the meager size of their homesteads precluded their making a living by farming, so they turned to raising small herds of cattle and grazing them on unclaimed public lands. But the fact that they were unclaimed did not mean that the western public lands were unused. Older, established livestock operations already depended on public-land forage to supplement what their small private holdings could produce. Once again, the western range was overstocked, and it was becoming more crowded with each passing year. The stage was set for another calamity, this one initiated solely by people.

Chaos erupted on the western range as established cattlemen collided with sheepmen and as both collided with the small homesteaders. Frontier violence, epitomized in the bloody episodes of Wyoming's Johnson County War and New Mexico's Lincoln County War, flared up across the West as each group sought to control and graze the open range to the exclusion of the others. Newcomers seeking public grass met staunch resistance from traditional range users, who considered the range theirs by custom if not by law. Frequently, violent confrontations occurred when nomadic sheep herds intruded on public ranges where cattle grazed. Along the Tongue River in southeastern Montana, an entire band of sheep was clubbed to death on December 28, 1900, when a herder brought his animals onto ranges that were fully stocked with cattle.[11]

Similar confrontations and outbreaks of violence took place in every western state and territory. Congressman Edward T. Taylor of Colorado, author of the 1934 Taylor Grazing Act, which ended once and for all open range conditions on public domain lands, characterized the chaos as a "free-for-all and general grab-and-hold-if-you-can policy." For too long, he lamented, "a kind of guerrilla warfare [has been] going on between and among the sheepmen and cattlemen with bitterness, strife, ill-will, and more or less litigation, and some sad killings."[12]

Overgrazing reached epidemic proportions by the early 1900s. Ranchers were powerless to protect what was not theirs. Even if they had wanted to (and many of them did), they could no longer graze their rangelands conservatively. Most of the rangelands they used were public, open to all citizens until they were homesteaded.

Bard Heaton, a rancher in Alton, Utah, herded sheep as a boy on what is now known as the Arizona Strip—a narrow band of BLM grazing land lying north of the Grand Canyon and west of the Colorado River. A number of ranchers on the strip had protected their rangelands from interlopers by grazing the grass so low that others could not use it.[13] A 1916 Department of Agriculture study reported similar occurrences elsewhere on the western range. "The only protection a stockman has," the study concluded, "is to keep his range eaten to the ground, and the only assurance that he will be able to secure the forage crop any one year is to graze it off before someone else does."[14] Albert F. Potter, first director of the Forest Service's Grazing Section, had observed much the same practice in Arizona:

> Flocks passed each other on the trails, one rushing in to secure what the other had just abandoned as worthless, feed was deliberately wasted to prevent its utilization by others, the ranges were occupied before the snow had left them. Transient sheepmen roamed the country robbing the resident stockmen of forage that was justly theirs. . . . [15] [As a result], class was arrayed against class—the cowman against the sheepman, the big owner against the little one—and might ruled more often than right.[16]

As one historian of public-land grazing phrased the problem, "nothing riled a cattleman any more than to try and save feed for later use, only to find from one to twenty bands of sheep on it, the range eaten bare and clean."[17] Clayton Atkins, a rancher on the Arizona Strip, had faced such a predicament as a young man on his father's cattle ranch, where forty separate herds of sheep wintered on the desert range that his family depended on for summer feed.[18]

Lloyd Sorenson, a prominent Nevada cattleman in the 1960s and 1970s, began his career as one of the many sheepherders who overstocked the strip rangelands that Atkins and other Arizona ranchers used for summer forage. The grass was on open, public range, belonging to no one, and Lloyd knew that if his sheep did not graze the last blade of grass, some other band of sheep would. He was eventually expelled from the Arizona Strip by established stockmen seeking to protect their public grazing lands.[19] But such protective measures did not alter the fact that western public rangelands had once again become dangerously overstocked. And they remained so until open range conditions were ended on forestlands in 1891 and on public domain lands in 1934.[20]

The events that made the history of the Arizona Strip occurred throughout the western range. A 1936 report by the Forest Service concluded that the western range "has been depleted no less than 52 percent from its virgin condition . . . [meaning] that a range once capable of supporting 22.5

million animal units can now carry only 10.8 million."[21] Although the precision of the Forest Service's figures is questionable, the relative magnitude of the percentage fits nicely with yet another observation by Albert Potter on the state of the western range:

> The grazing lands were stocked far beyond their capacity; vegetation was cropped by hungry animals before it had opportunity to reproduce; valuable forage plants gave way to worthless weeds and the productive capacity of the lands rapidly diminished. . . . [22] [Accessible forest rangelands] were denuded of their vegetative cover, forest reproduction was damaged or destroyed, the slopes were seamed with deep erosion gullies, and the water-conserving power of the drainage basins became seriously impaired.[23]

Overgrazing was rampant throughout the western range, but it continued longest on public domain lands—the lands that would later be entrusted to the BLM. Open range conditions on national forest lands had been dealt with by the creation of forest reserves in 1891 and the creation of the Forest Service in 1905. But the majority of the public's western range remained open and subject to the abuses that would mark its history and landscape for decades to come.

A QUESTION OF THE COMMONS

The tragedy of the commons, as described by Garrett Hardin,[24] is the environmental plague that infests and ravages common, or unowned, lands and resources. It begins when (1) the carrying capacity of an environment is exceeded and (2) a disparity arises between the private and social costs of exploiting an environment's resources. In the first instance, people's demands on common resources outpace the ability of the environment to supply them on a continued basis. This condition explains how and why resources are overused and exhausted. In the second, the benefits of exploiting a common resource accrue almost entirely to a handful of individuals, while the costs of exploitation fall unevenly on all of society. This condition motivates small numbers of people to exploit their environment.

Put into the context of livestock grazing, common lands under the proper preconditions "lock" each man "into a system that compels him to increase his herd without limit—in a world that is limited." "Ruin," Hardin writes, "is the destination toward which all men rush."[25] Graziers, locked into a system of common pasturelands, do what is in their rational self-interest. They exploit the land to the point of environmental destruction to obtain, before others can, forage to feed their animals. It matters not that every person's actions contribute to the overgrazing of the resource. What counts is that the individual receive as large a share as possible.

The tragedy of the commons, in Hardin's view, continues with full ferocity on public grazing lands. "Even at this late date," he contends, "cattlemen leasing national land on the western ranges demonstrate no more than an ambivalent understanding, in constantly pressuring federal authorities to increase the head count to the point where overgrazing produces erosion and weed-dominance."[26] They are, by Hardin's way of thinking, rational players in the tragedy of the commons, seeking to maximize their share of public forage at whatever cost it may exact from the land and society.

Both the ethical argument and the institutional argument rely heavily on Hardin's model to explain the fate of the western range. Proponents of the ethical approach find in the tragedy of the commons a vindication of long-held beliefs regarding the environmental ethics of public-land ranchers. The commons of the western range, writes legal historian George Coggins, was ravaged by the unconstrained greed of western stockmen seeking to appropriate vast public resources for private benefit. Between the efforts of ranchers to "monopolize use of the public lands" and attempts of homesteaders, nomadic herders, federal bureaucrats, and courts to "keep the public lands open," the environmental fate of the western range was sealed.[27]

A different twist is given to the tragedy of the commons from the institutional perspective. John Baden, founder and proponent of the new resource economics, uses Hardin's model to identify the institutional failing that culminated in the environmental decline of the western range. The first settlers to homestead the federal range found ample grass to feed their livestock, but as more settlers arrived, livestock numbers on the open range rapidly exceeded the land's carrying capacity. The overgrazing of the public rangelands was imminent, Baden writes, because

no property rights to this land were legally defined. Therefore, the benefit of adding animals to the range was received by the individual stockman while the cost was dispersed among all users. In this common property situation if the benefits of the stockman of adding one cow or sheep outweighed **his** costs, then additional animals will continue to be added. Thus, serious overgrazing resulted.[28]

Both the ethical and the institutional argument are correct when they equate the overgrazing of the western range with the expected environmental outcome of the classic tragedy of the commons. Certainly, what had happened on the English commons a century earlier is not substantially different from what occurred on the western range—at least in terms of results. Both were common properties; and despite their altogether different environments, they suffered the same malady of extensive overgrazing. Similar tragedies of the commons continue to this day, most conspicuously on desert grazing lands lying within the Sahelian zone of North Africa. But the events and outcomes of the first half-century of grazing on the western range cannot be fully understood by yielding to the intellectual temptation of Hardin's compelling essay. Beyond the obvious similarities of the model and the reality, the fact remains that conditions on the western range created a most uncommon commons.

Stockmen were not, as Hardin argues, "locked into a system" that compelled them to increase their herds without limits. At every step of the way, public-land ranchers strove to overcome the dilemma of the commons that made living and working on the western range so difficult. And the overgrazing they committed, with the possible exception of the brief years before the calamity of 1885–1887, reflected motivations and conditions other than Hardin's calculating rationalism or Coggins's scheming greed.

Establishment of formal property rights to all of the western range, as Baden implies, would have undoubtedly altered, for the better, the natural history of the land. But the institutional argument misses the most crucial point by focusing exclusively on the mechanism of private property ownership and pinpointing its absence as the causal factor in the environmental decline of public grazing lands. The root problem of the western range is traceable to another, more pernicious, source.

The lack of property rights and the questionable ethics of western stockmen were nothing more than symptoms—symptoms of the common denominator of landscape visions. One landscape vision, that of Jeffersonian agrarianism, laid the foundation and created the conditions for what would appear to later generations as a classic case of the tragedy of the commons. But what happened on the western range between 1885 and 1934 was more than the inexorable workings of Hardin's commons; it was the tragic unfolding of the environmental consequences of a single, intolerant vision.

ORIGINS OF THE AGRARIAN VISION

Levi Howes's fateful journey to Washington, DC in 1916 made sense, but it was a response to events that earlier generations would not have understood. To Americans enthralled by the promise of newfound independence or swept away in the democratic enthusiasm of the antebellum era, Levi's mission to keep the public lands of Otter Creek closed to homesteading would have seemed strange indeed. The message he brought to Congress would have been decried as undemocratic, and his motives would have been viewed with great suspicion.

What Levi was proposing was a denial of Jeffersonian democracy and a refutation of the Jacksonian Age of the Common Man. The western lands acquired by Thomas Jefferson and his presidential successors belonged to the people; they symbolized the democratic spirit of a young nation and represented the foundation upon which a unified people would prosper in equality. But Levi's purpose ran counter to the promise of the nation's first landscape vision. It would deny the hopes and aspirations fired by Jefferson's agrarian vision and held ever so tenaciously by Americans seeking the arcadian world of the nation's preeminent founder.

Jefferson's vision, at least as it appeared in his writings, was that of a virtuous and democratic republic—one in which the affairs of society were to be determined by the power of reason rather than the might of the sword. Such benign power, Jefferson believed, was best exercised by a "natural aristocracy." Members of that aristocracy, however, were not necessarily to be found among the privileged or highly educated classes. "State a moral case," Jefferson wrote, "to a ploughman and a professor. The former will decide it as well, and often better than the latter, because he has not been led astray by artificial rules."[29] His natural aristocracy— those who would continue what the American Revolution had begun— would be found among the cultivators of the earth.

"Cultivators of the earth," he wrote, "are the most valuable citizens" and the "most precious part of the state." "They are," he added, "the most vigorous, the most independent, the most virtuous, and they are tied to their country, and wedded to its liberty and interests, by the most lasting bonds."[30] Civic virtues, however, were not the only attributes that Jefferson ascribed to American farmers. They alone enjoyed and exercised the proper balance between mind and body. Their labors were in harmony with the designs of the Creator, and their works were the inspiration and sustenance of the moral sense. They would be the temporal depository of the "sacred fire" of truth and republican virtue. Their society would be "as a Citty upon a Hill"—not as designed by John Winthrop but as fashioned by human reason from the malleable soil of the new world.

Jefferson's yeoman farmers were the building blocks of what J. Hector St. John de Crèvecoeur described in *Letters from an American Farmer* as the most perfect society. "That of a farmer," Crèvecoeur wrote, "is the only appellation of the rural inhabitants of our country. . . . We have no princes, for whom we toil, starve, and bleed: we are the most perfect society now existing in the world."[31] Jefferson, an admirer of Crèvecoeur, was certain that the most perfect society would find fertile soil in the American heartland. A generous Creator had endowed the young nation with sufficient lands "to employ an infinite number of people in their cultivation."[32] This, he believed, was what distinguished the United States from the corrupt and vice-ridden nations of Europe.

It was with these convictions in mind that Jefferson set the course of federal-land policy. His Northwest Ordinance established the framework for westward expansion, opening the trans-Allegheny country to settlement and defining the ground rules by which public lands would be surveyed, conveyed to private ownership, and ultimately granted statehood. In 1803, Jefferson doubled the nation's land area with the purchase of the Louisiana Territory from France, justifying the transaction in part because it served the agricultural needs of an expanding republican society. A nation in which each family owned a plot of land—large enough to subsist on but not so large as to give the landowner undue power or influence—would, he hoped, remain virtuous and free.

Yet there was much that Jefferson neither understood nor anticipated as he took the fateful step to annex the Louisiana Territory. Beyond the western boundary of the Louisiana Purchase lay an equally immense territory, one fated to be consumed by an expanding nation. Jefferson knew of those lands, but he had little idea of how dissimilar they were from the world he envisioned. And he had no way of knowing the lasting imprint his agrarian ideal would leave on those landscapes.

VISION, POLICY, AND ENVIRONMENTAL HARM

Bringing the agrarian vision to western lands required more than the idealism of Thomas Jefferson and an enthusiastic popular following. It also required a policy of land disposal. In no uncertain terms, Jefferson opposed the sale of public lands as the principal means of their disposal. "Whenever there are in any country uncultivated lands and unemployed poor," he observed, "it is clear that the laws of property have been so far extended as to violate natural rights."[33] Jefferson's democratic and Lockean sentiments, however, did not immediately translate into a federal policy of free lands. Beginning with the Land Ordinance Act of 1785 and continuing to the start of the Civil War, federal-land policies were designed to raise revenues for the nation's treasury. Not surprisingly, those policies gave only nominal support to the goals and objectives of agrarianism. Jefferson's vision, too radical for a nation already at odds with tradition, awaited the democratic upheaval that would eventually thrust it upon the nation's conscience.

Land speculation and the amassing of huge tracts of land by unscrupulous companies revived the spirit of Jeffersonian agrarianism in the 1830s. The National Land Reform movement declared that every citizen had a right to a share of the nation's lands. Small homesteaders, not speculators or land capitalists, were the proper focus of federal-land policy. Horace Greeley added an additional wrinkle to the reform argument. He envisioned the public lands as a safety valve for unemployment and industrial discontent in the East. "Wages in many sections," he wrote, "are falling while rents and food grow dearer, and employment becomes more and more scanty and precarious." To sell public land in such troubled times was clearly a sin, Greeley argued. Americans, he believed, had a natural right to lands not already in use. Had not the time come, he asked, "when every free citizen shall have his own home if he will?"[34]

Support for land reform expanded in the 1840s and 1850s as Americans came to see landownership as the distinguishing mark between free and enslaved people. Free-Soilers and then Republicans inherited the mantle of agrarian reform and enthusiastically resurrected Jefferson's landscape vision. Republican victory in 1860 and the secession of southern states brought the vision to final fruition. Public-land policy would now assume the form and take the direction first urged by Jefferson and then sought politically by democratic reformers.

Passage of the Homestead Act of 1862 signaled the triumph of American agrarianism. The official policy of the U.S. government was now the creation of a western landscape subdivided into small farms owned by individual settlers. Reformers had achieved their objective of free lands for free people. Unfortunately for agrarian advocates, settlement beyond the 100th meridian proceeded slowly in the first two decades following the act's passage. This allowed the "forward fringe of frontier," the kingdom of cattle, to occupy western lands far in advance of the line of settlement.

The rapid and spectacular rise of the cattle kingdom on the western range threatened the central assumption of the reformers' vision and offered the frightening prospect of a new landed aristocracy. To bring in more settlers was the only practical antidote to the undemocratic rule of an emerging cattle barony. And for this reason, local and regional boosters established immigration commissions to attract homesteaders from the East as well as from Europe.

The culture of the stockman, it appeared, was not in keeping with the agrarian world envisioned in public policy and opinion. The livestock grower, as Walter Prescott Webb wrote in *The Great Plains*, was "a trespasser on the public domain, an obstacle to settlement, and at best but a crude forerunner of civilization of which the farmer was the advance guard and the hoe the symbol."[35] In 1887, the *Laramie Sentinel* reported that the conflict between cattlemen and farmers would be resolved when Cain, "the tiller of the soil," dealt the fatal blow to Abel, "the stock grower."[36] In less biblical terms, an 1889 Senate report concluded that it would be better if western lands remained forever an empty desert than that they become monopolized by the landed estates of powerful stockmen.

The secretary of the interior's annual report for 1902 left no doubt that such perceptions lay at the heart of federal-land policy. "The avowed policy of the government to preserve the public domain for homes of actual settlers," the report read, "has no more implacable and relentless foe than the class that seeks to occupy the public lands for grazing purposes."[37]

Gifford Pinchot, founder of the Forest Service, confirmed a decade later that "the single object of the public land system of the United States . . . is the making and maintenance of prosperous homes."[38]

Despite the aspirations of land reformers and the policy expectations of government officials, the Homestead Act of 1862 was sadly inappropriate to the environmental demands of the western range. A quarter-section of land was simply inadequate given the soils and climate of that region. And the expansion of the homestead unit, first to 320 acres and then, in 1916, to 640 acres, made little difference. Unless the land could be irrigated—and most of the western range could not—any amount of land was inadequate for cultivation. Without water, the land simply could not support crops.

The land would support cattle, however. To survive, many settlers turned to the only alternative available to them—the raising of sheep and cattle. But to raise enough sheep or cattle to support their families still required more than 160 or 640 acres. By necessity, settlers moved their herds onto the open range, antagonizing their neighbors and adding to overgrazing on the range. They became, by no fault of their own, victims of a land policy altogether unsuited to the arid landscape. As one official of the Colorado Stock Growers' Association testified in 1884, overgrazing and overpopulation had been a problem "ever since Mr. Jefferson began to attract immigration to this country by proclaiming to the world [America's great store of free land]."[39]

The events that transpired on the western range might have been different had John Wesley Powell's warning been heeded. In his 1878 *Report on the Lands of the Arid Region of the United States*, Powell made it quite clear that the homestead laws were ecologically inadequate. Most of the western lands, he noted, could not be farmed. Further, he wrote,

> the grass is so scanty that the herdsman must have a large area for the support of his stock. In general, a quarter section of land is of no value to him; the pasturage it affords is entirely inadequate to the wants of a herd that the poorest man needs for his support.[40]

Powell's solution was to expand the homestead unit to match the character of the environment. "Four square miles," he wrote, "may be considered as the minimum amount necessary for a pasturage farm, and still greater amount is necessary for the larger part of the lands."[41] The 1875 annual report of the commissioner of the General Land Office foreshadowed what Powell would report three years later. Except on irrigated lands, the commissioner warned, "title to the public lands cannot be honestly acquired under the homestead laws."[42] The legal units to be homesteaded were far too small to sustain families and communities on the western range. The only way for settlers to acquire additional land was to occupy the open range and prevent its settlement by others. But to do so, the commissioner knew, was contrary to law and policy. Politicians, attuned to public opinion, dismissed the commissioner's concerns and Powell's warnings and clung ever more strongly to the democratic illusion of the Homestead Act.

BEYOND THE TRAGEDY OF THE COMMONS

The failure of public-land policy to adapt to the environment of the western range did not prevent those who lived there from seeking solutions to the critical problem of control. Only with control could lands be managed, stocking held in balance with the growth of grass, and water resources developed. Stockmen adopted numerous strategies to achieve control on the open range, but the most important was the control of water. By locating their homesteads on or near water sources, stockmen could control miles and miles of waterless public land. Livestock belonging to other ranchers, of course, was free to enter the open range, but without water, its stay was necessarily short. "A custom has grown up and become thoroughly established among people of this community," one rancher wrote, "that where one stockman has developed water on and taken possession of the range by fully stocking the same that he will not be molested by other stockmen in his possession and enjoyment of such range."[43]

Waters not located close to deeded lands were more difficult to protect. Then development of barbed wire fencing gave stockmen a cost-efficient method for excluding outsiders from water sources and occupied rangelands. Ranchers erected miles and miles of fence line to protect valuable pastures and to demarcate the rangelands that custom, if not law, dictated as their own. These attempts at control became even more effective when done in the context of livestock or grazing organizations. These associations used the collective power of their membership to persuade—most often by peaceful means—potential interlopers to seek public forage on rangelands that were less congested.

The grazing association to which Levi Howes's father belonged relied on public notices to warn prospective graziers that the range and pasture-lands of Otter Creek were closed to further grazing. One notice informed the general public:

> We are certain that the placing of more stock upon the territory above named would not only prove destructive to the stock added but would produce great loss in the winter to stock already there, and for such reason we give notice to all that we will not assist any parties turning more cattle loose upon such territory. . . . We give this notice for the reason that we believe it is necessary to prevent great loss of property on the ranges indicated and we mutually pledge ourselves to each other to carry it out.[44]

Such notices were not nearly as effective as livestock associations wished. Part of the problem was that almost all efforts by stockmen to enforce closed-range edicts were unlawful. Indeed, Congress passed the Unlawful Enclosures Act of 1885 to stop the increasing efforts of stock-men to control the open range by fencing. The act declared that "all inclo-sures of any public lands . . . are hereby declared to be unlawful."[45] Stock-men were now powerless to control grazing on the public domain. They would no longer be allowed to restrict public entry onto the federal range or limit the use of its scarce waters and forage. Reasonable stocking rates that might have prevailed had stockmen been allowed to control their grazing lands would be replaced by stocking rates far in excess of the car-rying capacity of the land. For all practical purposes, the making of the tragedy of the commons was the official policy of the United States gov-ernment. But the tragedy that befell the public lands did not arise from some fatal flaw of common property. Rather, it arose from institutional and visionary barriers that prevented the residents of the western range from coming to terms with the land.

Recent studies of common resources cast a revealing, and interpretative, light on the early history of the western range. In particular, the theoretical claims put forward by Hardin have been tested and found deficient. One thrust of that critique has been aimed at Hardin's failure to take into ac-count the ability of resource users to regulate themselves and thus avoid the tragedy of the commons. A growing body of evidence suggests that communities, dependent upon common resources, frequently devise ways to limit overexploitation. In southeastern Montana, state grazing districts established common grazing lands and endowed their members with full authority to control and regulate livestock grazing. These districts prosper to this day, testimony not to the efficacy of common lands but to the ability of empowered people to arbitrate and adjudicate the use and management of shared resources.[46]

In a commentary published in *Nature* magazine, F. Berkes and several colleagues concluded that there are ways "to limit access or institute rules to regulate use [on common lands]."[47] Examples include lobster fishermen controlling access to lobster beds in Maine, native Indians in British Columbia curtailing state-authorized harvests of salmon, and hunting communities in Quebec regulating the trapping of beaver. These examples suggest that communities are fully capable of regulating the use of most common resources and protecting them from exploitation by outsiders. The only condition to their success is that the power to control and regulate resource use remain in the hands of actual users.

Not surprisingly, the fate of common resources worldwide has, more often than not, depended on how and by whom the power to control and regulate them is exercised. E. N. Anderson, in an essay published in *The Question of the Commons*, points out that a tragedy of the commons that devastated a Malaysian fishery in the 1970s was largely attributable to government intervention. In an attempt to quell conflict between communities sharing a common fishery, the Malaysian government stepped in to regulate and distribute fishing rights. Unfortunately, the government's action expanded, rather than constrained, pressure on the already overfished waters. "What the fishermen were trying to do," Anderson wrote,

> was "capture the commons" in the most literal possible sense: by use of force. Had they been allowed to continue, the fight would have been long and bloody and very possibly unsuccessful. But the government had even less to offer. . . . In the present case, the government choked off all efforts by the fishermen to help themselves or adapt to their situation. It replaced grassroots democracy in the cooperatives and elsewhere with appointed party men.[48]

What happened on the shores of modern Malaysia had also happened a century earlier on the arid western range. Western stockmen collided with an unyielding barrier as they strove to control a resource threatened with overuse. The federal government, hopelessly enamored by the homesteading myth, pursued policies and undertook actions to ensure that the designs of western ranchers were thwarted. By excluding ownership of larger tracts of land and by thwarting measures to protect the public range from overgrazing, the government usurped the vital component of local power. In so doing, it destroyed grass-roots democracy and left the western range defenseless, subject to the predations of the tragedy of the commons.

Bereft of the power to control, regulate, and manage their public ranges, stockmen acted as if guided by Garrett Hardin's model. But their actions were merely the darker side of a landscape vision that had failed to come to grips with the environmental reality of the western range. All along, the spectacle of Jefferson's agrarian dream had blinded policymakers to what was really happening on the public lands. They ignored or dismissed the presence of livestock producers and insisted that the public lands were empty—and would remain so until finally settled by the fountainhead of democracy, the virtuous farmer. Even today, that bias is perpetuated in the writings of public-land policy experts. "Even though Congress allowed homesteads larger than 160 acres between 1877 and 1934," writes George Coggins in a 1982 issue of *Environmental Law*, "most of the public domain remained vacant."[49]

But Coggins is wrong, as were those who presided over the tragedy of the western range. The fatal flaw of the Jeffersonian vision—its contribution to the environmental decline of the western range—lay not in its inability to people an arid landscape. Its misguided assumptions and its destructive power arose from the failure of its advocates to recognize that the public grazing lands had ceased to be vacant—that ecologically, the lands of the western range had already reached their carrying capacity.

CHAPTER FIVE

Progressivism's Response

*ising angrily from his seat and leaning slightly forward, the re-
gional forester for New Mexico and Arizona slammed his fist on
the table. The issue of building an access road to the western side
of the White Mountain Wilderness, he declared, was closed. There was
nothing else to talk about.* The 1986 Lincoln National Forest Plan *made
it clear that the road was in the public's best interest. The job of the Forest
Service was to weigh the needs and interests of all users and to arrive at a
decision for the greatest good for the greatest number. This had been done.
The road, which he considered the number one public-land access project in
the Southwest, would be built—and soon! And it would cross the Stephensons' I-Bar-X Ranch.*[1]

The I-Bar-X, which lies south of Carrizozo, New Mexico, is bordered
on the east by the White Mountain Wilderness. For Kelley Stephenson, the
ranch is the culmination of a lifetime of work. He earned it the hard way.
As a young man, he hired on at the I-Bar-X and, in time, became ranch
manager. Years of working another man's cattle, though, paid off when Kelley was able to buy the I-Bar-X.

Today, Kelley's son Bill, along with his daughter and son-in-law, run the
day-to-day operations of the ranch, sharing with Kelley only the major de-

cisions that arise from time to time. The access road is one of those decisions. For more than a decade, the Forest Service has sought a route across the I-Bar-X to one or more of the canyons dissecting the western slope of the wilderness. And for just as long, the Stephenson family has resisted the agency's plans.

From the beginning, the I-Bar-X road issue has differed strikingly from public-land access problems elsewhere in the West. It has never been a question of unlocking public lands enclosed by surrounding private lands. The White Mountain Wilderness lies in the heart of southeastern New Mexico's recreational belt and is accessible by five maintained roads. As one of the smallest wilderness areas managed by the Forest Service, no spot within its boundaries is more than a half-day's walk from an existing forest route. The problem is that its northwestern corner, which borders the I-Bar-X, is considered too far from the nearest public road. It is that area the Forest Service wants access to.

There are several reasons why the Forest Service wants the I-Bar-X road. Current forest plans call for additional campgrounds to be built at the boundary of the wilderness and the Stephenson ranch. The Forest Service would also like a northwestern entrance to the wilderness to attain a better distribution of hikers and campers. The road would also provide better access for sportsmen during the fall hunting season.

Bill and Kelley Stephenson take issue with Forest Service claims. They argue that the wilderness is already too accessible, that overcrowding plagues even the most remote areas of the White Mountains. Hunters have more than adequate access to the wilderness—even on the I-Bar-X side. Each fall, the Stephensons open their private road for public use so that hunters can reach a primitive camping site that the family, not the Forest Service, built and now maintains.

Both father and son feel strongly about keeping their land and the wilderness that lies beyond undeveloped. They fear that more people will lead to what has already happened on the eastern side of the wilderness: increasing congestion, widespread litter, and loss of solitude and beauty. Bill and Kelley are also acutely aware that their ranch is all that protects the wilderness from the subdivisions cropping up on the eastern side.

The Stephensons' greatest concern with the Forest Service plan is its potential impact on the land and their livelihood. They are protective of their thirty thousand private acres and the equal number of state-owned acres that are intermingled within the I-Bar-X. In their eyes, the access road is an assault on the integrity of both the ranch and the wilderness. Indeed, Forest Service threats to condemn parts of their property to build the access road have only stiffened their determination to protect the land.

Others have joined the Stephensons in opposition to the proposed access route. A sportsmen's organization in nearby Carlsbad fears that additional access to the White Mountains will inundate the area with hunters and destroy its reputation for trophy mule deer. The New Mexico Wilderness Coalition and the El Paso Regional Group of the Sierra Club also oppose additional access to the wilderness. The I-Bar-X side of the wilderness is the only area that offers relief—and relative solitude—from the crowds, campgrounds, and recreational facilities common to the eastern side. The New Mexico State Land Office has also joined the opposition. In 1987, it denied a Forest Service request to build a road to the wilderness through state lands because the route would cross environmentally sensitive wetlands.

It was this opposition that angered the regional forester and moved him to close debate on the road. But his anger revealed more frustration than confidence. He knew that the Forest Service would have to do a better selling job to show the public where its best interest lay. It would have to convince people that the agency's plan offered the greatest good for the greatest number.

Bill and Kelley were not at the meeting to witness the regional forester's anger, but they have no illusions about the Forest Service forsaking its original plans. They know that at any moment the issue may flare up again, and both men are prepared for when it does. They know that the conflict is a struggle between two visions, one of the land as a place to live and the other of the land as a place to engineer and plan for maximum social benefits.

COPING WITH THE OPEN RANGE: AN OVERVIEW, 1891–1934

The western range was under siege, assaulted by settlers, cattlemen, and sheepmen dedicated to one another's elimination. Federal action to curtail that chaos began with the designation of forest reserves in 1891. More than seventeen million acres of timberland were closed to homesteading, and millions of additional forested acres were withdrawn in subsequent years. A small portion of the western range had been shielded from the worst abuses of the open range. By 1894, that protection was expanded when the secretary of the interior prohibited "driving, feeding, grazing, pasturing, or herding of cattle, sheep, or other livestock" on reserve lands.[2]

Western anger over closed reserves, and support from key figures in the growing forest conservation movement, soon overwhelmed the vocal minority that opposed livestock grazing on forested lands. The no-grazing policy was reversed, and livestock was once again allowed on forest reserves. This time, however, only ranchers holding permits issued by the Department of the Interior could lawfully graze livestock on forested rangelands. That policy continued and strengthened with the transfer of all forest reserves to the Department of Agriculture in 1905. The Division of Forestry was given a new name and almost fifty million acres of national forest lands. The Forest Service was born, and a new chapter on public-land grazing began.

For the bulk of western public lands, however, a workable solution to overgrazing and violence was unlikely so long as Congress allowed federal-land policy to continue unchanged on the public domain. In an attempt to stir Congress from its inertia, stockmen and reformers escalated their lobbying efforts after 1900. The deteriorating state of the western range was publicized, and alternatives to the open range were publicly debated. Livestock associations petitioned the federal government to close the public rangelands to homesteading. They urged authorities to exercise control over grazing on the public domain. Above all, they recommended that existing grazing rights on public lands be acknowledged and enforced by federal law and regulation.

The solution sought by western stockmen, and shared by most public-land reformers, was to close the western range to settlement and to regulate its use by issuing leases or permits. Leasing would protect the interests of established ranchers and, at the same time, resolve the crisis of the open range. Persistent lobbying and a changing political climate culminated in the passage of the Taylor Grazing Act of 1934 and the end of the homesteading era. Under the new law, grazing rights to the public domain were allocated to traditional range users and authorized by legal permits. This meant that livestock on *all* federal ranges was federally controlled. The fate of the public domain now rested in the hands of the Grazing Service, an agency that in 1946 would be merged with the General Land Office and renamed the Bureau of Land Management.

THE PROGRESSIVE VISION

The making of a conservation ethic on the western range came as a natural—and logical—response to the intellectual milieu of the late nineteenth and early twentieth centuries. It bore the unmistakable signature of an emerging national progressive movement, a single-minded commitment to purging inefficiency, waste, and greed from society. And its conservation message spawned a progressive landscape vision, a vision of men and women assuming conscious and purposeful control over nature and directing its uses to the exclusive benefit of humankind. A progressive vision of this magnitude required no less than a complete revamping of American society.

No single person contributed more to the progressive vision than Gifford Pinchot, founder and first chief of the Forest Service. A confidant of presidents and a spokesman for the progressive conservation movement from 1891 to 1934, his vision of nature stood out in marked relief against the romantic and agrarian images of the past.

Nature's resources, Pinchot insisted, were to be treated in a businesslike manner, with forethought, foresight, and efficiency. "Conservation," he wrote, "stands for the same kind of practical common-sense management of this country by the people that every business man stands for in the handling of his own business."[3] The corporate standard would ensure "the wise use of the earth and its resources for the lasting good of men."[4] And to give content to that standard, Pinchot dictated the overriding goals of a national conservation policy. The prudent use and protection of natural resources was foremost. Next, and nearly as important, was the social necessity of controlling and using natural resources for the common good of all citizens, including future generations. Finally, special interests (such as those of western stockmen) had to be curtailed or regulated.

Adherence to these conservation goals was a patriotic duty of all conservation-minded Americans. "In dealing with our natural resources," Pinchot observed, "we have come to a place at last where every consideration of patriotism, every consideration of love of country, of gratitude for things that the land and this Nation have given us, call upon us for a return."[5]

The return that mattered most to Pinchot was selfless service to the nation through the honorable calling of public employment. Men and women dedicated to public service and trained in natural resource management, Pinchot believed, would objectively and efficiently discern, pursue, and implement the resource needs of the land and its people. The Forest Service would be an elite corps whose singular purpose was service in the national interest. The public spirit of the corps would be "the one great antidote for the ills of the Nation" and would create "the Kingdom of God on earth."[6] And its objectivity would ensure, Pinchot emphasized, that "where conflicting interests must be reconciled, the question will always be decided from the standpoint of the greatest good for the greatest number."[7]

ESSENTIALS OF VISIONARY REFORM

Pinchot's visionary zeal did more than inspire a generation of dedicated conservationists; it also profoundly touched the lands and people of the western range. From the outset, proponents of the new vision demanded sweeping change for public grazing lands. The disorder and inefficiency of market forces that had squandered the forage and soils of the arid West could no longer be tolerated. Those sentiments moved progressive leaders, most notably Theodore Roosevelt, to seek more orderly and efficient development of western rangelands. But above all else, saving the public grazing lands meant rescuing them from special interests. A small number of western cattlemen had monopolized the federal range and had laid waste to its considerable resources. It was all too evident to the progressive mind that certain stockmen had achieved dominance on the western range by claiming and controlling what rightfully belonged to all citizens. Pinchot declared in uncompromising terms, "The earth, I repeat, belongs of right to all its people, and not to a minority, insignificant in numbers but tremendous in wealth and power. The public good must come first."[8]

The antagonism Pinchot and other reformers felt toward land-rich stockmen was, in part, ironic. Unlike smaller farmers and ranchers who had also homesteaded the western range, only the more substantial stockmen had sufficient resources to achieve the conservation goals envisioned by progressive reformers—to conserve America's natural wealth and dedicate its use for the common good. Indeed, without the active support of these influential ranchers, the progressive vision would have met much stronger resistance as it settled upon the landscape of the western range.

In the context of progressive thinking, though, the antagonism was not ironic. Despite their personal resources—and their growing willingness to accept reform—western stockmen were not the elite corps envisioned by Pinchot. The logic of the progressive vision required that the application of science to technical problems occur within the orbit of a single authority—an authority untarnished by the economic interests of livestock raising and untouched by the political prejudices of elected office.

Progressive conservationists envisioned such authority residing within a federal agency empowered with the authority of the state, peopled by dedicated and technically proficient experts, and committed to the selfless and efficient management of society's natural wealth. The establishment of the Forest Service and the BLM met these goals admirably. They, along with other soon-to-be federal land agencies, would inherit the progressive mantle and pursue its vision across one-third of the nation's landscape.

REDEFINING DEMOCRACY

In contrast to Jeffersonian agrarianism, the progressive vision was void of sentimentality and nostalgia. It viewed nature neither as a fountainhead of republican virtue nor as a guide to moral behavior. Instead, nature was the material substance of national well-being, the rock-solid foundation of a society dedicated to efficiency, production, and consumption. The vision's broad and nationalistic sweep had little concern for the details of parochial democracy. Henceforth, democracy, spelled with a capital *D* and applied as national policy, would supplant the democratic thrust of a previous age. A vision that accepted no limits could not tolerate the narrow and seemingly selfish concerns associated with agrarian ambitions for self-sufficiency and local sovereignty.

"Conservation," Pinchot proclaimed, "is the most democratic movement this country has known for a generation. It holds that the people have not only the right, but the duty to control the use of natural resources. . . . "[9] Democracy would be the hallmark—and handmaiden—of a new progressive conservation ethic. But it would not be a democracy recognizable to Thomas Jefferson. Conservation was, in Pinchot's words, "the application of common sense to the common problems of the common good."[10] Natural resources, being the birthright of all, were rightfully the property of none. Their use would be determined by those most capable of exercising common sense and most certain of pinpointing common problems and the common good.

In a very real sense, the progressive vision signaled a profound loss of faith in the ability of all but a select few to steward and care for the western landscape. And that loss of faith did not change with the passage of time. Almost thirty years after its creation, the Forest Service had not deviated from its progressive roots. "The depletion of America's forest resources," the agency declared in its 1933 "National Plan for American Forestry," "may be largely attributed to the national conception of the rights of the private citizen and the policies set up to protect those rights even at the expense of the public welfare." The report continued: "Laissez-faire private effort has seriously deteriorated or destroyed the basic resources of timber, forage, and land universally." Private ownership, the Forest Service concluded, was the "most unstable form" for resource management.[11]

Progressivism's preference for public management and ownership of western grazing lands, however, did not include participatory democracy. Not until the passage of The National Environmental Policy Act of 1969 did the BLM and the Forest Service open themselves to the influences of grass-roots democracy. But the passage of legislation that required public review and public participation gave no guarantee that the decision-making process in land management agencies would become more democratic. True, federal agencies would henceforth have to listen to, and even consider, public opinion in all future public-land plans and actions. But the roles of the Forest Service and the BLM remained well within the parameters of their progressive vision. Both agencies still occupied themselves with discerning and implementing the public good, and final responsibility still lay in the hands of a few.

"We cannot allow the uninformed public to make management decisions on our forests and ranges" is the 1986 declaration of a Forest Service employee and candidate for office in the Society for Range Management.[12] A vision of a planned environment on the western range remains unshaken by the legislative developments of the 1970s and 1980s. Those developments, if anything, have strengthened the progressive vision and magnified its effects on the land. The western range, as before, remains entrapped by the rapture of a solitary landscape vision.

As the progressive vision has matured, though, its content and direction have changed dramatically. Science and public administration, once the means to attain rangeland conservation, have become the ultimate objectives of public-land ownership. Values once beyond the scope of science and bureaucracy have been quantified, analyzed, and dryly summarized in mandatory environmental impact statements and detailed in national forest and resource management plans. What were formerly the purview of personal visions have become the subject of management alternatives and cost-benefit analyses.

Science and public administration have, with deliberation, become the embodiment of the progressive conservation spirit and the rationale for its continuance. Neutral by design and objective in theory, land management agencies on public grazing lands have changed their purpose from serving the public good to determining precisely what the public good should be. That not-so-subtle change underlies and highlights the saga of the modern western range: the methodical displacement of Jefferson's noble farmer from the plains and mountains of the western range by an enlightened technocracy. In the name of the public good, a land dedicated to grass-roots democracy has been transformed into the province of bureaucracies.

CHAPTER SIX

The Grassland
Experiment

*B*ordered on the east by the 100th meridian and wedged between
Pierre, South Dakota, and Interstate 90, the Fort Pierre National Grassland stands sentinel over the easternmost edge of the
western range. Encompassing one hundred and sixteen thousand acres, it is
one of the smaller grasslands managed by the Forest Service. Its verdant,
rolling hills support a wide diversity of life, and its quiet serenity hides a
rich and controversial past.

Before 1930, hundreds of small farmers eked out a living on 160- and
320-acre homesteads on what is now the Fort Pierre National Grassland.
But depression, drought, and the New Deal changed the face of the land.
Well-intentioned federal programs purchased failing homesteads and offered
homeless families a second chance. Under the tutelage first of the Soil Conservation Service and then of the Forest Service, Jefferson's prided yeomanry
became wards of the state.

Driving along one of many dirt roads dissecting the grassland, I could
only imagine how much the land and its people had changed. Only a half-
century earlier, hundreds of families had called these fields and pastures
home. Now, only a handful of ranchers lived here. A Forest Service publication explained that most of the Fort Pierre National Grassland "was pur-

chased by the U.S. Government because a yearlong livestock operation could not be supported." [1] *I found that difficult to believe as I drove up to a small wood-framed house at the end of a grassy pasture. South Dakota was in the midst of severe drought, yet the pasture was alive with tall, waving grass. Cattle grazed in the distance—part of the year-round livestock operation run by Donna and Dwayne Slaathaug.*

Donna greeted me before I reached the front porch. Dwayne was still cutting hay and would not be home for at least another hour. But that did not matter; Donna had something to tell me, and it would be simpler with just the two of us.

Donna's grandparents had arrived in the area in the early 1900s and had claimed 320 acres not far from the Slaathaugs' house. Their homestead was adequate at first, but a growing family quickly stressed the land to its limits. Donna's grandfather purchased additional lands to supplement their half-section. By then, land was available and inexpensive as neighbor after neighbor succumbed to the deepening agricultural depression of the early 1920s.

More acres cushioned the family against the economic collapse of the Great Depression and lessened the calamity of the drought and Dust Bowl that followed. Enough land and a little rain made it possible for them to persist through the most difficult years. But what should have been a triumph of human endurance ended when a government purchasing agent told Donna's grandfather that he would have to sell his lands to the U.S. government.

The sale was part of a federal relief program aimed at bringing economic stability and land conservation to the region. The program created "land utilization projects" to rehabilitate displaced farmers and abandoned croplands. The social and economic plans of the area's local project called for buying the surrounding farms. Donna's family had to go, assured that they could repurchase the farm once prosperity returned to the region. The New Deal had achieved what years of depression and drought had failed to do.

Donna and Dwayne's circumstances were much different, living and working in the shadow of an agency they could not control. Their cattle depended on public range managed by the Forest Service. They had no choice but to adapt to a landscape vision that viewed them as peripheral to the nation's needs for resources, recreation, and space.

For Donna, that vision entailed an element of betrayal—not only for herself and her family but also for friends and neighbors who had also lost their homes. They had come to the land in good faith, expecting the dignity and independence that came with hard work and ownership of property. Instead, their homes had been taken away and their families uprooted. In exchange, they were offered graz-

ing permits. But Donna could not forget that the land had once belonged to her family; nor could she ignore the pain its loss entailed. She knew that each additional law, regulation, and plan increased the distance between herself and the land, between the present and her past. Despite the memories and the changes she faced, she could not imagine any other home for herself or her children than here on the rolling plains of central South Dakota.

BOOM AND BUST ON THE GREAT PLAINS

Except for two small units in Oregon and Idaho, the national grasslands are unique to the Great Plains. They are the scattered and broken islands of federal domain that dot the rolling prairies of the Dakotas, Nebraska, Kansas, Oklahoma, Texas, Wyoming, Colorado, and New Mexico. Their four million acres straddle the 100th meridian, with their bulk lying solidly within the western range.

Circumstance and climate conspired to set these lands apart from public lands in the mountains and deserts of the arid West. Unlike the national forests and the BLM's public domain, the grasslands were not always public. Between 1900 and 1915, tens of thousands of settlers from the Midwest poured onto the prairies of the Great Plains seeking free land on which to raise families, crops, and livestock. They came at the best of times, when land laws were most liberal and climate was most kind. The Kinkaid Act of 1904 and later the Enlarged Homestead Act of 1909 offered 320 to 640 acres to farmers ready and willing to apply Midwest agriculture to the high plains environment. Generous rainfall convinced settlers that farms would prosper and gave credence to claims of the prairie's unbounded fertility. All one had to do, promoters claimed, was plow the sod, sow the seed, and await a bountiful harvest. And for years, that is just what happened.

Boom times settled on the Great Plains, spurred by the rising prices created by a world at war. Farmers mortgaged their land and took out personal loans to finance new homes, build barns, and purchase farm equipment. Rural townships became bustling centers of economic and social activity. But the Great Depression of the 1920s, followed by the economic collapse and severe drought of the 1930s, plunged the Great Plains into social and environmental crisis.

Improvident land policies, propped up temporarily by an inconstant nature, had encouraged too many people to settle on the grassy plains of the western range. Prairie soils that had nurtured productive grasslands for centuries could not sustain the culture of wheat or the pressure of too much livestock. And drought and wind stripped the plowed and over-grazed lands of topsoil.

The land and people of the Great Plains might have weathered drought and depression better had the land remained in native grass. That would have been possible if settlers had raised cattle instead of crops. But ranching was not a viable option in a region subdivided into 160- and 320-acre holdings and lacking open range. Without additional range and forage, homesteads could sustain no more than a handful of cows and a few goats, pigs, and chickens, not enough to support a family.

Illogical settlement patterns made cultivation the only choice many settlers had in making a living from the land. Often, they broke and plowed the high plains sod to supplement the little domestic stock their lands could support. And when cultivatable lands were scarce, they overstocked their homesteads. The homestead laws, after all, required them to improve their claims and to devote their lands to the exclusive industry of raising a family. It was an economy that an agrarian vision had encouraged and one that the kindness of nature would make possible for a few years.

One quite ordinary and unremarkable township in northwestern North Dakota reveals the settlement patterns and conditions that prevailed throughout much of the Great Plains before the 1920s and 1930s. Described simply as Tier 148N, Range 103W, the township encompassed thirty-six sections. Except for nine sections owned by the Northern Pacific Railroad and two assigned as school lands, the remaining twenty-five sections supported seventy families, most of whom lived on 160-acre plots.[2] By growing crops on what level land existed and raising farm animals on the rest, the residents of Tier 148N, Range 103W eked out a subsistence living during the best years.

Looking at the same township today, it is hard to imagine that so many people could once have lived there. The landscape is hilly and strewn with boulders and rock outcroppings. Level bottomlands are scarce. Now part of the Little Missouri National Grassland, the township supports only the Anderson, Greenwood, and Severson ranches. Sadly, what happened there also happened elsewhere on the Great Plains. Lives and lands were ruined as too many people settled on too little land for too long.

NEW DEAL DIRECTIONS

The Great Depression did not discriminate between rural and urban areas. Human suffering was the same wherever it occurred. From New York City to Tier 148N, Range 103W, evictions, unemployment, and bankruptcy wrecked lives and plunged families and communities into social turmoil. Just surviving became the only occupation for almost forty million Americans.

But the Great Plains differed from the rest of the country in one important aspect. Severe drought exposed its fragile and broken prairie sod to the ravages of hot, dry winds. "Submarginal lands" that should never have been cultivated or heavily grazed bore the price of an inflexible agrarian vision. Topsoil was carried aloft by the searing prairie wind, depleting the rich grassland soil and darkening the midday sun from Colorado to the eastern seaboard. The Great Plains suffered the unbridled fury of depression and drought.

Eroding submarginal farmlands and desperate farm families touched the heart of the nation and moved social and conservation reformers to action. Four million acres of Great Plains were earmarked for special treatment by Franklin D. Roosevelt's New Deal. These were the lands on the eastern edge of the western range, the lands most in need of restoration.

The progressive vision, still struggling for control elsewhere on the western range, found fertile soil for its aspirations on the drought-stricken plains of middle America. And from those aspirations, a grassland experiment of unheard-of proportions evolved. The New Deal began its work on the submarginal lands of the Great Plains, lands that would be, in the words of the U.S. Department of Agriculture, the "proving grounds for social, economic, and educational programs."[3]

"Land utilization projects" were the heart and soul of New Deal programs on the Great Plains. They were pieced together from millions of acres of private lands previously abandoned or purchased between 1933 and 1946. Their goal, as the preamble to the Bankhead-Jones Farm Tenant Act would reaffirm in 1937, was "to promote more secure occupancy of farms and farm homes, to correct the economic instability resulting from some present forms of farm tenancy, and for other purposes." Most important among those "other purposes" was the development of "a program of land conservation and land utilization, including the retirement of lands which are submarginal or not primarily suitable for cultivation."[4]

Organized first under the Resettlement Administration, then transferred in 1938 to the Soil Conservation Service (SCS), "land utilization project" lands—called LU lands—were divided into grazing and conservation districts. Their landscapes were returned to grassland cover, and their uses were restricted mostly to grazing. Of the settlers whose homesteads became LU lands, some were fortunate enough to receive grazing permits to use the lands they had once owned. Many others were resettled elsewhere, to farmlands that would support them or to towns and cities where employment and relief could sustain them until better times.

Purchase and reclamation of LU lands and resettlement of their residents were done with the best of intentions. But the times and the people were not always inclined to caution and restraint. The progressive vision, by circumstance and by choice of its followers, was not shackled by the limitations that a deeply rooted population had forced upon it elsewhere on the western range. It faced no constraining obstacle, short of financial means, as its followers applied it to the inhospitable lands of a parched and seemingly vacant prairie.

If federal documents are to be trusted, LU lands were acquired voluntarily. A 1964 USDA report states that "all sales made to the Federal Government [by settlers] were voluntary . . . limited to poor land used in agriculture, *except* that intervening or adjoining land could be purchased in order to allow efficient conservation and use of the area as a whole [emphasis mine] ."[5] The "exception" provided an enticing loophole in an otherwise elective program. It gave enormous discretion and cause to federal agencies whose job was to apply the progressive vision. It persuaded well-intentioned reformers, now in federal employment, to exceed the limits of voluntarism and to resort to tactics that only a vision's religious fervor could justify.

Stories like Donna Slaathaug's were repeated across the Great Plains as LU lands were consolidated. Ingebert Fauske, a rancher on the Buffalo Gap National Grassland and a member of the 1964 Public Land Law Review Commission, was a young man when government agents came to his father's homestead and demanded that 160 acres of their property be sold. His father finally agreed to sell, but only under duress.[6] Congressman A. L. Miller of Nebraska conveyed a similar experience. "I owned some land down in Colorado," he testified at a 1954 congressional hearing, and raised a considerable amount of wheat, but the Federal Government came along and insisted upon buying the land. In fact, I still have letters in my files saying if I did not sell they were going to condemn the land, and it was a question of either selling it to the Government at that time or going through some condemnation proceedings, whose costs were to be assessed back to me, and I eventually gave up land which was producing at one time 30 bushels of wheat to the acre.[7]

Miller's concerns over condemnation were not unwarranted. Although formal takings of settlers' lands were the exception, they did occur with unsettling frequency. Warranty deed records from Fall River County, South Dakota, for example, include numerous entries of lands condemned by the federal government, lands that are now administered as part of the Buffalo Gap National Grassland.[8] Further, there were methods to force compliance from recalcitrant settlers. Veiled threats of closing public schools, for example, strongly influenced the decisions of families living on what is now the Fort Pierre National Grassland. More frequently, the shadow of delinquent taxes and the threat of foreclosure persuaded unwilling farmers to accept grudgingly the inevitability of government-financed resettlement.[9]

Among homesteaders who voluntarily relinquished their lands, the decision to leave was no less difficult. "I am still haunted," Fauske lamented in a recent memoir, "by the scene of a family sitting on boxes and furniture, weeping, because the Government [Works Progress Administration work crews] had just burned their homes. If a veteran from the Civil War could have viewed the area with its dots of ashes where buildings had been, he would certainly have thought it was a part of General Sherman's march to the sea."[10]

Once the LU projects were in place, an interlude of calm and rebuilding settled on the prairie landscape. Administration by the SCS from 1938 to 1954 encouraged local grazing districts and their user associations to assume management responsibility for LU lands. Being an educational and advisory agency, the SCS defined its mission on the Great Plains as one of assistance rather than management and enforcement. Its goal, defined by the Bankhead-Jones Act, was to help ranchers reclaim and conserve their permitted grazing lands and to achieve economic and social stability for their communities.

A 1941 report by the SCS summed up the agency's philosophy toward the land and the people of the high plains. The federal government, the SCS claimed, had intervened to preserve "a basis upon which to reconstruct a more stable and permanent agriculture for the area. . . . It was also of national concern," the report continued, "that the Government had unwisely permitted the settlement of this area on an impracticable basis and should, therefore, assume responsibility for assisting those destitute stranded families during this period of extreme distress. . . ."[11]

NATIONAL GRASSLANDS IN TRANSITION

The gentle demeanor of the progressive vision under the tutelage of the SCS ended in 1954 with the transfer of the majority of LU lands to the Forest Service. Management of those lands changed dramatically to reflect their new status as national grasslands. Dale Greenwood, a rancher on the Little Missouri National Grassland, described the changes that ensued: "[Since] 1954, when the Soil Conservation Service relinquished their responsibility to the Forest Service, [the role of administration] has gone from 'advising' to 'regulating,' to 'policing.'"[12] The progressive vision had returned with full force to the Great Plains, no longer apologetic for the failed policies of the past.

Renewal of the progressive vision had sweeping ramifications. History was rewritten as the Forest Service interpreted the tragedy that had befallen the national grasslands. An early narrative for a national grasslands brochure placed the blame squarely on the shoulders of farmers and small ranchers and reaffirmed the necessity of federal ownership. According to the brochure, land managers

> observed that farmers had ignored the advantages of planting trees for windbreaks, and that extensive tilling and overgrazing had removed the precious grasses whose debris and tangled roots prevented the evaporation of precious moisture. . . . The land managers recognized that this was a situation that called for immediate action, and that the results of their efforts had to be lasting, for they wished to avoid further destruction of the plains during future drought.[13]

While the Forest Service sought greater control, the 1964 Public Land Law Review Commission argued for disposal of the national grasslands.

In its 1970 report to the president, "One Third of the Nation's Land," the commission refused to accept the argument that the former LU lands could be protected only through federal ownership. Conservation programs begun by the SCS, the commission insisted, were "sufficient insurance against the repeat of the 'dust bowl' conditions that led to the acquisition of much federal lands."[14] Despite the commission's recommendation, new amendments were added to the Bankhead-Jones Act, augmenting the power already held by the Forest Service.

The agency's mandate was legislatively expanded from the narrow focus of grazing and social stability to recreational development, soil and water conservation, and wildlife protection. Elaborate environmental planning documents replaced the localized decision-making processes encouraged by the SCS. Grass-roots democracy gave way to the national democracy envisioned by Pinchot, and the benign and informal social engineering of the SCS yielded to the scientific and formal environmental engineering of the Forest Service. The national grasslands would be engineered in strict accordance with the progressive vision, and their rangelands would be managed for the good of *all* the people.

The changes that have occurred on the national grasslands because of that management have been costly to both the land and its people. To obtain its objectives, the Forest Service has diminished the power and integrity of local grazing associations.[15] Traditionally, grassland associations distributed and regulated grazing privileges on common grazing lands and oversaw the details and demands of daily management. Because of their success, the soils and vegetation of the original LU lands have stabilized and healed. But grassland associations, formerly the primary tools of land conservation under the SCS, are now perceived as barriers to the agency's calling. By supervising their meetings and changing their traditional roles, the Forest Service has diminished their importance. In the words of one association president, the agency has "gradually increased [its] control and eroded ours."[16]

The new vision of control, expertise, and engineering dictates that national interests take precedence over those of individuals and communities. It has made the Forest Service increasingly intolerant of limits to its authority and unwilling to share with associations the exercise of power and control on the prairie landscape.

But this kind of thinking overlooks the fact that permittees' contributions to land conservation and improvements on national grasslands have declined precipitously over the years. As the power of associations and their members diminishes, more and more ranchers are refusing to invest in stewardship of the national grasslands. Today, less than a third of range improvements are paid for by the people who benefit from them the most.[17] Sadly, Forest Service monies intended to make up for declining private expenditures are unable to keep up with the conservation demands of the land. And the public monies that are expended tax unfairly a public whose interests lie more in the reduction of national debt than in the subsidization of livestock production on federal lands.

Moreover, the disincentives that have persuaded ranchers to spend fewer dollars on their public lands have unwittingly made them less caring. Because associations have lost their effectiveness, grassland allotments grazed by multiple permittees are more neglected today than in the past. The chronic problem of the uncontrolled commons is repeating itself on the Great Plains, offset only by the policing activities of a well-intentioned Forest Service. For all these changes, the land has benefited little.

Contradictions permeate the progressive vision, affecting both the land and the conservation practices of land users. In 1964, the USDA praised LU lands for giving people "a chance to observe good land use practices and efficient management of forests, grasslands, and recreational and wildlife areas."[18] Twenty years later, the Forest Service repeated those sentiments in "The National Grasslands of the Rocky Mountain Region": "The role of the National Grasslands in demonstrating proper management on the Plains is just as important today as it was when these lands were purchased half a century ago."[19]

Yet recent management decisions by the Forest Service have not been consistently benign in what they have demonstrated and caused to happen. The phasing out of traditional cutting and haying practices on the national grasslands, for example, has compelled some ranchers to plow and cultivate their private rangelands to grow replacement forage. Because of that, the purpose of the national grasslands has been subverted, as fewer submarginal lands remain in native grassland. The message of "proper management on the Plains," it would appear, has been tarnished in the translation from good intentions to public policy and practice.

Ironically, the gravest threat to the conservation message of the national grasslands has come from the well-intentioned wildlife plans adopted by the Forest Service. Those plans have stopped haying and cutting and levied significant livestock reductions in an effort to enhance wildlife habitat on federal rangelands. But in devising its wildlife plans, the Forest Service has forgotten that the national grasslands are complexes of public and private lands where decisions and actions taken on one affect the other. As a result, agency decisions and actions have unwittingly reduced the wildlife potential of private lands that are rich in habitat. Above all, they have diminished the willingness of public-land ranchers to cooperate in wildlife programs—programs perceived as threats to their livelihood.

Dwayne Slaathaug considers the Forest Service's wildlife plans an affront to himself and to the grasslands.[20] When he joined Operation Stronghold, a wildlife conservation alliance, he did so because its goal of managing private lands for wildlife fit with what he had already done with his own land. It reinforced what he knew to be true, that public and private lands are indivisible ecologically and indistinguishable to the wildlife who depend upon them. But being a grassland permittee is teaching him a different lesson. The agency's plans are forcing public and private lands into contrasting management regimes, emphasizing wildlife on one and livestock on the other. By so doing, Dwayne believes, the Forest Service is promoting land uses that are harmful to wildlife and discouraging to a conservation ethic.

Dwayne is angered and saddened that some of his neighbors plowed their fragile rangelands to make way for cultivated forage crops, crops needed to replace native grassland lost because of Forest Service wildlife plans. And he is worried that livestock reductions made on national grasslands to enhance already abundant wildlife habitat will force ranchers to graze their private lands to the exclusion of wildlife or to the detriment of the soil and vegetation. It makes no sense to him that national grasslands committed to saving the prairie sod from the plow and too many cattle should be the cause of the land's cultivation and overgrazing—even if that land is private rather than public. From the Forest Service's view, the shift may appear beneficial. Public lands will gain at the expense of private lands. But ecologically, none will win. The ecosystem will lose an element of complexity as land uses are unnaturally segregated and as economically strapped ranchers seek marginal solutions on marginal lands. Well-intentioned plans will succumb as the harm done to private lands rebounds to the detriment of the landscape at large.

Forgotten in the closing circle, where loss feeds upon loss and diminishment hastens diminishment, are the social motives and conservation ideals that first fired the progressive vision: the dream of rebuilding lands and communities damaged by ill-conceived settlement policies. As the national grasslands have changed, the vision has narrowed, turning in upon itself until its continued existence has become its sole rationale.

A DIFFERENT PATH:
THE NEBRASKA SANDHILLS

What becomes immediately apparent as one surveys the national grasslands is the absence of features that distinguish them from the millions of acres of privately owned grasslands. This is not to say that the national grasslands are commonplace or that they lack the solitude characteristic of the Great Plains. It is instead an observation on their striking historical, social, and environmental similarity to those private lands that share their quiet beauty, though not their public purpose.

Simply stated, there is no ecological rhyme or reason to the seemingly erratic scattering of national grasslands on the prairie. Their randomness is the polar opposite of the logical, and oftentimes necessary, pattern of landownership that arose elsewhere on the western range. In the Rocky Mountain West, productive bottomlands were homesteaded, leaving the more arid and less productive uplands as open range. But because of a uniformly more moist and productive environment and a history that is unique, similar contrasts do not exist on the Great Plains. For those lands, drought and depression provide a better explanation for patterns of landownership than do ecology and landscape features. Yet the confluence of drought and depression in the 1930s does not give a complete and satisfactory explanation for the creation of isolated pockets of publicly owned grasslands. Despite almost identical historical experiences, abundant prairie rangelands have remained in private ownership.

Examples drawn from privately owned lands argue against the conservation and social necessity of the national grasslands. The most productive grasslands of the Great Plains—the Nebraska sandhills—suffered all the problems that depression, drought, and bad homestead policies could offer. Yet because of their early settlement in the late nineteenth century, they followed a path far different from the trail blazed by the New Deal. They were able to weather the crises brought on by people and nature and to emerge from the 1930s essentially intact.

Although separated by two decades, the early histories of the sandhills and the rest of the Great Plains closely resemble each other. Homesteading

93

subdivided the sandhills into increasingly smaller land units, just as it would elsewhere on the Great Plains during the boom years before and immediately after World War I. But the Kinkaid Act of 1904 intervened at a critical moment, moving the sandhills onto an altogether different historical track. Applicable only to western Nebraska, and the sandhills in particular, the act allowed 640-acre homesteads for the first time. Its intent was to encourage sustainable crop farming rather than livestock raising, but its long-term effect was quite different.

Nebraska cattlemen, frustrated by their inability to fence the open range and control water resources, turned the law to their own advantage. Having settled the sandhills first and having the most to lose by its fragmentation into small cultivated parcels, they used the act to enlarge their private holdings and to secure control over the range. Marie Sandoz, a witness to the opening of the sandhills under the more liberal terms of the Kinkaid Act, observed just that. She watched as eager settlers lined up, waiting for the magic moment when they could rush forward and claim their section homesteads. But on "the day of the opening," she later wrote,

long queues of homeseekers waited for hours, only to find that even the sad choice of land that was free had been filed earlier in the day. There was talk of cattlemen agents who made up baskets full of filing papers beforehand and ran them through the first thing. One woman was said to have filed on forty sections, under forty names, at five dollars a shot. The land was covered by filings that would never turn into farms.[21]

Almost overnight, the open range of the Nebraska sandhills had been legally divided and formally closed. Much of it was claimed by stockmen who considered it theirs by prior use. Those lands remained in native grassland.

Even so, significant portions of the Nebraska sandhills succumbed to the farmer's plow. Settlers who lacked sufficient land and capital to ranch, and who were still enticed by the allure of the agrarian vision, cultivated their homesteads in cereal crops. But once the sod was broken, the structure of the soil disintegrated. Sand that had been held in place by fibrous grass roots for centuries was free to drift with each gust of prairie wind. As one sandhills historian succinctly noted, "the crops blew out, and little was harvested."[22]

Disappointed and ruined farmers abandoned their homesteads or had them confiscated by banks and county governments. Most simply sold their failed farms to eager stockmen for $1,000 to $5,000 a homestead. The faltering economy of the sandhills, though, managed to escape the fate reserved for other submarginal lands. The people were able to sort out, on their own, the social and conservation ills created by inappropriate land policies. And it all happened without federal relief—the outcome of tenacious residents acquiring vacated lands and combining them into substantial ranches. "Since the 'kinkaider' days," as reported by a rural economist in a 1928 study,

> individual holdings of the [Sand Hill] land have been enlarged by purchase and lease and attempts at cropping operations have been abandoned. Fenced pastures have replaced the open range and private control of the land is the rule. The final result is a cattle industry established on a much sounder basis than in the days of free grass.[23]

When depression and drought finally came in the 1930s, ranches ranging from ten thousand to sixty thousand acres dominated the landscape of the Nebraska sandhills. The luxury of abundant land, of course, did not protect stockmen from the plagues of rainless skies and economic recession. Grass was still overgrazed, soils were swept away in massive "blowouts," and many families teetered on the brink of bankruptcy. But additional acres allowed long-term survival for the grasslands and the people of the sandhills. They permitted what would be denied elsewhere on the Great Plains: viable ranches.

One-half century after depression and drought, the Nebraska sandhills stand out as some of the most productive grasslands on the western range. Their productivity and beauty, unexcelled elsewhere on the Great Plains, do not rely on public ownership for preservation. It is true that as irrigated agriculture infringes on native rangeland—an invasion encouraged by federal crop subsidies and price supports—the lands are being threatened. But the sandhills are still cattle country, private and prosperous.

A different future was in store for the four million acres that were first ravaged by a stubborn agrarian dream and then fatefully labeled by conservation reformers as submarginal LU lands. But the sandhills offer persuasive evidence that alternatives existed, that the national grasslands were not destined to be public by some deterministic confluence of depression and drought. What happened on the sandhills also suggests what might have happened on the greater western range had men and women been free to accommodate the demands and limits of nature.

What made the difference between private rangelands like the sandhills and the public grasslands at Fort Pierre and elsewhere was a third factor in the equation of depression and drought. It was the form and substance given to the progressive vision by the unprecedented conservation and social programs of the New Deal. Those programs, built on the historical coincidence of drought and depression, altered the landscape of the Great Plains far more than did the combined forces of economy and nature.

CHAPTER SEVEN

Technocracy and Empire

*A*lton, Utah, is located midway between Zion and Bryce Canyon national parks at the end of a narrow county road several miles east of Highway 89. Because of its isolation, it has no gem shops, pottery stores, or cafes. All that distinguishes it from the sagebrush and juniper countryside are a few aging homes and cultivated hay fields. It offers nothing that might attract tourists in their passage between parks. But for those who know Alton, there is an unforgettable feature: Bard Heaton.

By Utah standards, Bard is a relative newcomer. His family settled in Alton around 1900, long after the first wave of Mormon settlers had peopled, irrigated, and tilled the western slope of the Wasatch Range. His father and grandfather had come to southwestern Utah to ranch, not to farm. They had made Alton their headquarters and built a substantial ranch of eighteen thousand acres.[1]

At first the Heatons raised sheep, grazing them on open winter range in northern Arizona and moving them north, in late spring, to the family ranch. Bard's earliest memories are of herding sheep on the Arizona Strip and following them to the high country near Alton. But what caught his attention most were the overgrazed rangelands of the 1920s and 1930s, the valley bottoms and flats unnaturally barren of grass.

The Landscape Visions

Those early years on the open range left their mark on Bard Heaton. They became haunting memories of past wrongs and reminders of the debt he owed to the land. They nurtured a simple philosophy: One should take from the soil only enough to live, leaving the rest for the land to prosper. He has ranched by that dictum, trusting that the land would benefit from his stewardship, as he had benefited from the land.

Over thirty years, he has reclaimed nearly fifteen thousand acres of the Alton ranch and spent most of his personal fortune in the process. He did so mindful of the environment and attentive to the economics of his investment. He focused on the best sites, where soils were most stable and productive and where his dollars would go furthest. He protected areas critical to soil and water conservation and vital to wildlife habitat. And because of his vision, diversity thrives where thickets of sage and juniper once dominated. Islands of trees and brush now commingle with stands of mixed grasses and wildflowers. Gullies that once cut across the landscape, draining the land of its topsoil, are green and healing. And deer and elk numbers are up dramatically.

Bard's commitment to the land has not stopped at the boundaries of his deeded property. Like his father, he depends on BLM grazing lands to supplement his private range. Those lands are, in Bard's mind, part and parcel of his operation and no less deserving of his care. His permit to graze, he believes, entails responsibility and accountability. As with his private lands, he has felt an obligation to leave the public domain in better condition than he found it.

Caring for public lands the same way he has cared for his own ranch has not been easy for Bard Heaton. The BLM has complicated and unduly postponed his proposals. In the mid–1970s, Bard proposed to the agency that he extend his range improvement work onto his grazing allotment. He offered to pay the several hundred thousand dollars it would cost to return landscape diversity to public rangelands strangled by excessive juniper and sagebrush. He pointed out that deer and elk would benefit, as they had on his private range. He also reminded the BLM that his public lands had been ignored since the closing of the open range. It was time that someone be accountable for the environmental damage of the past.

Bard's request was denied. His grazing management, the BLM acknowledged, was unmatched by that of other ranchers in the area, and his permitted lands had improved markedly under his care. But many in the agency feared that such a large investment would give Bard too much vested interest in lands that were not his, would usurp responsibilities that Congress had reserved exclusively to the BLM. Bard's plan was viewed as a challenge to the power and authority of the agency. The issue of who controlled the land was more important than the fact that someone was willing to improve it. Bard was angry and frustrated. The BLM had done nothing for his allotment, and there was no reason to believe that it ever would.

Local managers in the BLM suggested that Bard might get around the agency's resistance by agreeing to cost-share the project through a cooperative agreement rather than financing it from his own funds. But Bard was not interested in cost-sharing. He had managed his permitted lands quite well in the 1960s, when the local BLM office had only three employees and little money. Just because its ranks and funds had swollen to seventy five employees and many more dollars, he saw no reason to abdicate his conservation role. He knew his responsibility. He had always paid his way in the past, and now would not be different. It was a matter of principle. It was part of caring for the land.

Ten long and frustrating years after his initial request, the Department of the Interior inaugurated a "good neighbor" program, and Bard was given a chance to pursue his dream. Since 1985, three thousand public acres have benefited from his vision of a richer, more diverse rangeland. But those three thousand acres hide the thousands more that might have been improved had time and opportunity not been lost—or the thousands that will never be improved because of environmental impact statements (EISs), lengthy planning processes, and a myriad of new laws and regulations. Each year, Bard finds more reasons to keep his money closer to home, using it to improve lands he owns.

Standing in a grass and juniper savannah rooted securely in that soil, Bard Heaton surveys a landscape that stands in sharp contrast to the accidental workings of nature that have molded the nearby Zion National Park. His Zion is a vibrant and thriving testament to human purpose, an act enriching the diversity of a western range tragically diminished by a less than gentle history. But it is also, as Bard Heaton has painfully learned, a testament constrained by political and bureaucratic obstacles, one isolated from the public's western range by a vision blind to Bard's land ethic and hostile to his lesson of individual accountability.

THE BUREAUCRATIC IMPERATIVE FOR CONTROL

Conservation reform did not end the reign of intolerant visions on the federal range. As on the national grasslands, one dominant vision simply supplanted another, leaving the land and its people still captive to a sweeping ideology, one that held sway because of the power of national politics, not the persuasion of ideas. The passage from agrarian to progressive ideals, though, was not without consequence. In the wake of changing values, a marked shift occurred in how, and by whom, visions were to be realized on the public grazing lands.

The shift toward bureaucracy was the most immediate and enduring social and political consequence of the progressive vision. It highlighted a key tenet of conservation reform and signaled a profound change in the use of the visionary tools of control and implementation. Those tools, so integral to the workings of landscape visions in general, gave scope and substance to the visions that have dominated western grazing lands. They were the means for attaining the agrarian ideal, and they remain the means for pursuing progressive conservation reform.

Control is the most basic of the two visionary tools. But more than control is needed to attain the goals of landscape visions. For visions to have substance, humans must translate wishful aspirations into concrete results. Together, human action and effective landscape control have made the reign of intolerant visions on the western range possible.

Motivating people to act and achieving landscape control were simple matters for an agrarian vision that enjoyed broad popular support. Homestead acts reserved huge expanses of the western range for sturdy yeoman farmers. The laws also frustrated efforts by ranchers to control more land than agrarian democracy deemed proper. They kept the western range open, despite tremendous social and environmental costs. But controlling the open range was only half the task. Applying agrarian values across the width and breadth of the western range was the necessary second step, one reserved for the cultivators of Jefferson's yeoman republic.

After 1862, law and policy made it clear who would carry the agrarian vision to fruition on the western range. Small farmers were compelled by a perceived manifest destiny to subdivide the nation's western third into thriving homesteads. The same law and policy left no doubt that small farmers were also the vision's final object and purpose: the making of a virtuous agricultural republic.

Conservation reform changed everything. Authority to control the federal range was taken from the province of failed homestead laws and put squarely into the hands of the Forest Service and the BLM. Those agencies became the vehicles for implementing the progressive vision and began to manage the western range in a way more suitable to the needs and aspirations of youthful bureaucracies. Thoroughly dedicated to the ideals of conservation and public service, they turned their attention to the pressing problem of securing control.

But securing control was a much different matter for conservation bureaucracy from what it had been for agrarian democracy. Its progressive vision was not rooted in a broad political consensus but rested in the hands of a small circle of elite scientists and administrators. For that reason, control required extraordinary effort—a commitment to bringing the public interest to bear on lands victimized by self-interest. Only by imposing the public will on a western people unaccustomed to such power—and often antagonistic to its conservation goals—could land management agencies hope to pursue policies and programs central to their progressive vision.

Options existed from the beginning as to how control might best be exercised. On the national grasslands, the Soil Conservation Service set the framework for grassland management by forming local grazing associations, then dedicating itself to overseeing and monitoring their operation. Apart from that, the SCS operated mostly in an advisory and educational capacity, in keeping with its legislative mandate. It left the care and use of the land to those who were closest to the soil and whose livelihoods were most affected by the decisions of daily management.

The Grazing Service, predecessor of the BLM, pursued a similar course on the lands closed by the Taylor Grazing Act of 1934. With the assistance of grazing advisory boards (made up of ranchers elected from each grazing district), it divided the western range into allotments and set authorized livestock numbers. It then assumed a strictly custodial role, delegating much of the day-to-day supervision of public lands to ranchers and their elected boards.

But advisory and custodial roles did not suit the ambitions of the Forest Service or the Bureau of Land Management. The BLM, burdened by the do-nothing reputation of its parent agency, the Grazing Service, was eager to erase its image of subservience to mineral and livestock interests and was determined to emulate the visionary zeal and professionalism of its sister agency. For both organizations, stricter control over the use and management of public grazing lands was needed to attain the full potential of scientific land management.

In part, the drive for more control rested on the progressive vision's optimistic assumption that people and nature were malleable building blocks readily shaped and formed by engineers. But to forge from these blocks a healthier and more productive western range, one attuned to the needs of society, required control far beyond what had been exercised by the SCS and the Grazing Service. Trained engineers had to have the power and authority to regulate what people did and to direct the uses of natural resources. Only then could the greatest good be ensured for the greatest number.

Conservation reformers, such as Gifford Pinchot, understood that changing the land ethic of the very same western stockmen who had over-grazed the public range required more than laws demanding conservation; it also called for intervention, regulation, and close supervision. Laws could not perform what only dedicated and trained scientists could do in their capacity as civil servants. So the Forest Service and the BLM supple-mented law with a more direct and certain means to power and authority: They expanded agency staffs and developed new programs. An enhanced bureaucracy, a force then alien to the West and still novel to the American experience, would secure control and impose the progressive vision on the federal range.

Building a bureaucracy was a response to the compelling vision set forth by conservation reformers. But the Forest Service and the BLM did not depend solely on the moral fervor of visionary conservation. Other, more mundane, motivations also explain the growth of the two agencies and account for their dominance over a third of the nation's land and almost all of the public's grazing lands. Parochial concerns for prestige, position, and raw power drove the expansion of both agencies as much as the power of visionary idealism did. This gives additional perspective on how and why fledgling bureaus with only a handful of employees could by 1990 become massive bureaucracies employing nearly forty thousand full-time and thousands more part-time workers.

Seen from the "public choice" perspective of the new resource econom-ics, bureaucracy building was not an unexpected behavior for land man-agement agencies; it was merely an unconstrained one. Organizations like the Forest Service and the BLM are creatures of self-interest, and they share many of the attributes and strivings common to the private sector. Growth is the measure and reward of success. It is also the means to even more power and the stepping-stone to greater success.

Federal land agencies differ from private sector businesses in one crucial aspect. Their ambitions are not constrained by the natural limits of a com-petitive marketplace. The Forest Service and the BLM enjoy what is de-nied to nonpublic bureaucracies: immunity from the consequences that come with accountability. The budgets that have built their staffs and ex-panded their offices have relied not on customer satisfaction but on political lobbying and the forging of special interest alliances. Protected by law from going out of business, both agencies have focused on maintaining or increasing their share of an ever-expanding federal budget. Growth is more than the normal course of business; it is the logical outcome of the incentives provided by a progressive vision.

A more skeptical view comes from Robert Kharasch in *The Institutional Imperative*. He spares no energy to discount the role of idealism or the place of reasoned self-interest in the workings of bureaucracy. He reduces the aggrandizing motives of large institutions to a series of self-evident propositions. Among those principles are three simple axioms:

First Axiom: Any institutional action is merely the working of the institution's internal machinery.
Second Axiom: Institutional existence depends upon the continual working of the internal machinery.
Third Axiom: Whatever the internal machinery does is perceived within the institution as the real purpose of the institution (i.e., function is seen as purpose).[2]

Based on these principles, Kharasch arrives at what he terms the law of institutional self-occupation: "If an institution can generate the subject matter of its operation, it will." Bureaucracy building and the imperative for control are, by this thinking, the outcomes of a narrow institutional logic, one that drives growth for no other reason than simply to attain it.[3]

Whether or not the bureaucratic strivings of the Forest Service and the BLM can be reduced to the absurd level of circular reasoning or explained by the motives of idealism and rational self-interest, one essential fact stands out. Starting with the establishment of the Forest Service in 1905 and escalating with the formation of the Bureau of Land Management in 1946, the imperative of control has dominated the agenda of federal land management agencies. It has persuaded the Forest Service and the BLM to forgo long-term conservation goals for the short-term objectives of building organizations and asserting power. Their scientific mandate has evolved through the various logics of bureaucracy into a modern technocracy seeking a landed empire on the western range.

BUILDING A GRAZING BUREAUCRACY:
THE BLM

In 1947, a year after its creation, the BLM enjoyed a modest budget of almost $4 million to cover the care and management of renewable resources on public lands. In 1991, that budget had swollen to over $135 million. During the same period, the BLM's total operating budget increased nearly thirtyfold, from $30 million to approximately $900 million. Agency staff also multiplied, though at a slower rate. Full-time BLM personnel grew from a mere one thousand employees to almost ten thousand.[4]

In just over four decades, the BLM—created from the merger of the Grazing Service and the General Land Office—went from the status of a fledgling agency to the status of a well-financed land management bureaucracy. It successfully shed the image of simple land custodian and assumed the stature of progressive manager of natural resources. But the significance of those four decades goes beyond the birth and growth of an agency. What matters most in the saga of the BLM is *why* that growth occurred. Did it happen because the BLM wanted to improve its management of western lands, or did it reflect the agency's desire for power and control? And who benefited from that growth: the land or the bureaucracy?

One way to answer those questions is to look at the agency from the vantage of 1967, the midpoint of its first four decades. Before that date, the BLM's annual grazing program was modestly funded, remaining well below $20 million each year. Most of that money went for staff salaries and agency administration. Virtually no funds were allocated for on-the-ground land improvements. In 1967, for example, $14 million was invested in the improvement of public grazing lands. Only $1 million of that money came from the BLM; the remainder was invested by public-land ranchers. For every $0.10 the government invested in the care of the federal range, stockmen spent over $1.25 in the construction of fences and the development of water resources.[5] Before 1967, the government's share of rangeland investments was even less.

By all indications, rangeland conditions were not suffering from the paucity of government expenditures. BLM figures, for example, substantiate a slow but steady improvement in range conditions on public lands from 1936 to 1966. A 1976 report released by the Council on Environmental Quality supported that conclusion. The report's authors, renowned range scientists, wrote:

> In the next 30-year period, between 1936 and 1966, we believe that the federal rangelands improved some. Although there appears to be little or no difference in the percentage of good or excellent range, the amount of range considered to be in poor or bad condition was estimated to have declined from 58% to 33% in 1966. At the same time, the amount of fair condition range increased from 26% to 49% . . . . This shift from poor to fair condition was more pronounced on the [BLM's] Public Domain lands . . . . We believe that the reported overall response of Public Domain ranges was small because they were extremely depleted by excessive "free range" use at the beginning of the period, and the arid nature of most of the Public Domain ranges does not allow them to respond quickly to management. A move of one condition class in 30 years can be considered a successful response to management.[6]

The "management" referred to in the report entailed, at the very most, two major efforts. Closing of the open range in 1934 was the first and probably the most important. It reversed the intolerable conditions that underlay the tragedy of the western commons and gave stockmen the opportunity to protect their permitted public lands from excessive overgrazing. The second effort came mostly from permittees, who invested most of the labor and almost all of the money expended on rangeland improvement prior to 1967.

For the BLM, however, the results were not all that encouraging. Despite its steady growth since 1946, the agency still faced an uncertain future. Its job was to oversee and manage the public domain for the purposes set by the Taylor Grazing Act. But that act had only temporarily withdrawn public domain lands from homesteading. In a very real sense, the BLM was an interim caretaker for lands still targeted for disposal. If the public domain were reopened to settlement or purchase, the BLM would no longer have a land base.

Beginning in the early 1970s, the BLM sought a legislative solution—a federal statute that would permanently withdraw public domain lands, place those lands permanently in the agency's custody, and provide adequate funding to build a stronger Bureau of Land Management. A first step was taken with the issuance of the 1975 Nevada Report, formally titled "Effects of Livestock Grazing on Wildlife, Watershed, Recreation and Other Resource Values in Nevada."[7] In that report, the BLM criticized the broad discretionary powers allowed permittees under existing laws and warned of the effects of bad grazing practices on other rangeland resources and uses. The BLM also released a study showing that range conditions on public domain lands had actually declined since 1966.[8] The Senate Appropriations Committee, which had requested the 1975 range condition study, reacted to the agency's findings in a way most favorable to BLM's ambitions. "Range conditions are deteriorating at an alarming rate," the committee concluded, "and budget estimates repeatedly do not meet the Federal responsibility in this area."[9] In response to the committee, the BLM testified:

> Analysis of data shows that range conditions are deteriorating except under *intensive* rangeland management practices. Significant decline may continue. BLM believes the best solution for significantly correcting these deficiencies is acceleration of the *intensive* management and development program to arrest deterioration and increase the productivity of the public lands for a multitude of uses [emphasis mine].[10]

The BLM's message was clear: the public range could be improved, but only under strict BLM administration and only with sufficient funding. Intensive management required many times the budget allocated to the agency in the past. It also demanded permanence and authority to realize the agency's conservation mandate.

The BLM got what it was looking for, and more. The Federal Land Policy and Management Act of 1976 (FLPMA) permanently withdrew public domain lands from future disposal and greatly enhanced the power of the BLM to control and regulate grazing on the federal range. Two years later, after a stern warning from the General Accounting Office (GAO) that "forty-nine million acres [of BLM land] were subject to destructive continuous grazing," the Public Rangeland Improvement Act of 1978 (PRIA) was passed by a Congress eager to meet BLM's requests for greater funding.[11] The 1978 act authorized massive expenditures for range improvements.

Almost immediately, the BLM reaped the fruits of its political labors. Its overall operational budget almost tripled in the four years following 1976, and agency investments on public rangeland improvements skyrocketed. They doubled with the passage of FLPMA, received a major boost from PRIA, and reached their highest level in the early 1980s. By 1982, annual agency expenditures on range improvements totaled just over $13 million, a figure overshadowed only by an even greater budgetary expansion in range staff and administration.[12] And even better, the infusion of funds was proving what the BLM had long claimed. Rangeland conditions were improving at an unprecedented rate.

The agency's 1984 report showed that rangeland in excellent and good condition had doubled and that only half as much land was in poor or bad condition—all in the brief period since the critical 1975 Senate report![13] Even more remarkable, the 1975 Nevada Report was reviewed internally by BLM scientists and discredited—a belated reaction to mounting criticism of the report's faulty methodology. In retrospect, things were not nearly so bad in Nevada—or, for that matter, elsewhere on the western range.

On paper, the BLM was proving its point. Building bureaucracy was good for the land. But the figures supplied by the BLM did not tell the whole story. Permittee investments for range improvements, for example, had fallen almost as quickly as government expenditures had increased. Where ranchers had once outspent the government by as much as twelve to one, by the late 1970s they were paying for less than 20 percent of all public rangeland improvements.[14] Moreover, the precipitous fall in private expenditures after 1976 eroded the windfall effect of an expanded agency budget. Total annual investments (public and private combined) on BLM grazing lands during the ensuing years were not substantially greater than what they had been during the 1960s. In other words, the BLM may have spent more money, but the net total expended on the land had not changed significantly. In fact, it may have actually fallen. Contrary to the intent of Congress, the BLM had funneled monies targeted for on-the-ground range improvements to personnel. Between 1975 and 1979, the BLM had diverted as much as $2.5 million per year into staff salaries from "8100" dollars—the 50 percent share of grazing fees retained by the BLM and earmarked for range investment.[15]

The BLM's optimistic report on range recovery was also deceptive. In 1988, a GAO study on BLM range conditions challenged the accuracy of BLM range condition estimates.[16] It offered evidence that percentages of excellent- and good-condition range may have been overestimated in official reports. The GAO's conclusion is not surprising. The marked improvement in range conditions between 1975 and 1984 makes little biological sense, given the true picture of land investments and the inherent resistance of the land to rapid improvement. If anything, BLM range condition data reflect the political investment made by an agency more eager to enhance itself than to attend to the needs of ailing rangelands. And the investment paid off, earning the agency a grazing budget well in excess of $40 million by 1991.[17]

Four decades after its creation, the BLM firmly controlled a major share of the western range. Its success, though, did not rest on earned and proven laurels. Certainly, soil and vegetation on the public domain had changed for the better since the closing of the open range. But most of that change had occurred long before the BLM had begun its ambitious drive toward bureaucracy. What came out of the 1970s and 1980s was not a western range restored to the promise and ideal of conservation reform. What emerged was empire, pure and simple, the landed domain of a technocracy true to its progressive origins.

BUILDING A GRAZING BUREAUCRACY: THE FOREST SERVICE

The BLM was not alone in its manipulation of range condition data to meet agency demands for resources and power. Well before the closing of the public domain, the Forest Service was issuing dire warnings of resource damage and depletion in national forests to bolster its cause for more funds and more staff. Many of those warnings were based on expediency rather than fact. Henry Clepper, a historian otherwise sympathetic to the Forest Service, found evidence of fabricated range condition reports coming out of the early years of the agency's grazing program. Those reports, he regretfully noted, were among the few means available to agency range staff to gain control of forest grazing in an environment of rancher hostility. Clepper wrote:

> early reports of range conditions were on occasion distorted and technically in error. The angry concern of those charged with the protection of the public lands may have led to exaggeration, but it demonstrated the need for improved management to prevent destructive grazing . . . sensationalism helped overcome the apathy and indifference of the responsible policy makers.[18]

Manipulation of early range data was symptomatic of the effort being made by the Forest Service to promote its larger, and more important, forestry program. The specter of timber famine, raised first in 1868 by the General Land Office, became the agency's battle cry for more authority and funding. In 1910, the Forest Service warned that "the United States has already crossed the verge of a timber famine so severe that its blighting effects will be felt in every household in the land."[19] Later, in 1919, the agency predicted that "within less than 50 years, our present timber shortage will have become a blighting timber famine."[20]

Predictions of timber famine intensified in following years, culminating in the controversy-ridden Copeland Report of 1933, which attributed "practically all of the major problems of American Forestry . . . [to] private ownership."[21] Before national forest inventories fell any further, the report warned, Congress should attend to the reform and regulation of America's private woodlands. Not surprisingly, the reform and regulation envisioned in the Copeland Report bore all the traits of progressive conservation. The job of salvaging America's extensive timber resources belonged to the nation's forestry elite.

Had Congress followed the recommendations of the Copeland Report, the Forest Service would have extended its control over timber resources far beyond the boundaries of national forests and well into the heartland of privately owned woodlands. But neither Congress nor the American people were ready for a progressive vision on the scale sought by the Forest Service. Indeed, the public's refusal to be swayed by predictions of an impending timber crisis proved wise and prudent. Forest inventories increased in subsequent years, making the issue of timber famine essentially irrelevant.

Warnings of forage famine and rangeland depletion, however, continue to play a crucial role in the making of the Forest Service's grazing program. After suffering attempts during the Hoover administration to dismantle it and losing its bid for public domain lands to the Department of the Interior, the Forest Service wanted to restore its image. The agency needed to reestablish its political clout and reaffirm its scientific credibility as a leader in rangeland management. To do so, it needed an issue as compelling and urgent as timber famine.

Publication of "The Western Range" in 1936 gave the Forest Service the issue it needed. The agency's report announced that America's private and public rangelands, with the notable exception of national forest grazing lands, were on the verge of environmental catastrophe. "There is," the report observed, "perhaps no darker chapter nor greater tragedy in the history of land occupancy and use in the United States than the story of the western range."[22] Whereas the Forest Service had corrected the overgrazing of the past and begun a policy of sound land management, other property owners and managers of the western range were lagging far behind.

Besides a sensational depiction of plundered resources, the report offered the most comprehensive compilation of data ever assembled on western grazing lands. It presented Forest Service estimations of range conditions on national forest, public domain, private, and state grazing lands. Although only 30 percent of Forest Service rangeland was described as being in poor condition, the majority of all other rangelands were classified as severely depleted. The report showed 75 to 90 percent of all public domain, private, and state grazing lands declining in condition. On national forest ranges, 90 percent of all grazable land was judged to be stable or improving in condition. No source for the estimates was given.

The American National Livestock Association concluded that the report was a "self-serving compilation of falsehoods"[23] with one goal in mind: extension of the Forest Service bureaucracy over the public range. Clarence Forsling, chief of Forest Service research in 1937, gave substance to the criticism.[24] He acknowledged that one purpose of the report was to point out the weaknesses of the Taylor Grazing Act as a solution to the problems of the public domain. A different solution—the Forest Service—would have been far more preferable.

Adding insight into the report's motives were allegations by Walt L. Dutton, a range specialist and forest supervisor in the Pacific Northwest Region.[25] Dutton sharply attacked the report, claiming its data had been manipulated to sharpen the contrast between national forest ranges and public domain lands. There was no question that public domain lands were in bad shape, he said, but Forest Service lands were not substantially better. They were certainly not shining examples of superior land management.

Despite the criticism, the report gave the Forest Service its best forum for advancing the progressive vision. It provided the blueprint for "management which will restore and maintain in perpetuity on a sustained yield basis, and utilize, all of the resources of the land."[26] For Earle Clapp, associate chief of the Forest Service and prime mover behind the report, the Forest Service was the proper agency to tackle range improvement on all public grazing lands. "Restoration during the next 50 years," he wrote, "should make it possible for these [forest] ranges to carry 20 percent more stock than the present grazing capacity of the range." On the public domain, he continued, Forest Service management should bring the land's carrying capacity up "to the point where it can carry safely the livestock now being grazed."[27]

Depression and war put the report and its proposals on hold for more than a decade. By official accounts, the delay was not a problem: Forest rangelands were doing quite well without the programs envisioned in "The Western Range." Department of Agriculture figures for 1940 showed a 29 percent improvement in the productivity of forest ranges since 1905.[28] But many members of the agency's range staff looked at the past thirty-five years and perceived little change. If the progressive vision was to work, they believed, more money and people were needed to broaden agency range programs and expedite range investments.

In written testimony before Congress in 1949, the Forest Service described land rehabilitation as envisioned by its range staff. Given sufficient funds, "the depleted range and watershed areas can be restored to productivity within 2 to 4 years and made to support 5 to 10 times the number of livestock now being carried."[29] And ranchers who might otherwise face livestock reductions would, as a result, reap the benefits of better range and more cattle and sheep. The agency's proposal was almost too good to be true. In its bid for additional funding, the Forest Service had shortened the predicted time for range recovery from fifty to four years and upped the livestock advantage from 20 to 1,000 percent.

Ranchers eager to avoid reductions in carrying capacity and western congressmen looking for quick fixes to western rangeland problems bought the Forest Service proposal. Passed in October 1949, the Anderson–Mansfield Act authorized the Forest Service to spend up to $133 million on reforestation and range revegetation over a fifteen-year period. What had begun on the note of range depletion ended in a crescendo of congressional generosity. Just as the Forest Service had profitably tethered its forestry program to rising fears of national sawtimber shortages, it successfully linked its embryonic range program to predictions of forage famine and imminent livestock reductions. With $133 million in hand and a record-high 1949 range improvement budget, the agency was well on its way to testing the tenets of scientific land management on national forest rangelands.

What followed was the most ambitious program of land rehabilitation ever attempted. Millions of acres of forest rangelands were plowed, sprayed with herbicides, bulldozed, chained, and reseeded. From New Mexico north to Oregon, sagebrush and scrubby woodlands were erased from the landscape and replaced with monocultures of crested wheatgrass. Three million acres of pinyon-juniper woodlands were mechanically scraped from the soil surface of national forest lands and, to a lesser extent, from public domain lands.[30] Large chains dragged between pairs of tractors cleared the land of unwanted brush and prepared the land for a new and more promising vision.

Throughout the 1950s and 1960s, range rehabilitation continued, funded at a level far beyond the BLM's meager pre-1967 grazing management budget. But the promises of range rehabilitation went unfilled. Fifty years after "The Western Range" was published, and twenty-five years after the Forest Service's promise to improve carrying capacity on depleted range, national forest livestock numbers had fallen from 12,216,000 animal unit months (AUMs) to 8,702,842 AUMs.[31] And by 1989, the Forest Service was openly admitting that the future might offer only more of the past. In its "Draft 1990 RPA Program," the agency projected that grazing on forest ranges could fall by as much as 10 percent over the next half-century.[32]

Armed with the studies and reports of the 1970s and 1980s, the Forest Service has repeatedly raised the specter of forage shortages and massive livestock reductions in order to acquire additional money for range management. The agency has even resorted to data manipulation to persuade Congress of its financial needs. By changing the way cows and calves are counted (from 1 to 1.32 AUMs per cow-calf unit), the Forest Service's range division has turned a decline in grazing use on national grasslands into an apparent increase. Robert Williamson, head of the range division, explained the agency's paper manipulation at the 1989 National Cattlemen's Association meeting in Phoenix, Arizona: It was needed to win congressional support for an expanded grazing budget.[33] More livestock on national grasslands, he insisted, showed what could be done with more dollars and made clear what might be lost without additional funding.

Adding to the questionable economics of agency range management is the fact that each year, the Forest Service has spent nearly twice as much on grazing management as it has received from grazing fees. And its total level of range investment since 1950 has more than exceeded the total value of livestock forage in national forests.[34] Massive amounts of taxpayer dollars have been invested in public lands to support less and less livestock and to achieve, at most, minimal improvements in range conditions.

In 1987, over half of all national forest rangelands were reported to be in fair or poor condition—a statistic surprisingly unchanged from the condition estimates first provided in 1936 by "The Western Range." Even more significantly, the percentage of forest range reported in 1987 as declining in condition represents an increase over 1936 figures, going from an estimated 10 percent to 14 percent.[35] Complicating the picture even more, a 1988 GAO report has criticized the accuracy and completeness of Forest Service range condition data.[36] It has raised the prospect of fifty years of range improvement work without any documented evidence of success except for a bureaucracy expanded far beyond its modest origins.

This is not to suggest that decades of infusion of federal funds onto national forest rangelands did not bring some beneficial results. They caused positive change in many cases, at times transforming marginal rangelands into highly productive grasslands. Yet benefits gained in one arena were all too often offset by losses in another, frustrating the agency's promise and mission to restore depleted rangelands. In the Carson National Forest in New Mexico, for example, thousands of acres of sagebrush were plowed and reseeded to crested wheatgrass in the 1960s. An extensive and highly productive grassland was created in order to maintain and enhance livestock numbers. Today, the crested wheatgrass range is dying from inadequate grazing use.[37] Ungrazed plants are choking themselves in the debris of previous years' growth. Not only are ranchers denied the benefit of the monoculture created for their use, but the use of once productive and diverse winter range has also been denied to the area's deer and elk population.

Similar situations exist in most western national forests and cast doubt on the ecological and economic wisdom of a half-century of Forest Service range improvement programs. Conservation and environmental groups have questioned the ecological effects of massive plowing, chaining, herbicide spraying, and reseeding on wildlife habitat, water quality, soils, and range vegetation. They fear that as much harm as good may have been created by transforming diverse native rangelands into unbroken expanses of biologically simplified range. Economists have challenged the economic viability of spending enormous sums of money on projects that appear to have benefited neither the land nor its users. They point out that the environmentally questionable activities of brush control and reseeding would not have occurred on the scale that they did without the help of Forest Service subsidies. Had public-land ranchers borne the costs instead, the results of range reclamation would have been ecologically more palatable and economically more prudent. The technology of range reclamation was, and remains, simply too expensive for most ranchers to have done otherwise.

Like the Bureau of Land Management, the Forest Service has sought and achieved bureaucracy in the name of an enticing landscape vision. And like the BLM, it has been rewarded with larger and larger budgets for performances far below the standards of its progressive vision. The conservation goals that should have directed the agency's attention toward meeting the needs of the land have motivated the Forest Service to seek more staff and larger budgets. Had the results of bureaucracy building been more favorable toward the lands of the western range, a kinder assessment might be possible.

TESTAMENTS TO TECHNOCRACY

Progressive reform on federal rangelands required more than the brute force of bureaucracy to succeed. Policing, after all, could only restrain western stockmen from injuring the land. It could not stop them; nor could it contribute positively to the recovery of depleted rangelands. To be effective and lasting, conservation and renewal of public lands had to be based on control over the users as well as over the many uses of the federal range. Only by applying their progressive vision to both land and people could the Forest Service and the BLM hope to reverse the environmental damage of the past.

Reversing the damage began with policies and programs rooted in progressive standards of technical expertise and centralized control and planning. Three of those policies and programs are particularly notable. One is a tool: the system of grazing permits intended to regulate the users of public grazing lands. The other two are principles: the ideals of sustained yield and multiple use, which set the direction for future management and use of the federal range. Together, the tool and the principles energized conservation reform and enhanced its grasp on the federal range. They came to symbolize the heart and soul of a progressive ideology confident of its ability to manipulate people and nature to the mutual benefit of both.

Grazing permits were the first, and easiest, step toward applying conservation reform and controlling the federal range. They were the means by which the open range was closed. Issued initially for national forests and after 1934 for public domain lands, permits determined which stockmen and how much livestock could graze the public's range. In so doing, grazing permits ended the worst abuses of an unregulated federal range, bringing relative economic and ecological stability to lands and people exhausted by decades of overgrazing. Permits gave selected stockmen exclusive rights to forage from the public's range and created a modicum of incentives encouraging wiser use of the resource. And by offering an alternative to historical overgrazing, permits allowed space and time for the healing of severely depleted ranges. As a result, western rangelands stabilized and staged a modest recovery.

Unlike the leasing system preferred by public-land ranchers, grazing permits also maximized the authority and control of federal land agencies. "Under the permit system," a USDA agricultural bulletin reported in 1922, "a man receives a permit to graze a definite number of animals for a definite period of time on certain specified lands, with priority right to consideration for renewal at a future time, while under the other system [leasing] a man gets the use of a definite number of selected areas of land [for any number of livestock] for a definite period, usually also with priority consideration for renewal."

"At first sight," the bulletin observed, "there is no difference in the effect [of the two systems]." Yet at closer examination, the differences were marked. First, "the permit system normally results in slight understocking of the range . . . while the lessee of an area is almost sure to overstock in order to be sure that he 'gets his money back.' . . . *Especially is this true if his tenure of the land is for a short period only* [emphasis mine]." Second, and most important, "any sort of permit system makes it *necessary for capable officials* to determine with reasonable accuracy the grazing capacity of a large region and formulate a plan for the region during a given season before they can begin to allot animals to specific areas [emphasis mine]."[38]

The grazing permit system established by the Forest Service, and later adopted and continued by the Grazing Service and the BLM, provided for only ten years' tenure—too brief a period, as the bulletin noted, to be workable under a lease arrangement. By the later reckoning of some public-land ranchers, it was too brief even for a permit system. In Australia, public grazing lands are leased for periods of no less than thirty years. The Australian government relies on the incentive of secure tenure rather than the administration of trained experts to steward and conserve its nation's rangelands. The system has encouraged Australian leaseholders to treat rangelands as resources to be conserved for long-term use rather than short-term exploitation.[39]

But such solutions were not desired when the Forest Service was founded or even when the Grazing Service and the BLM were created. Part of the reason lay in a lingering sentiment for the democratic aspirations of the agrarian vision. During the early years of both the Forest Service and the BLM, the possibility of reopening portions of the federal range to settlement or purchase was real. Public-land ranchers were still temporary residents, and ten-year permits were quite adequate for people and livestock considered neither permanent nor representative of the democratic destiny of the public's land. And when the last of the federal lands were permanently withdrawn from settlement with the passage of FLPMA, short-term permits fitted nicely with the abbreviated role accorded stockmen and the rededication of the western range to progressive democracy.

But the failure to establish a lease system on the federal range (beyond isolated tracts of public land assigned to the BLM) was more a function of conservation ideology than of lingering agrarian sentiment. Only a permit system provided the authority by which land management agencies could impose their progressive vision on the western landscape. It granted them the power to determine numbers of grazing animals, seasons of use, and systems of grazing management. It was the administrative tool by which scientific land management could be practiced; it acknowledged the unique role to be played by trained experts and dedicated administrators.

As affirmed by *Natural Resources Defense Council v. Interior Secretary Hodel* in 1984, which denied the legality of the BLM's cooperative management agreements (CMAs), the permit system and the statutory authority behind it were "intended to preserve and improve the ravaged commons through intensive management and ongoing governmental rights of reentry."[40] To the extent that CMAs extended grazing permits beyond ten years and allowed ranchers to set stocking rates and seasons of use, they were incompatible with basic federal responsibilities. They abdicated the duty of land managers to prescribe the numbers of animals and seasons of use and "fail[ed] to retain necessary governmental authority to enforce" the terms of grazing permits.[41]

That decision reaffirmed the commitment of conservation reform to bureaucracy and the imperative of control. By nullifying a management program intended to simulate the positive incentive advantages of leasing systems, the purpose and intent of the permit system was made clear: regulation first, stewardship second. Vesting private citizens with interests in the public's land, even when done for conservation purposes, violated the letter of the law—and, most certainly, the spirit of the progressive vision. Indeed, the court's 1984 decision only reinforced what had been practical policy since the closing of the western range. Pinchot's elite, not the citizens who made their homes and livelihood on the land, were the proper stewards of the federal range.

By fostering agency control over public rangelands, grazing permits enabled the Forest Service and the BLM to take the second step in scientific land management: setting the carrying capacity for livestock on the federal range. "Carrying capacity," under the principle of sustained yield, stood for the maximum level of stocking consonant with the long-term productivity and health of the land. It expressed an intuitively simple and logically sound idea: The forage grazed from a unit of rangeland should not exceed the biological capacity of the land and its vegetation to renew itself. Even with the recent expansion of the sustained yield concept to encompass all resources and their uses within a grazing unit, its implications remained unchanged. Livestock should be grazed only in the numbers compatible with the sustainability and ecological integrity of the entire land unit.

Sustained yield practices were implicit in the goals and objectives of the Forest Service's early range program and in the adjudication of grazing privileges by the Grazing Service after 1934. But the principle and practice of sustained yield remained embryonic until the passage of the Multiple Use–Sustained Yield Act of 1960 (MUSYA) and FLPMA in 1976. Those acts, lobbied for by the Forest Service and the BLM, gave authority for a more rigorous and scientific application of sustained yield practices on public grazing lands.

Sustained yield has been, and remains, the crucial factor separating past and present uses of public lands. In an important sense, it is the feature that makes federal land management scientific—or, more correctly, gives it the appearance of scientific objectivity. Such appearance, however, obscures the practical problem of applying sustained yield policy. Carrying capacities under sustained yield management are set as fixed, discrete numbers; but grazing systems are dynamic, and their carrying capacities are not reducible to single numbers. Seasonal fluctuations in weather, changes in management regimes, and the vigor and health of an ever-changing forage base combine to make carrying capacity a function of the moment. Attempts to define carrying capacity as a set number for more extended periods—as the agencies do—can be defended only on pragmatic, not scientific, grounds.

The objectivity and scientific credibility of agency estimations of carrying capacity break down even further when the methods of their calculations are considered. For example, range scientists at New Mexico State University calculated carrying capacity on the same unit of land using four separate techniques commonly used by the Forest Service and the BLM. They arrived at carrying capacities varying by as much as 100 percent.[42]

Perhaps the greatest obstacle to estimating meaningful carrying capacities on public lands has been the problem of defining the parameters of sustained yield. Grazing management that provides sustained forage production for a given number of livestock, but not for a herd of elk or deer, may be an acceptable definition of sustained yield to some but certainly not to those who place higher value on wildlife and the aesthetics of recreation.

The principle of multiple use has evolved as the agencies' guide for setting the parameters of sustained yield and for determining just what should be sustained and in what quantities. Just as sustained yield provided the biological direction for making grazing permits the vehicles of scientific land management, multiple use has provided the political means to the Forest Service and BLM for defining the place of livestock grazing on the federal range.

Mandated under the same acts that gave political clout to the practice of sustained yield, and sharing a similar heritage, multiple use has become integral to public-land grazing management. Its roots, like those of sustained yield, are traceable to the early writings of Gifford Pinchot. But unlike sustained yield, multiple use has acquired a special connotation in the minds of those who regularly use America's public lands. It continues in symbol, if not in fact, the legacy lost with the failure of Jefferson's agrarian dream. Multiple use has kept the western range open to people other than resident stockmen. And though settlement on the federal range is no longer possible, multiple use has sustained the democratic myth first begun by the homestead acts, the belief in a western landscape capable of fulfilling the physical and spiritual needs of all Americans.

Beyond its cultural symbolism, multiple use also represents the fulfillment of the progressive promise—Pinchot's commitment to delivering the greatest good for the greatest number. Defined in FLPMA as "the management of the public lands and their various resource values so that they are utilized in the combination that will best meet the present and future needs of the American people," multiple use embodies the highest ideals of conservation reform.

Through multiple use, scientific expertise is theoretically able to extract the optimum mix of resources and uses from the land. In so doing, the wastefulness and inefficiency of the marketplace are avoided and resource benefits to all of society are maximized. All Americans find their resource needs and uses on the public lands met by bureaucracies dedicated to the public's interest. Multiple use, in this sense, is an almost unlimited expression of faith and confidence in the powers of technical and social planning and engineering. It so elevates the ability of well-intentioned men and women to discern and attain what is best for others that it also borders on wishful thinking, if not outright arrogance.

An overbearing optimism in the beneficence of land bureaucracy, however, is only half the story of multiple use. From its inception, multiple use represented more than a symbol of progressive conservation; it was the means by which the Forest Service and the BLM could secure more certain control over the rangelands. Starting in the late 1940s, both agencies found themselves under frequent assault from livestock interests whose political clout far exceeded their numbers. More than once, the Forest Service and the BLM fought back attempts by public-land ranchers to have their management authority curtailed or, even worse, their land base diminished by privatization.

Multiple use turned out to be one of the most useful political tools in the arsenals of the Forest Service and the BLM. Passage of MUSYA created a formidable barrier between the Forest Service and vocal livestock interests. Now mandated by law to give equal attention and consideration to other users and uses of the federal range, the Forest Service was in a much better position to ward off the political intrusions of ranchers. Similarly, FLPMA's multiple use provision provided what the BLM had implicitly sought in its 1975 Nevada Report. It gave the agency the political means to escape from the shadow of livestock interests and achieve the institutional autonomy it had sought for years. Its control of the public range ensured, the BLM was free to pursue its vision of grazing management on the western range. With the passage of FLPMA and MUSYA, the BLM and the Forest Service found their management positions greatly enhanced and their future on the western range virtually guaranteed.

Multiple use, sustained yield, and grazing permits all contributed to the tightening grasp of land management agencies on the land and people of the western range. They began as promising responses to the environmental waste and inefficiency of overgrazing. Yet they evolved into testaments to a land management technocracy attuned more to the bureaucratic imperative of control than to the urgent needs of a depleted landscape. The Forest Service and the BLM indeed relied on multiple use, sustained yield, and grazing permits to contain overgrazing and to structure grazing management on the federal range. But the land did not improve as quickly or as dramatically as their application might have suggested—or as the agencies' common vision predicted.

Instead, grazing policies and programs unwittingly locked the western range into a second, more pernicious, commons. This time, however, it was not a commons of ruthless exploitation and destruction of natural resources but a commons remindful of banality and lost opportunity. Progressivism's visionary harvest lacked the vitality and spirit of its agrarian predecessor. It moved the western range toward neither the extreme of excellence nor that of degradation but rather submerged it in a wallowing sea of mediocrity.

CHAPTER EIGHT

The Visionary Harvest

U ntil 1971, Joe and Susan Fallini's Twin Springs Ranch was a
model of good management. Its rangelands, stretching across
665,700 acres of central Nevada, testified to what caring stewardship could do for the land. Hard work and a willingness to invest in the
land's improvement had left a legacy of healthy plants, stable soils, and
abundant wildlife. Because of its good condition, the range could easily support two thousand head of cattle and still have ample forage and habitat for
125 wild horses and thousands of antelope and deer.

For the Fallinis, Twin Springs was the culmination of a dream begun one
hundred years earlier when Joe's grandfather stepped off Ellis Island and
headed west.[1] News of gold and silver bonanzas in Nevada had captured his
imagination, luring him to the bustling mining town of Eureka. There, he
went to work hauling mining supplies to outlying settlements. Honest labor
and prudent saving quickly changed his status from immigrant and freight
hauler to American homesteader and rancher.

Twin Springs, some seventy-five miles south of Eureka, could not have
existed without the legacy left by Joe's grandfather. Yet it was not until Joe
and his brothers pieced together several smaller ranches that Twin Springs
was born. Since that time, Joe and Susan have run the ranch, and until

1971 they were able to manage it on their own terms, remarkably free from the dictates and supervision of the BLM's district office in Tonopah.

During those years of relative freedom, Joe and Susan grazed livestock on their public rangelands lightly, always keeping a two-year reserve of forage in case of drought. They also developed waters for good livestock distribution and built fences for proper grazing management. They spent as much as $150 per year for each cow grazed on BLM lands—a rate twenty times greater than that of other public-land ranchers and infinitely more than the zero sum invested by the local office of the BLM.

An important part of Joe and Susan's management was keeping the wild horse population under control. Each year, they went to the county commission and requested approval to gather and remove wild horses. Their goal was to keep the herd stable at its historical level of 100 to 125 head. They put excess horses up for adoption and sale—and even slaughter. The few that had to be killed seemed a small price to pay for avoiding mass starvation on an overgrazed and depleted range.

Everything changed with the passage of the 1971 Wild Horses and Burros Protection Act, which shifted responsibility for managing wild horses from the state to the BLM. The act obligated the agency to keep wild horse numbers at levels and locations existing at the time the statute was enacted.

Despite the best of congressional intentions, agency control of wild horses spelled environmental catastrophe for the Twin Springs Ranch. The problem was not what the BLM did with the new law but what it did not do. Strongly influenced by wild horse advocacy groups, the agency did nothing. Consequently, by 1973, there were 260 wild horses on Twin Springs, horses that were roaming well beyond their customary range and drawing down the forage reserves intended for drought years. The Fallinis asked the BLM to manage the Twin Springs' herd, to bring the number of horses in balance with historical levels and to restrict them to traditional locations as required by law.

Despite the Fallinis' appeal, the BLM continued to do nothing. Wild horse numbers exploded over the next decade, reaching a peak population of twenty-three hundred head in 1984. The Fallinis' forage reserves were exhausted, and the annual forage base that supported their livestock teetered on depletion. Moreover, annual costs for pumping water and maintaining water lines and troughs quadrupled during those ten years to almost $200,000. Half the increase was caused by wild horses.

The land bore the greatest costs. Photographs taken at fixed points graphically documented the conversion of once vigorous and healthy rangelands into beaten-out *patches of weed and barren earth. State game surveys substantiated the precipitous decline of antelope and deer.*

Joe and Susan Fallini, joined by the state of Nevada, filed suit in federal court against the BLM as part of an appeal process begun in 1973. When the case was finally heard in 1986, the BLM denied that overgrazing was a problem and testified that forage was adequate on Twin Springs for both cattle and wild horses. The Sierra Club, siding with the agency, acknowledged that some range damage had occurred but placed full blame on the Fallinis. But telling photographs, reams of data, and expert witnesses brought a court decision favorable to the Fallinis and the land. The BLM was ordered to reduce wild horse numbers to historical levels and to restrict them to traditional ranges.

Two years later, wild horse numbers were finally under control. The herd had been culled to 370 head and would be reduced even more. But Joe and Susan's problems were not over. The BLM, freed from the pressures of wild-horse lobbyists, changed its mind on the Twin Springs Ranch. Past data, the agency conceded, had been in error. Twin Springs had been seriously overgrazed and its ranges drastically depleted by wild horses. Consequently, cattle numbers on the Fallinis' allotment would have to be cut by 20 percent because "land use plan objectives [for Twin Springs] are not being met under current stocking rates."² With the damage done, and at no risk or cost to itself in the process, the BLM assumed the belated role of resource protector.

Adding insult to injury, the agency denied the Fallinis' request to develop more private waters on Twin Springs as a means to speed up range recovery. The BLM would authorize more water developments, but only if the Fallinis agreed to open their new waters permanently to wild horses. Joe and Susan were stunned. The herd had no need for additional waters; the growth of the herd was proof of that. Also, it would be the Fallinis, not the BLM, who would have to pay the cost of watering the horses.

Like a scene from a Kafka novel, Joe and Susan Fallini found their lives uprooted by a bureaucracy shielded from accountability and out of touch with the land and its people. Almost twenty years of frantic struggle to save Twin Springs had earned them nothing but accusations that their stewardship was failing. Their ranch, once a model of good management, now bore the scars of abuse and depletion.

What had been a plague for the Fallinis turned out to be a blessing for the BLM. As the rangelands of Twin Springs were grazed and beaten to dust, the agency thrived and grew stronger. In 1985, Congress appropriated $17 million for the BLM's wild horses and burros program. That sum, basically unchanged to this *day, equaled twice the agency's budget for all range improvements and nearly half of its grazing budget.*³ *Henceforth, the BLM would have more incentive to control wild horses and to protect the fragile rangelands entrusted to its care. For Joe and Susan, that thought offered little consolation.*

FORGING A NEW COMMONS

Two features distinguish the western commons of the homestead era: a lack of control and an absence of caring. A lack of control was the outcome of laws and policies designed to create an agrarian society on an arid and inhospitable landscape. An absence of caring was the price of no control. The futility of open-range conditions and the frustration felt by stockmen powerless to act made conservation an irrelevant issue on the federal range, at least until the creation of forest reserves and the closing of the public domain. But even with the cessation of homesteading, the design of public-land law and policy did not change in a way that might have fostered a conservation ethic among western stockmen. Their good stewardship was welcomed, to be sure, but in no way was it considered necessary.

An unfamiliar dichotomy emerged on the federal range. One group, the livestock producers, was assigned the task of using the resource; the other, the federal agencies, was given the job of conserving the resource. Such an arrangement, it was assumed, would provide the necessary checks and balances to contain the narrow economic interests of ranchers and to reach the goals of progressive conservation. It would be the ideal strategy for putting an end to the tragedy of the western commons.

But beneath the veneer of progressive optimism lay a disturbing reality—one that would frustrate agency ambitions to heal past environmental ravages. The tools and principles that empowered the Forest Service and the BLM to control and care for the federal range did not encourage good management and better stewardship among public-land ranchers. Instead, the permit system and the principles of sustained yield and multiple use perpetuated an environment in which ranchers lacked control and incentive and left untouched the conditions underlying decades of misuse of federal rangelands.

What happened was simple. The tragedy of the western commons was formalized into law and implemented as the official policy of the Forest Service and the BLM. With alarming consistency, the distribution of grazing privileges simply froze customary use at levels beyond what the forage could support. "In most [grazing] districts," Wesley Calef writes, "permits had been issued for many more livestock than the range could properly support."[4] Tragically, stockmen who wanted to stop overstocking of public ranges were dissuaded from doing so for one reason: protection of individual grazing permits and the use rights that were tied to them.

OWNING NUMBERS, NOT LAND

From the perspective of federal law and agency policy, the rights claimed by stockmen to public grazing lands are controversial. Accepted by the Internal Revenue Service but denied by the Forest Service and the BLM, they reflect the unique nature of the permit system and the reality of intermingled landownerships. They rest, in part, on the ownership of "base lands" (private lands sufficiently adequate to support a rancher's livestock when not on public range) and "base waters" (waters controlled by the rancher that make arid federal ranges usable by domestic stock). Only by controlling such lands and waters can ranchers qualify for the ten-year grazing permits issued by the Forest Service and the BLM.

Preference ownership is a by-product of those requirements. As long as public-land ranchers hold on to their base properties and abide by agency regulations, they enjoy indefinite preference in the renewal of their ten-year grazing permits. Federal lands, attached to private holdings in this manner, have given stockmen what amounts to transferable rights in publicly owned property. Today, those rights are key assets that can be sold in conjunction with base properties, used as collateral for loans, and even assessed by state and federal authorities for taxation.

But grazing permits entail more than preference ownership. Because of the below-market grazing fees historically charged by the Forest Service and the BLM, permit value has been added to the privilege of public-land grazing. That value reflects the difference between what ranchers pay for public-land forage and what they would have to pay if they leased equivalent private lands. In other words, permits grant stockmen the right to graze public lands at below-market rates—a subsidy that enhances the asset values of their permits and the base lands and waters linked to them. Together, permit value and preference ownership have created readily marketable, although legally tenuous, property rights in public grazing lands.

Ranchers who were granted the first grazing permits acquired those rights without cost. As a result, the worth of their ranches skyrocketed far beyond the value of a few acres of private property or several acre-feet of water claims. They enjoyed substantial windfall profits. For the majority of permittees who have purchased public-land ranches, however, those profits have inflated the cost of federal grazing. Today, stockmen wishing to graze public lands pay far more than subsidized grazing fees; they must purchase the preference and subsidy rights that were free to original owners. Grazing of public lands, at least from a buyer's point of view, is not merely a privilege granted by federal agencies; it is a right purchased on the open market and valued as much as real property.

Assuming that stockmen perceive public-land ranching as a property right, the question remains why the permit system should discourage rather than promote conservation and improvement of federal rangelands. At the very least, a property interest in the federal range would be expected to give stockmen a substantial stake in the continued well-being of the land. Certainly, that would be true if ranchers' interests were vested in the land and its resources. But the informal rights created by grazing permits have nothing to do with the land or its resources.

Strictly speaking, all that public-land ranchers *own* are permits to graze fixed numbers of livestock. They have no absolute claim to the land or exclusive use of its forage. Their interests, and their informal rights, are vested in a single, administratively derived number. What counts most is the sheer magnitude of the grazing permit, not the condition of the range and its vegetation. The reason is clear. Livestock numbers issued by an agency can be controlled and cared for and their benefits defined, captured, and enjoyed. In contrast, the physical features of public lands, and the array of benefits linked to them (such as deer, elk, and trout), are more elusive. They are largely beyond the control of permittees, and their care—except as it affects the grazing permit—is a matter of considerably less concern.

Ecologically unsound as it may be, the grazing permit system encourages stockmen to attend more to the preservation of their herd sizes than to the well-being of the land. It is the logical outcome of a system of incentives that makes artificial numbers, not the resource base that must support them, the focus of attention. Environmentally, the effects are far from desirable. Socially, the results are costly, depriving the nation of the land's potential and barring public-land ranchers from playing a more productive role in its stewardship.

By comparison, private-land ranchers can afford to reduce livestock numbers without diminishing the value of their rangelands. In fact, they have incentives to reduce livestock numbers to improve range conditions and enhance the future economic value of their property. Most important, private owners can capture the benefit of their stewardship, whether in the form of increased livestock carrying capacity or a higher sale price for their properties. Environmentally, the odds are greater that private-land ranchers will consider the needs of deer, elk, and trout in the management of their lands.

At the heart of the problem are the many meanings of carrying capacity. From the permittees' perspective, it is a matter of property rights—rights that are unnaturally severed from the ecological well-being of the land. For the Forest Service and the BLM, it is a matter of scientific determination, a setting of some fixed number safely wedged between the yearly fluctuations that characterize a site's ability to support livestock. To private-land ranchers, it is less tangible, being influenced by a wide range of economic and biological factors.

A 1922 study of ranching behavior among tenant and landowner ranchers on the exclusively private Edwards Plateau of Texas captures the essence of the different outlooks on carrying capacity and sharpens the contrast between the private and public sectors. Privately owned lands, the study observed,

> are not always handled exactly like they would be under government control, because the private individual is seeking the greatest net return from his investment. Thus while a ranchman may decide that the normal carrying capacity of the range is a certain number of animals, he does not limit himself rigidly to the grazing of that number . . . . For example, a rancher may relatively overstock his ranges under conditions of abnormally high prices with the idea of understocking to rebuild them when prices are low.[5]

Quite possibly, the tendency of private ranchers periodically to exceed average or normal stocking has influenced agency commitment to fixed carrying capacities. Certainly, progressive conservation's original fear that the narrow economic interests of individual stockmen were responsible for the degradation of western rangelands still holds sway within the Forest Service and the BLM. Yet it is doubtful that even the narrow economic interests of such private-land ranchers, unless bolstered by hefty subsidies, could long ignore the personal costs of sacrificing future forage for present consumption. A successful ranch, as measured across generations, requires that its owners attend to the same considerations of sustained yield that occupy government agencies. The only difference between the two is that one reaches sustained yield by adjusting carrying capacity each year and the other sets it as a fixed number.

More to the point is the study's conclusion regarding the marked distinction between stockmen who ranch by lease and those who ranch by virtue of landownership. The two groups, whose analogy to public- and private-land ranchers, respectively, is clear despite the private status of the Edwards Plateau, perceive carrying capacity in entirely different terms. Their perceptions are shaped largely by contrasting relationships to the land. Where the tenant rancher focuses on the carrying capacity of the lease, the landowner rancher focuses on the carrying capacity of the land. For example,

> in Texas a tenant [read: public-land rancher] usually thinks of carrying capacity as meaning the number and kinds of livestock which a given ranch will presumably carry during the period of the lease. He is more likely to over-estimate and, therefore, overstock the ranch than not. The owner of a ranch in Texas [read: private-land rancher] usually thinks in terms of annual carrying capacity. On an exceptional year he may say that the carrying capacity is 80 heads of cattle per section, on an average year 40, and on a poor year 20 . . . . [6]

Not surprisingly, public-land ranchers' perceptions of carrying capacity conflict just as markedly with those of the Forest Service and the BLM—though for far different reasons. Agency calculations of carrying capacity are closely linked to the concept of sustained yield. Fixed numbers of livestock are set and authorized based on the biological potential of the range. For public-land ranchers, however, such a method conflicts with both their perceived interests and the practical aspects of their daily management. Permitted numbers in excess of a particular year's carrying capacity are not seen as harmful—certainly not if the rancher is given the stocking flexibility and discretion enjoyed by private-land ranchers.

But sustained yield, as applied and enforced by land agencies, has intensified the stewardship disincentives of the grazing permit system and made them more glaring than ever. The permit system, by creating rights in artificial numbers, and sustained yield, by reducing those artificial numbers to a fixed quantity, have narrowed the options available to public-land ranchers and stiffened their opposition to land conservation.

WHAT THE RANGE CAN BEAR

Sustained yield as a biological concept is not the problem. The problem lies in the way the Forest Service and the BLM have envisioned and applied the concept—as a fixed number intended to control stockmen and accommodate the logistics of too few managers for too many lands. Yet by tailor-fitting a naturally dynamic and scientifically elusive ideal to the body of laws, regulations, and policies guiding land management, agencies have given a not-so-subtle twist to its meaning and use. Rather than being a goal for good management, the principle of sustained yield has evolved into a set of practices that have discouraged good management among stockmen who use public lands.

Grazing nonuse practices point to the problems associated with sustained yield. Both Forest Service and BLM permittees are allowed to reduce stocking voluntarily for designated periods. They can take nonuse for a variety of purposes: to relieve livestock pressure on overgrazed lands; to adjust to adverse market conditions; or to accelerate range improvement. This allows public-land ranchers a semblance of the management flexibility enjoyed by stockmen in the private sector. But appearances can be deceiving. In practice, sustained yield policies of the Forest Service and the BLM have either lessened or eliminated the stewardship potentials of nonuse.

Ranchers who practice grazing nonuse to enhance the condition of their rangelands have frequently collided with the political realities of sustained yield. For example, a rancher in southern New Mexico took grazing nonuse for four years as a conservation practice on a BLM allotment she acquired in 1982. After five years of intensive monitoring, BLM analysis showed that range conditions had improved and carrying capacity on the allotment had nearly doubled from the originally permitted 125 head to 225 head. The rancher, eager to profit from her investment in grazing management, asked that her permit be increased by 25 head. The agency denied her request, insisting that sustained yield concerns other than of livestock—in this case, management of the allotment for possible wilderness designation—took precedence.

The fact that the allotment would not have improved as markedly as it did without the rancher's voluntary reduction in stocking had no bearing on the BLM's decision. Indeed, the BLM discounted the permittee's conservation efforts with a frivolous observation. "Over the past four years," the BLM wrote in its final decision on the rancher's request, "your actual use . . . has been less than the authorized use. This could raise the question as to whether or not an increase in grazing use is *actually needed* [emphasis mine]."[7] Not only was the BLM penalizing the rancher for good stewardship, but it was also playing politics with sustained yield to avoid a sensitive decision on carrying capacity in a potential wilderness area. Sustained yield, as this example suggests, is not necessarily the hallmark of good conservation science or the most certain path to restoration of the western range.

Questions and concerns about the health of the land have been overshadowed by a narrow institutional vision of using neat and tidy numbers for controlling the federal range. Agency regulations, for example, limit the number of consecutive years during which ranchers can take grazing nonuse. During the early 1980s, when livestock prices were depressed, many ranchers took significant voluntary reductions in stocking. Although their reductions were motivated by economic considerations, few permittees had allotments in such good condition that plants and soils could not have benefited from extended rest. But agency regulations prevented them from taking as much nonuse as they might have wished. Moreover, both the Forest Service and the BLM, intent on sustaining fixed numbers of livestock on federal grazing allotments, took steps to discourage ranchers from taking voluntary nonuse at all.

In southwestern national forests, the Forest Service told ranchers taking more than 20 percent nonuse that their allotments would be stocked with outside livestock to ensure full utilization of available forage. The reason given to one group of permittees from the Gila National Forest went to the heart of the issue of sustained yield:

> [Your] allotments run over 12,000 head of yearlings and generate over $100,000 worth of grazing fees to the United States Treasury . . . [but] over the past several years . . . one-third to one-half of these allotments have been vacant in any given year. We also have a

problem of keeping some of our yearlong allotments stocked to their approved capacity.[8]

Many of the same concerns played a key role in making sustained livestock numbers a priority on public domain lands. Specifically, the BLM was forced to revise its policy on nonuse when confronted with a critical report prepared by the Office of the Inspector General in the Department of the Interior. According to the 1986 report, the BLM had allowed excessive grazing nonuse, with the result that "available grazing AUM's [animal unit months] are unused with a possible loss of revenue."[9] In response, the director of the BLM authorized agency personnel to issue temporary grazing permits to stockmen wishing to graze underutilized allotments.[10]

Nationwide, grazing nonuse on the federal range has been significant, averaging almost 15 percent on national forest lands and 22 percent on BLM lands.[11] Reports from agency field staff suggest that nonuse may actually be greater than reported. For many public-land ranchers, however, the dangers of taking nonuse frequently outweigh the advantages. Just the threat that their allotments might be stocked with outside livestock is sufficient cause for most permittees to graze the federal range to the maximum limit allowed. Just as on the open range of a hundred years before, they must use the existing forage for no other reason than to prevent others from later exploiting it.

Many public-land ranchers are aware that authorized livestock numbers on their allotments exceed current carrying capacity. Forage is simply inadequate. The BLM's 1975 Nevada Report criticized the unusually high level of grazing nonuse (28 percent) in Nevada because it was indicative of a national problem of overstocking due to inflated grazing permits. A 1988 GAO report sounded a similar theme by suggesting that too many Forest Service and BLM allotments had authorized stocking in excess of carrying capacity.[12] In both instances, nonuse was not considered an appropriate response to the problem—even though many of those "overstocked" allotments were being used properly because of voluntary nonuse. Instead, nonuse was and is viewed in the vein suggested by public-lands legal scholar George Coggins: an "elaborate scheme" to avoid coping with overstocking on federal ranges.[13]

Such a conclusion, however, overlooks the role of nonuse in mitigating one of the worst flaws in the grazing permit system. Historically, nonuse has been the only option available to public-land ranchers for resolving the dilemma of owning livestock numbers rather than owning the grazing lands themselves. It has allowed many permittees to reconcile their property interests with the well-being of the land. But agency policies are becoming increasingly intolerant of that strategy. Both the Forest Service and the BLM have regulations and policies that dictate alternative solutions. In most instances, this means reduction of authorized livestock numbers rather than continued reliance on voluntary nonuse. Again, agencies prefer to establish a fixed number consonant with sustained yield.

Unfortunately, agency policy on nonuse has at times crossed the fine line separating bad sense from nonsense. On a small ranch in the Lincoln National Forest in south-central New Mexico, a rancher chose not to stock her recently permitted forest rangelands. She did so because she was aware of the prevailing drought and conscious of the need to rest forest rangelands damaged by decades of overgrazing. On May 8, 1984, she received a letter from the Forest Service addressed to all permittees requesting that they reduce stocking on their lands due to the severe drought. She had, of course, already taken this action on her own accord. But the Forest Service wrote directly to her a day later, on May 9, 1984, warning that she had taken nonuse without proper authorization. The agency informed her that she would have to fully and immediately stock her allotment or face a penalty for disobeying the terms of her grazing permit. Her willingness to care for her permitted grazing lands did not seem to matter. What counted instead were the demands of the agency for control and an institutional vision committed to sustaining the livestock yield of her land. Not surprisingly, the rancher's forest rangelands are far from healed. To this day, arroyos continue to deepen, soils still erode, and the plant life that remains holds on tenuously to what little is left.[14]

DIVVYING UP THE WESTERN RANGE

Multiple use, like sustained yield, is a cornerstone of public-land policy and management. It is, from a biological perspective, an extension of the sustained yield principle. A myriad of products and uses can be taken from the land indefinitely only if each and every one of them is stewarded in concert. In other words, the long-term supply of such things as forage for livestock, timber for homes, recreation for urban dwellers, and habitat for wildlife depends on the integrity of the ecological system. In this regard, multiple use is hardly disputable and most certainly is not an idea that should be exclusive to the federal range.

But there is another dimension to multiple use on public lands. Multiple use is the quintessential expression and achievement of the progressive vision. Above all, it is conservation reform's declaration of omniscience, a bold statement of the ability and power of select people to plan the precise mix of public-land products and uses that will maximize social welfare and benefit the greatest number of people. As such, it addresses people and nature on the western range with the optimism and arrogance of confident ideology rather than the cautious neutrality of good science. It boldly goes where science has feared to tread, deep into the realm of human values and forward into the engineering of human happiness.

By virtue of its unchecked aspirations, its wanderings from scientific objectivity, and the various meanings it conjures, multiple use is a formidable force. It has been, and continues to be, a crucial factor in the complex equation of public-land grazing. It has, as will be explained, exacerbated the conservation flaws of sustained yield and the grazing permit system and formalized the most offensive attributes of a failed commons.

At the very least, multiple use has spawned a tragic waste of natural and social resources. It has pitted special interest groups against one another in the struggle to influence the mix of uses that come off the federal lands. Each year, national environmental organizations, local citizen groups, and traditional public-land users (e.g., ranchers, loggers, miners, and oil and gas drillers) spend more money in arguing their points of view to land agencies, Congress, and the federal courts than either the Forest Service or the BLM invests in the management of federal rangelands.[15] When the equally enormous sums expended by the two agencies in multiple use planning are added to that total, it becomes evident that only a small fraction of the money and effort directed toward the public's western range ever reaches the ground.

In 1983, the Grace Commission estimated that planning was costing the Forest Service $200 million per year, more than the agency spends on its recreation, wildlife, grazing, soil, and water programs.[16] And except for fire control and timber sales, planning also costs more than any other line item in the Forest Service budget. Economist R. W. Behan considers such planning expenditures extremely wasteful. In the October 1989 issue of *Forest Watch,* he posed an intriguing hypothesis:

Suppose we bought $200 million worth of direct investment in forest land resources each year, instead of $200 million in planning activities and documents. Could we anticipate a lessening of resource use conflicts, accordingly, as the resulting cornucopia of forest goods and services washed across the land? I suspect we could.[17]

Decision making in national forests and BLM districts, however, is not aimed at creating the cornucopia Behan envisions. Its practical goal is to divvy up a resource pie, unnaturally constrained by ever-expanding overhead costs, among warring interest groups. How that pie is divided, of course, is the end result of costly political and judicial lobbying and intervention. Each group strives to capture the biggest piece of the public resource pie by whatever means available, unaware or unconcerned that under Behan's scenario there could be enough for all without internecine warfare.

As wasteful as such a process may be, it is the only practical and effective option available to special interest groups to influence a decision-making process that is inherently political. But wastefulness is the least of the problems attending multiple use on the federal range. A more urgent concern is the crisis of accountability that its practice has created. Multiple use has rekindled with democratic passion the agrarian commitment to keeping the western range open. But it has done so against the agrarian grain of localism and apart from the Jeffersonian vision of a landscape dedicated to independent families and sovereign communities. Not unexpectedly, its triumph has been the re-creation of a western commons.

Absent from the attributes of the multiple use commons are the unity and harmony that Jefferson ascribed to man and nature. Jefferson's belief that people, their rights, and their lands were somehow inseparable and indivisible has become archaic. A new vision has come of age, one in which lands and people are seen as uses and users, readily separable and conveniently divisible. That vision, so integral to progressive reform, has transformed the face of the western range by reducing the complexity of the land and the diversity of the American people to discrete sets of commodities and user groups amenable to measurement and management. In the process, sentiments regarding human freedom and the proper relationship of people to nature have been dismissed for the immediacy of mixing and matching public-land commodities with public-land consumers. The everyday demands of divvying up nature have become the business of the

Forest Service and the BLM, who plan nature's multiple uses for the multiple satisfactions of society at large.

Among the special interest groups that stand to profit from the practice of multiple use on public lands, only the Forest Service and the BLM have known consistent success. Whatever the issues have been, from closing the open range to writing environmental impact statements to managing wild horses, the agencies have profited handsomely in terms of budgets, programs, and employees.

Profitable as multiple use management has been for these agencies, the public lands remain a gigantic commons in which more and more participants compete for finite natural resources—the commodities of the progressive vision. But the rules governing the federal commons now differ markedly from what they were a hundred years ago. Users—to borrow the vernacular of multiple use—have no choice but to restrict their activities to capturing the specific commodities that public-land law allows. Only the uses and products of the land, not the land itself, are up for grabs. As a result, it is in the self-interest of user groups to maximize their "take" of specific bundles of uses and products. At the least, such a parochial outlook makes resource users indifferent to the fate of the rest of the environment of the public lands. At the most, it compels them to fight alternative uses and users of the federal range that pose threats to, or compete with, their special interests.

Consumers of natural resources, by focusing on the multiple uses of land rather than on the land itself, are encouraged to do what homesteaders before them had to do for survival. Animal rights activists, for example, have pushed their cause of wild-horse preservation on public lands with such intensity that rangelands have been overgrazed, horses have been starved, and BLM stock pens have been packed with homeless mustangs, costing taxpayers millions of dollars each year.[18] Off-road vehicle enthusiasts have also pursued their chosen use at the expense of the land. The Erosion Allotment in the Santa Fe National Forest is one example. The Forest Service, unable to keep local motorcyclists out of the area, has surrendered the land to abuse. In turn, the bikers, who have no interest in the land except as a source of casual recreation, have seen more beauty than environmental harm in the scarred hillsides that their motorcycles have created.[19]

Environmentalists have been equally susceptible to the narrow logic of multiple use. On the Diamond Bar Allotment in the Gila Wilderness, for example, livestock grazing is part of the land's natural history. There, decades of intensive grazing have turned productive streamsides into sparsely vegetated watering and bedding grounds for cattle. The current permittee, hoping to reduce livestock pressure on riparian areas, has offered to develop upland waters to distribute his cattle better. But local wilderness groups have opposed the plan, fearful of the precedent that would be set by adding range improvements to an area meant to be primitive. Today, the streamsides on the Diamond Bar Allotment continue to degrade, victims of a multiple use commons where parties have been able to seek their narrow interests to the tragic exclusion of the land's best interest.[20]

Some public-land groups have used examples like the Diamond Bar to make a case against further designation of wilderness. Organizations like People for the West and the BlueRibbon Coalition have raised the banner of multiple use in a crusade to keep public lands open for all uses and all users. More wilderness, even though legally recognized as one of many valid multiple uses of federal lands, is unacceptable to them because of the restrictions it entails for such activities as motorized travel, logging, energy development, and mining. Not surprisingly, members of the two groups view the motives of environmentalists, particularly wilderness enthusiasts, with suspicion. As one full-page advertisement in the Blue-Ribbon Coalition's monthly publication *BlueRibbon* makes clear:

> The Wilderness issue has been used by the so-called environmentalists to virtually "lock us out" of many areas that were once open to motorized recreational vehicles. Snowmobilers, trailbikers, power boaters, hunters and others have formed the *BlueRibbon Coalition* to protect our rights against these "land grabbers." By joining the *BlueRibbon Coalition* you can help stem the tide and return our country to a sensible policy of multiple use of our public lands.[21]

Conspicuously missing in the vision of multiple use advocates, and too often overlooked in the visions of well-intentioned wilderness groups, is concern for the biological health and ecological integrity of the western range. Locked in political combat, and attentive only to the uses of the land that concern their separate visions, they are compelled to replay the tragedy of the western commons, though with one ironic twist. Public-land ranchers, once victims of an open range and targets of the epithet "land grabbers," now join People for the West and the BlueRibbon Coalition in calling for an open range and in angrily denouncing environmentalists as land grabbers. The tragedy of the commons that their forefathers experienced and suffered from is sadly forgotten in the urgency of protecting their slim hold on a hotly contested federal range.

Multiple use and the permit system have desensitized stockmen to the interests of the land and, in the process, have given them false reasons to justify their place on the federal range—false because multiple use and the permit system are excuses, not reasons, for continuing public-land ranching. They have persuaded ranchers, for want of any viable alternative, to persist in land practices that are economically marginal, ecologically unsound, and out of step with changing cultural mores.

Under the schemes of multiple use and the permit system, public-land ranchers have been forced to choose between their own survival and the needs of wildlife, fisheries, and recreation. All too often, ranchers see elk and deer as threats to their private and permitted lands. In the Apache Sitgreaves National Forest in Arizona, burgeoning populations of elk are threatening jealously guarded livestock numbers as the Forest Service shifts more and more public forage from traditional to wildlife uses. Permittees in that forest are using every technical and political tool available to fight the change, even though it is clearly favored by the vast majority of public-land users.[22]

Even though stockmen's strongest incentives are to hold on to or increase their livestock numbers, some public-land ranchers have attempted to make the shift from ranching for domestic stock to ranching for wildlife. Dayton Hyde, a rancher in southeastern Oregon, asked permission from the Forest Service to reduce stocking permanently on his allotment to allow for more elk and deer. Anticipating agency reluctance, he even offered to pay the grazing fee for the cattle he hoped to take off his allotment. The Forest Service, guided by laws and regulations demanding multiple use, denied his request, warning that understocking for the purpose of wildlife enhancement could result in the revocation of his grazing permit.[23]

More often than not, wildlife has simply meant economic loss for public-land ranchers. For Sterling Carter, a permittee in the Black Range of southwestern New Mexico, it has meant near bankruptcy.[24] After acquiring his allotment in the early 1980s, he invested enormous amounts of time and money in developing rock-header dams to increase water on his allotment and to attain better livestock distribution. Because water had been a limiting factor not only for livestock but also for wildlife, his efforts helped make possible a rapid expansion in deer numbers. Ironically, the very range improvements intended to benefit his permitted lands led the Forest Service to reduce his grazing permit. For the agency, more deer meant less forage available to cattle. For Sterling's bank, that translated into a loss of the very assets backing up the ranch mortgage. And for Sterling, it meant operating further in the red. More deer, which to a private-land rancher might have offered a promising recreational opportunity, represented only a problem to the Forest Service, the bank, and the permittee.

Riparian concerns have presented similar dilemmas to public-land ranchers. For all practical purposes, grazing permits and agency policies of multiple use have limited stockmen to treating streamsides and lakes only as rich sources of livestock feed and water. Unable to control or capture the recreational, wildlife, and fishery values of such areas, they do just what is allowed and expected of them: they take the forage and consume the water. Neither Forest Service nor BLM policies have ever accommodated any use of riparian areas by ranchers except consumptive use.

This is not to imply that all permittees ignore wetland maintenance. Dayton Hyde, at least on his privately owned lands, has maintained and restored wetlands on a landscape conspicuously void of water.[25] He has transformed the bottomlands surrounding his headquarters into rich and productive marshlands. And by prudently grazing his cattle on them, he has successfully preserved them as habitat for a diversity of wildlife. Further, the pools and streams dissecting the marshland contain some of the finest trout fishing in southern Oregon—a contributing factor to the economic success of his ranch. What is most striking about his conservation efforts, however, is what lies on the other side of the fence separating his wetlands from Forest Service land. The abundance of wildlife, the bounty of vegetation, and the quality of fishing are simply not there.

If this sketch of individual stewardship points to a particular lesson for public lands and public-land ranchers, it is this: Except for the persuasion of an ingrained land ethic, which too often is defeated by circumstance, incentives for stockmen to steward resources for uses other than livestock are sadly lacking. Whether those resources fall in prized riparian zones or in remote wilderness areas, public-land ranchers are guided by laws and policies that motivate them to consume forage and water to the exclusion of all other concerns.

Locked into livestock production, they must graze the lands to maintain their permits and to hold on to their share of multiple use. Yet by so doing, stockmen have unintentionally diminished the very qualities that make public lands so attractive to other Americans. That fact alone has sparked the escalating drive among some environmentalists to expel ranchers from the federal range. It highlights the urgency expressed in the increasingly common slogan "Cattle Free by '93."

THE COMMONS IN PLACE

Looking back to the commons born and nurtured by an agrarian vision, it is all too apparent that the tools and principles of progressive reform—the trinity of grazing permits, sustained yield, and multiple use—have continued the tradition with vengeance. But still unresolved are the environmental ills passed from one vision to another, the ills that now symbolize the failure of the progressive commons. In a world that is interconnected, Hardin reminds us, "ruin is the destination toward which all men rush."[26] The tools and principles of progressive conservation reform, intended to bring efficiency and democracy to the western range, have made control more fractured than ever and caring more difficult than before. People and their activities remain pitted against a landscape short on stewardship yet long on exploitation.

CHAPTER NINE

Demise of Stewardship

*lizardo Vigil is in many ways typical of permittees in the Santa
Fe National Forest in northern New Mexico.[1] Livestock raising
is part of his family heritage, a way of life stretching back centuries to an era of conquistadores and Spanish land grants. His Grass Mountain Allotment is also part of that history. Sheep and cattle owned by his
ancestors grazed its grassy slopes long before Congress added it to the National Forest System. Its ownership has changed in the interim, but Elizardo
and his family still recall the generations of Vigils who used the land and
made a modest living from its grass.*

*Today, Elizardo holds a forest permit that allows him to graze fifteen
cows for four months on the Grass Mountain Allotment—a stocking rate
that equates to five head on a year-round basis. That stocking rate is modest,
given the thirty-five hundred acres of forested range and scattered grasslands
that make up the allotment; it is also far fewer than the 250 sheep his father
grazed before the allotment became part of the Santa Fe National Forest.*

*Under normal circumstances, five cows on thirty-five hundred acres would
not be a problem. But in northern New Mexico, few things are normal, and
even fewer things do not at some point constitute a problem. Elizardo's
problem is a small mountain meadow lying in the center of his allotment.*

Besides being a choice grazing spot for his cows, it is also part of a well-traveled route for people and elk going to and from the Pecos Wilderness. Its prominence to passing tourists and its importance to elk in winter has made the Grass Mountain Allotment a sore point in the relations between Elizardo and the Forest Service. And for the Forest Service range conservationist who has overseen the allotment's management for twenty years, the meadow has come to symbolize an Armageddon of sorts for scientific land management.

The problem is this: Although the allotment has ample grass throughout its range, Elizardo's cows prefer to camp on the small mountain meadow, where they can find all the grass and water they need. As a result, the meadow is weedy, trampled, and excessively dotted with the unpleasant aftereffects of fifteen bovine factories. Hikers and backpackers are understandably upset with what they see and smell, and the elk are discouraged from using it by the lack of winter forage. The Forest Service range conservationist in charge of the Grass Mountain Allotment does not believe cows should be grazing in such close proximity to one of New Mexico's premier wilderness areas. He also believes the meadow would be best used if left exclusively to the elk herd that resides on Grass Mountain in winter. On both counts, he is probably right. Even Elizardo does not dispute his conclusions. But grazing is part of the multiple use mixture that the Forest Service has planned for Grass Mountain. It has been that way for decades and will probably continue to be that way for years to come. The only issue is what will become of the small mountain meadow.

In 1986, Elizardo had an idea. Why not fence the meadow to keep his cattle out for at least part of the summer? That way, they could graze the plentiful grasses found elsewhere on Grass Mountain, and the meadow would be able to rest. Hikers and backpackers would have a more enjoyable experience, elk would have more winter feed, and the Forest Service would have the landscape it wanted.

But in 1986, Elizardo could not afford the cost of range improvement. His allotment was so small that even a few hundred dollars spent on fencing would eat up whatever profit he could expect from his fifteen cows. And fencing was not all that was needed. Once his cattle were excluded from the meadow, he would have to develop at least two springs to water them and to disperse them throughout the allotment.

Elizardo had a solution to the cost problem. He offered to fence the meadow and develop the necessary waters if the Forest Service would agree to increase authorized stocking on his allotment by four head: the equivalent of one more cow on a year-round basis. He also requested that the Forest Service monitor Grass Moun-

tain to determine the effectiveness of his management and to increase his stocking by another five to ten head if data supported such action.

The Forest Service range conservationist refused the proposal, not because it would not work but because it would increase the number of cows on an allotment he had already judged as inappropriate for livestock grazing. The conservationist knew he could not remove the few cows permitted on Grass Mountain, but he could prevent their number from increasing. It did not seem to matter to him that abundant forage existed on the allotment or that the herd, even when increased by four head, would be less visible once it was excluded from the meadow. What mattered was his vision of how the allotment should be, not how it could be given the right incentives and a receptive permittee.

Nothing has changed on Grass Mountain. Fifteen cows are camped on the small mountain meadow for four months each summer. Hikers and backpackers still pass through the meadow, disgusted and angered by what they see and smell. Elizardo is doing nothing, and so is the Forest Service. And nothing has changed for the elk that arrive each winter seeking grass.

LAYERS OF DISINCENTIVES

The plight of the western range is a favorite theme of congressional reports and environmentalist critiques. Entire forests have been felled and turned into reams of paper to tell Americans that *All Is Not Well on the Western Range;* that *Our Ailing Rangelands* are sad remnants of a once bountiful nature. But the stories these documents tell address only one side of the public-land equation, the well-known side of rangeland users and their disappointing record of stewardship. Other than a scornful recognition of human greed, no thought is given to the variables that have driven the history of public-land grazing and that have often compelled western stockmen to act against the best interests of the land. Also ignored are the workings of landscape visions and the twists and quirks they give to human action. Public-land ranchers have always worked and lived in an environment of ecological as well as ideological complexity. As such, their desires and abilities to care for public grazing lands have been profoundly conditioned by the visions of Jefferson and Pinchot. For ranchers like Levi Howes and Marc Stevens, those visions have hindered but never prevented good land management. For many others, however, the incentives offered by agrarian and progressive ideals have made the simple act of caring too costly.

Between the two landscape visions, progressive conservation reform has most affected personal stewardship by entangling public grazing lands in layers of disincentives. One layer, its features rooted in the system of grazing permits and the principles of sustained yield and multiple use, has already been explored. But the disincentives that shroud public grazing lands are far more profound and pernicious than those discussed so far. As standard-bearers of the progressive vision, the Forest Service and the BLM have enjoyed the time and freedom to forge the tenets of scientific land management into concrete programs and practices. The fruits of their labors have been the mechanics of grazing management, the guidelines for public-land investment, and the size and membership of grazing allotments.

MANDATE FOR GRAZING MANAGEMENT

Managing livestock grazing to conserve and improve rangeland resources is a premise of good land stewardship. Students are taught it in natural resource colleges, ranchers believe in it, and the Forest Service and the BLM are committed to it by law and regulation. If anything, good grazing management should be common ground between agencies and permittees, giving each the incentives necessary to promote a healthier western range. But positive incentives have not been the most consistent outcome of federal programs and practices on public grazing lands. Allotment management plans (AMPs) are a case in point.

In the simplest terms, AMPs are blueprints drafted by the agencies that spell out the details of ranch management. They prescribe grazing regimes, range improvement programs, and divisions of responsibility. Ideally, they set allotments on the path toward sustained yield and work out the fine points of multiple uses of resources. Unfortunately, AMPs are not nearly as benevolent as their description would indicate. Among other things, they diminish the flexibility that lies at the heart of successful grazing management. By setting fixed numbers of livestock, specific times to graze, and patterns or rotations of livestock use, they make it difficult for ranchers to adjust to the changing environmental conditions characteristic of arid lands.

In the 1960s, the BLM adopted the Hormay Grazing System after the Forest Service pioneered it on northwestern rangelands. Despite warnings from the Council on Environmental Quality and the Council for Agricultural Science and Technology that the Hormay system "is unfortunately not a panacea to all grazing problems" and that it "has great potential for range destruction," the BLM adopted it as standard grazing practice in the untested environment of the Southwest.[2] Public-land ranchers, spurred on by agency enthusiasm for the new rest-rotation grazing system, signed AMPs, making Hormay a household word on desert rangelands. At the same time, and on similar southwestern ranges, private-land ranchers experimented with an identical system.

In the BLM's Roswell District in south-eastern New Mexico, results were discouraging from the start.[3] Almost everywhere the Hormay system was tried, on both public and private lands, livestock and plants fared poorly. Private-land ranchers abandoned or modified the system once its flaws became apparent, but it remained in effect on BLM ranges for an additional decade. Ranchers and federal managers, both committed to AMPs for fixed periods, simply could not abandon a grazing program for which substantial federal dollars had been invested. Their flexibility compromised, they were either unwilling or unable to change a system that had not matched expectations. As a result, public lands and public-land ranchers bore the environmental and economic costs of a grazing system that hung on by virtue of administrative inertia.

Many of the same problems have occurred on national forest ranges when AMPs have rigidly enforced otherwise ill advised grazing schemes. In the Burro Mountains of southwestern New Mexico, a permittee and the Forest Service signed an AMP committing the Walking X Allotment to a five-year grazing system. After the first two years, poor cattle performance and overgrazed pastures demonstrated that the system had failed. Despite complaints from the permittee, the plan continued in full force for the entire five years. Today, the allotment is in poor condition and faces severe reductions in livestock numbers.[4]

Limitations and flaws in AMPs are also products of conflicting allotment goals, the discordance common to such plans when the broad landscape goals set by federal agencies (increasingly in the context of expanded public review and participation) fail to mesh with the more personal and limited objectives sought by permittees. Any divergence between the two lessens the chance that ranchers will care for the land or that agencies will attain the landscapes they envision. In many cases, colliding visions not only doom an AMP to failure but also preclude its being tried and tested. This may seem to be a blessing in disguise, but for grazing lands in need of improvement, the lack of a signed AMP precludes in many cases the option of positive management. Unable to come to terms on what should be done, permittees and agencies simply retire to the sidelines to wait for concessions that may never come. And the land continues to deteriorate.

For Elizardo Vigil and the Forest Service, their conflicting visions on the future of the Grass Mountain Allotment have made a mutually agreeable AMP impossible, stalling much-needed range improvements. Similarly, the BLM's insistence that Joe and Susan Fallini agree to develop waters for wild horses as a precondition for water development for cattle makes it unlikely that anything will happen to benefit the land. Conflicting goals undermine good land stewardship, making it unlikely that an ecologically coherent and economically viable solution will ever happen.

Practical problems aside, there is a more profound reason why AMPs do not promote better land management. They are, first and foremost, *administrative* tools that have only incidental bearing on the environmental state of western rangelands. Their main contribution to public-land grazing has been to give the Forest Service and the BLM a tangible measure of administrative success, one quantified by the sheer number of allotments enlisted in AMP programs. And the agencies, by equating the count of AMPs with superior stewardship of public rangelands, have been able to showcase their management prowess to Congress and back up their pleas for additional range appropriations with seemingly solid results.

But statistics on the gross numbers of AMPs are deceiving. The story they tell is one of bureaucratic functioning rather than of concrete advancements in land stewardship. The BLM, for example, reported in 1975 that AMPs were enjoying remarkable success on public domain rangelands. "Implementation of the AMP program by the year 2000," the agency noted, "will result in a reversal of declining trends."[5] That optimistic prediction was based on trend studies showing that 54 percent of agency rangelands covered by AMPs were improving in condition, compared with a dismal 17 percent among non-AMP lands. Moreover, grazing statistics taken from a 1988 General Accounting Office (GAO) study on public grazing lands seem to substantiate the BLM's positive claims. Most of the one-third of BLM allotments having AMPs were shown to be properly stocked and in a condition that was improving. The 66 percent without AMPs were reported to contain a disproportionate number of overstocked and declining ranges.[6] A 1990 Department of the Interior solicitor general's report on BLM grazing lands in New Mexico concluded that deterioration of rangelands was largely attributable to the agency's failure to implement AMPs on all grazing allotments.[7]

Robert Nelson, senior economist in the Department of the Interior's Office of Policy Analysis, disputes the validity of the BLM's claims. He attributes the success of AMPs to the simple fact that they were "implemented on the better rangelands grazed by more energetic and progressive ranchers." The BLM's philosophy, he notes, was to apply sophisticated grazing management on areas that were highly productive from the start. "Hence," he concludes, "the better condition of rangeland with AMPs compared with all BLM rangeland might very well show merely that these areas had better condition to begin with."[8]

Closer scrutiny of the GAO's 1988 grazing statistics lends credence to Nelson's contention. Among BLM grazing districts investigated by the GAO, all were shown to be spending a disproportionate amount of range improvement funds on allotments with AMPs—allotments that were generally in better than average condition from the start. In New Mexico, the causal link between AMPs and range conditions is no less tenuous. One resource area manager put it most succinctly: The solicitor general's report testified more to the budgetary ambitions of the agency than to the efficacy of AMPs.[9]

AMPs have been equally advantageous for the Forest Service, although in a somewhat different fashion. Unlike those of the BLM, Forest Service statistics show no advantage accruing to the 75 percent of forest allotments that operate under AMPs. GAO figures for 1988 indicate no significant difference between allotments with and without AMPs in terms of levels of stocking or rangeland conditions.[10] This finding is striking, given the Forest Service's historical proclivity to draft AMPs for better allotments and its long-established policy of limiting federal investments to allotments having AMPs. One possible explanation for this apparent anomaly is that forest allotments without AMPs have a narrower range of management options. When problems occur, livestock numbers are slashed rather than dollars being invested to uphold them. As a result, overstocking is quickly resolved, and in some cases, deteriorating range conditions are reversed. In contrast, allotments receiving AMPs enjoy the full benefits of

Forest Service spending, particularly investments aimed at lessening the need for drastic livestock reductions.

This may explain, in part, the GAO's most surprising finding. Forest allotments with current AMPs (drafted within the past ten years) have a one-third greater chance than allotments without AMPs of being over-stocked or being in declining condition. This raises serious questions about the efficacy of federally financed range improvements tied to Forest Service AMPs. Are such investments being made to improve overgrazed rangelands or to placate ranchers and boost Forest Service range programs and range staff? Evidence suggests the second possibility. The Forest Service has argued on several occasions that Congress should dedicate a fixed percentage of Range Betterment Funds—the dollars intended for on-the-ground range improvements—to the development and administration of AMPs. The agency's argument is that a backlog of AMPs is delaying range improvements on needy allotments and preventing expenditures of federal range dollars—dollars that come primarily from Range Betterment Funds. Only by expending dollars on Forest Service expansion—*dollars otherwise earmarked for range improvements*—can the business of public-land management be expedited.

A telling example occurred in the Lincoln National Forest when a permittee agreed to an AMP in 1985 as a precondition for controlled burns on weed-infested pastures—a simple and inexpensive project intended to invigorate native grasses. After three years of excluding stock on those pastures to build up surface fuels, the permittee still had not received the agency's approval or assistance.[11] According to Forest Service staff, a lack of funds is preventing completion of his required AMP. Yet without the AMP, the permittee is powerless to act. The stewardship that he might bring to public lands must await the bidding of an overtaxed bureaucracy.

If anything, AMPs are a drain on the limited resources available for both forest and public domain rangeland improvements. They consume enormous sums of money that might otherwise be spent on land stewardship. Forest Service and BLM expenditures on rangeland improvements, for example, were $15.3 million in 1982 and $16.7 million in 1983. In comparison, $10.5 million in 1982 and $8.7 million in 1983 were spent on allotment planning—amounts equal to 60 percent of the total expended for on-the-ground improvements for the same years.[12] As large as that percentage may seem, it will in all likelihood increase.

Expanded planning processes being adopted by both agencies—such as the Forest Service's Integrated Resource Management Program—virtually guarantee the budgetary eclipsing of range improvements by allotment planning. In fact, the Forest Service has already made significant strides in this direction. In early 1990, the agency implemented a new policy requiring that all future AMPs be subject to public review and comprehensive environmental analysis. The BLM is implementing a similar, and predictably costly, policy.

The bottom line is that AMPs have made better public relations instruments with Congress than stewardship tools and incentives for public rangelands and their users. Both the Forest Service and the BLM have looked to AMPs for the power and control they offer over western rangelands rather than for the stewardship potential they might provide. As a result, the pursuit of AMPs has become a consuming activity, one too often overshadowing what should be the first and only priority of land agencies: the well-being of the western range.

Corby and Miles McGinnis are a case in point.[13] As part of their Kemmerer, Wyoming Diamond H Ranch Company, they purchased a small livestock operation in and near the Bridger-Teton National Forest. The ranch includes two sections of grazeable Forest Service land, three sections of BLM land, and almost five sections of fenced-off private land. For administrative convenience, the BLM granted supervisory control over its lands to the Forest Service.

When the allotment was purchased, Corby and Miles were told that they needed an AMP before any grazing could begin. Because two forty-acre parcels of BLM land were located in the McGinnises' three-thousand-acre private pasture, the Forest Service was able to make the AMP mandatory for the entire ranch, not just for the public land portions. It made no difference that the two parcels were being sold to the Diamond H Ranch or that the private pasture contained most of the ranch's carrying capacity. An opportunity for extending Forest Service control had offered itself, and the agency acted to the extent allowed by law.

During the first year of grazing, the McGinnises applied for 30 percent voluntary nonuse. Given the limited carrying capacity of the Forest Service portion of the ranch, they preferred to keep the allotment unstocked, using it as a buffer against trespass on their private land, but that did not conform to Forest Service regulations. Corby and Miles did have one consolation, though. After lengthy protests, the BLM agreed to abandon its supervisory agreement with the Forest Service, forcing a revision of the AMP. Today, the three thousand private acres are the McGinnises' to manage and steward according to a vision that comes from caring, not a bureaucratic agenda.

Not far from the McGinnis ranch is a BLM allotment permitted to Jim Gould, a rancher headquartered in Meeteetse, Wyoming.[14] His allotment, like the McGinnises', is surrounded by private holdings. Several years ago, Jim asked the BLM for permission to lay a half-mile of small-diameter pipeline across his allotment so that a remote area of his private range could be better watered. His plan entailed no expense for the BLM or any changes in his use of public lands. At the least, his private range would benefit from the plan, and if the agency were willing, waters could even be developed where the pipeline crossed the allotment. His request was straightforward and routine. But in Jim's case, strings were attached to the easement. Before he could begin the project, he would have to sign an AMP. Jim agreed, believing that what mattered most was getting the pipeline installed, not quibbling over whether or not his grazing management was formalized.

The BLM then tossed another obstacle in Jim's path. His construction of the pipeline—indeed, his watering of both private and public lands—would require a modification of the AMP that was already signed. The agency insisted that he enter into a cooperative agreement in which he would pay for the project and the BLM would share control over both the pipeline and the privately owned waters passing through it. As much as Jim wanted to improve his private and public rangelands, the price demanded by the BLM was simply too high. Because of his refusal to participate in the agreement, Jim's allotment faces a reduction in stocking, and his private lands remain poorly watered.

What has happened to Jim Gould is not unusual. AMPs do not stop at the boundaries of public lands. Their effects are broadly ecological, spilling over onto adjacent properties and propagating the vision of scientific land management. The unfortunate harvest is one more layer of disincentives, one more wedge between people and the natural environment.

For caring ranchers like Marc Stevens in Montana, Joe Fallini in Nevada, and Bard Heaton in Utah, AMPs are stumbling blocks to good management. For the vast majority of public-land ranchers, AMPs and the restrictions they carry are one more reason not to care so much, not to take the time and effort needed to meet the needs of the land. And for a small minority, AMPs are excuses not to care at all; they are incentives to leave the responsibility for the land to the agencies that devised the AMPs in the first place. In whatever light AMPs are viewed, their effects on stewardship have been stifling and their promotion of mediocrity on the western range shameful.

VANISHING ROLES AND INCENTIVES: THE PLIGHT OF CARING

Range investments have always been a source of contention between public-land ranchers and public-land agencies. For the Forest Service and the BLM, investment by permittees has raised the specter of vested interest, the likelihood that ranchers might use the leverage of personal investment to wrest control of federal lands from federal managers. An internal memo prepared for the assistant secretary of the interior in 1945 warned:

> It is inevitable . . . that a permittee who expends his own money to improve the range . . . will feel that the Government is under some moral or equitable obligation to renew the permit or accord him a preference right of one kind or another.[15]

Agencies have not been alone in their suspicion of the connection between rancher investments and vested interests. During the 1940s and 1950s, conservation organizations, such as the Izaak Walton League of America, argued against ranchers paying for range improvements on public lands. The league urged the federal government to assume full responsibility for range expenditures, warning that ranchers' investments "would only serve to support the argument of the stock associations that grazing national forests was a permittee's right instead of a privilege . . . ."[16]

Narrow concern over vested interests has kept conservationists and land agencies from focusing on the positive side of private investments, from seeing that much more than ranchers and their sense of tenure can benefit. Undoubtedly, dollars spent by permittees have contributed to both the perception and the reality of their tenure on and control of public grazing lands. Grazing permits have led to marketable rights in federal forage and perceived ownership in permitted livestock numbers. Ranchers' claims of preference rights and permit values, despite their questionable legality, often influence, if not constrain, the Forest Service and the BLM in matters of public-land management. But private investments have also helped the land.

C. W. Hudson, one of the first forest supervisors of the North Platte National Forest, acknowledged that he actively encouraged permittees to build and maintain range improvements. By doing this, he wrote in 1909, "each permittee is then working for his own interests and at the same time developing the range."[17] Unfortunately, most forest administrators took a more cautious approach. William Rowley, in his history of the Forest Service grazing program, noted rising concern "that stockmen were becoming too cooperative, too devoted to making improvements on the range."[18] Even range projects built in partnership were viewed by many as giving stockmen prescriptive rights to forest grazing lands.

BLM's water- and land-based allotments are most instructive when it comes to unraveling the incentives for and reasons behind permittee investments. For example, from 1940 until the Federal Land Policy and Management Act of 1976 (FLPMA) was passed in 1976, ranchers' investments on water-based allotments were more than double those on land-based allotments. After 1976, investments on water-based allotments fell twice as quickly, until by 1986 private expenditures on both allotment types had reached historical lows as well as approximate parity. Instead of outspending their land-based counterparts by an average of $4.20 for every cow grazed, ranchers on water-based allotments were now spending only $0.60 more—a decline of 700 percent.[19]

Control best explains the spending discrepancy between allotment types and the narrowing gap between them. Quite simply, water-based allotments have given permittees far greater control over grazing management in the past. Water-based allotments are exclusive to the arid Southwest, where water is at a premium. Because ranchers must control base waters to graze those allotments, they often are able to monopolize the only water sources that make public lands usable by domestic stock. Further, given the intermingled land status of most southwestern rangelands, stockmen who have water rights on scattered private lands can effectively "lock up" massive portions of federal property. Their grazing permits may be privileges, but their ownership of scarce waters gives them considerable advantage.

For those reasons, BLM permittees in the Southwest have until recently enjoyed relative autonomy in the operation of their public-land ranches.

The benefits of that autonomy have been private rangeland investments far in excess of those made by other public-land ranchers or by the federal agencies in charge. In fact, a jealous desire to protect historical autonomy and the control it allows has compelled stockmen in general to vigorously oppose federally financed range improvements—at least in the years before 1976.

For example, proposals by the Grazing Service in 1945 and the BLM in 1952 to have Congress fund range rehabilitation projects simply fell on deaf ears. Whether out of principled opposition to government subsidies or pragmatic calculation of their effects, ranchers feared that federal dollars spent on public ranges would expand the powers of the BLM and result in more federal control. As a result, writes Phillip Foss, stockmen "settled for a most limited range improvement program as the price for retaining relative freedom from regulation and supervision of their grazing activities."[20]

The freedom was illusory. By the mid-1970s, an array of environmental and public-land laws made it clear where control rested on the federal range. Statutes such as the Multiple Use–Sustained Yield Act, the National Environmental Policy Act, the Forest and Rangeland Renewable Resources Planning Act, the National Forest Management Act, and the Federal Land Policy and Management Act signaled a one-way transition of power and control from ranchers to land management agencies. Hastening the erosion of ranchers' traditional powers and perceived arenas of control was greater citizen participation in public-land affairs—a process symbolized by Earth Day in 1970, implemented by the 1974 *Natural Resources Defense Council v. Morton* ruling on grazing environmental impact statements, and realized in the increasingly detailed participation of the public in allotment management planning.

Public-land ranchers responded as expected to the planning and regulatory environment that was in place by 1976: Their investments on public rangelands fell to a fraction of what they had been. An immediate result was that their resistance to federal programs lessened. No longer willing or able to spend as much on their allotments, stockmen had to either accept federal range improvement funds or face the possibility of stocking reductions. The overall effects were less pronounced on national forest lands, where permittees had never enjoyed the autonomy of BLM ranchers. Not surprisingly, their share of total forest range investments hovered at 25 percent during the 1960s, when BLM ranchers were outspending their agency by as much as ten to one. And their loss of control was less obvious. The Forest Service had long held the power and authority that became the BLM's only during the 1970s.

Permittees of both agencies, faced with dwindling control over their allotments and increasing uncertainty as to their tenure on the federal range, did what their ancestors had done on the open range of the nineteenth century: They took the maximum they could from the land and returned the minimum needed to get by. The political reality of environmentalists seeking ways to restrict or eliminate domestic livestock on public lands and the broadening discretionary powers of the Forest Service and the BLM made investments on public lands a risky venture.

The willingness of ranchers to invest in public lands has not declined solely because of resignation to modern politics and bureaucracy. Permittees like Jim Gould and Bard Heaton have demonstrated that they want to invest in public lands if only the agencies will allow them. But as the Public Land Law Review Commission reported in 1969, "the lack of increase in private expenditures reflects the policy of the major land agencies to undertake most of the capital investment themselves in order to prevent the permittee from gaining any feeling of a property interest." [21] Today, the BLM is doing just that; it is moving toward mandatory cooperative agreements, such as cost-share range improvement programs.

For the most part, these kinds of agreements have displaced Section 4 permits, relics of an almost forgotten provision of the Taylor Grazing Act authorizing exclusive private investment and ownership of range improvements. For many stockmen, Section 4 permits have long held a special attraction. They not only allowed permittees to pay the full costs of range improvements but also gave them full title to the final products, such as fences, wells, pipelines, and water tanks. At the minimum, Section 4 permits provided the element of control and predictability conducive to permittee investment and stewardship, features largely lacking in cooperative agreements.

It was for these reasons, plus an ethic of self-reliance, that Bard Heaton insisted on a Section 4 permit for doing his range improvement work. After ten years of battle with the BLM, he got what he wanted. But his neighbors to the south, who ranch the BLM's Arizona Strip, have not been so fortunate. Stockmen like Clayton Atkins relied on Section 4 permits to build the fences that ended the open range and allowed him to develop the water resources that made grazing management possible. But Clayton's son, Brent, is frustrated by the BLM's resistance to additional Section 4 permits.[22] If Brent wants to improve his permitted rangelands, his only alternative is to enter into cooperative agreements. His stewardship is necessarily constrained. Without ownership, Brent is unlikely to invest as heavily in public lands as his father did a half-century earlier.

Forest Service practices offer similar disincentives, motivating permittees to invest as little as necessary in their permitted rangelands. But unlike the BLM, the Forest Service has never allowed rancher ownership in fences, pipelines, wells, drinking tubs, and storage tanks. As a consequence, most range improvements are paid for by the agency or, at most, cost-shared with permittees. That has been true on national forest ranges ever since their withdrawal from the public domain.

Forest ranchers who want to spend their own dollars on physical range improvements can do so, but there is little incentive for it. Title to their improvements simply reverts to the government. And even if their rangelands improve as a result of their private efforts, there is no assurance that the benefits will accrue to them. More and healthier plants does not guarantee greater livestock numbers, since other multiple use objectives may require allocation of new forage to wildlife or recreation. Or, as in the case of Sterling Carter on the Black Range, new improvements may make the allotment more attractive to wildlife, calling for reductions rather than increases in permitted stock.

Herb Metzger is a prime example of how Forest Service policy discourages and even disallows permittee investment and stewardship. Herb ranches south of Flagstaff, Arizona, in the Coconino National Forest.[23] His family settled there in 1914, when the range was mostly open grassland and pine and juniper were restricted to rocky outcrops. Over the years, improper grazing management and fire control allowed trees to encroach on the grasslands, and by the time Herb took over the ranch the damage to the range was extensive. Tree invasion had transformed thousands of acres of healthy desert grasslands into woodlands of marginal use for both cattle and wildlife. In the 1970s, Herb drafted a plan to restore his allotment to more pristine conditions—a project that he wanted to finance himself. The Forest Service ignored his offer. A decade later, with a rangeland now infested with mature trees, the agency undertook an identical program, but this time with its own staff and equipment and at a cost 300 percent greater than Herb's estimate—and all with taxpayer dollars. Failure to encourage or allow permittees like Herb Metzger to invest on public lands has been costly to the American public, but it has also proven costly to the land.

Until control is shared and incentives are provided, the stewardship potential of public-land ranchers will remain untapped. In the meantime, the agencies will seek appropriations that will never be adequate to do the work needed. And for every dollar spent by the taxpayer on range improvements, an equivalent dollar will be squandered in the quest for mediocrity on the western range. Uncaring ranchers will do as little as they must, and the agencies will be their accomplices. A perennial battle between visions seeking control will dominate the federal landscape, with the advantage shifting steadily from individuals and the strategy of localism to bureaucracies and the rule of centralism. And the principal losers will be not the ranchers who graze the land but the land itself and the diversity of life supported by its water, soil, and air.

REFLECTIONS OF THE FAILED COMMONS

The worst of the rangeland commons persists on grazing allotments that are either too small to warrant caring or too crowded to instill individual responsibility. Small allotments are a legacy of the homestead era, when too many people and too many cattle settled on too little land with far too little forage. But they are also the outcomes of the laws and policies that imposed progressive conservation on the western range. The Taylor Grazing Act, for example, merely formalized the chaos of excessive numbers of ranchers by dividing the range into as many allotments. Its objective, after all, was "to stabilize the livestock industry dependent upon the public range." Today, the BLM is committed to preserving a landscape of small allotments, an inheritance stemming from past mistakes but upheld in the name of social welfare.

Small allotments are also the product of national forest policy. From the beginning, the Forest Service envisioned its task in terms of both conservation and social reform. Certainly, overgrazed and deteriorated forest ranges needed rest, but of equal importance was the need to extend the benefits of range resources beyond a handful of powerful western stockmen. Making national forest lands the province of the independent small rancher was, according to Phillip Wells, chief law officer in the Forest

Service under Gifford Pinchot, the factor "which in the past made the Forest Service a shining example in the dispensing of social justice."[24] Social justice, in this context, meant creating grazing opportunities.

Well into the 1940s, forest permittees found their livestock numbers routinely reduced to make way for new allotments. Buyers of public-land ranches were most often affected, learning only after purchase that the ranch's authorized capacity had been cut by 10 percent or more and that portions of the allotment had been distributed to other stockmen. In some cases, reductions struck established ranchers, especially when the imbalance of grazing privileges was most blatant or the demands for redistribution most urgent. For Herb Metzger, the Forest Service's push toward social democracy cost him 10 percent of his allotment, which went toward forming several small grazing allotments.

More often than not, social justice meant preserving the pattern of small allotments that characterized many national forests. In the 1940s, for example, limits on maximum allotment sizes were established westwide. In New Mexico, the limits were as low as one hundred head in the Santa Fe National Forest and as high as eight hundred head in the Gila National Forest. The limits were ostensibly set to protect the economic interests of permittees, to make an equitable division of forest range resources, and to prevent monopoly. Nothing has changed since then. Small allotments remain the rule throughout the National Forest System. Today, in New Mexico, their prevalence is most conspicuous in the Santa Fe National Forest, where more than four hundred permittees graze twelve thousand head of cattle, less than thirty head per rancher. According to the 1986 *Revised Draft Environmental Impact Statement, Santa Fe National Forest Plan,*

> livestock production is often a secondary source of income and favored as "a traditional way of life" by permit holders. The Forest seasonal permit is vital to a year-round operation. Current range management policy recognizes the importance of the smaller permit in supporting the socio-cultural environment of northern New Mexico.[25]

Supporting that environment has meant authorizing more livestock than the forest can carry. Moreover, small allotments have made the resolution of past overgrazing more complicated. "In some areas," the Forest Service reports, "more complex management practices are needed [to end overgrazing], which will require additional time, effort, and funds to implement because of local cultural, social, and economic situations." [26] In other words, small allotments have not only contributed to the overgrazing of the forest but also now demand a disproportionate share of agency resources.

Only a difference in magnitude separates the Santa Fe National Forest from other public grazing lands. Westwide, both Forest Service and BLM ranges are dominated by small allotments. Over half of them contain fewer than two thousand acres—significantly less than the minimum acreage deemed appropriate by John Wesley Powell for viable homesteads. Moreover, 43 percent of all public-land ranchers running cattle graze fewer than one hundred head; 90 percent graze fewer than five hundred head. Sheep operations, which account for only 21 percent of livestock forage consumed (compared with the 78 percent of cattle), exhibit similar trends. [27]

These figures reveal much about the nature of modern public-land grazing and the predicament of stewardship on the western range. Studies out of New Mexico State University, for example, show that cattle ranches with fewer than three hundred head are marginally profitable at best and may entail net losses as great as $60 per head. [28] Estimates made by the National Cattlemen's Association place the break-even point for cattle ranches even higher, at approximately five hundred head. [29] If these sources are correct, the majority of public-land ranches cannot be sustained without outside financial support. As a result, many public-land ranchers are occupied with activities other than ranching, and their limited financial resources are stretched so far that they are of little use to the grazing lands. Small grazing allotments are simply not good investments for permittees.

Several studies confirm the problems attending small grazing allotments. In a study of community grazing in New Mexico, Clyde Eastman and James R. Gray conclude that "the better-managed livestock operations tend to occur in the communities with larger landholdings." [30] Likewise, a 1985 Australian study examining the influence of ranch size on vegetation condition reported that "the vegetation on smaller properties, those which have the potential to produce less income for their owners, tends to be in poorer condition than larger properties." [31] Excessive stocking on smaller properties was the primary cause. Many of the same conclusions and observations hold for small allotments on the federal range. As long as more is taken from the land than is returned, static to deteriorating range conditions are almost inevitable.

An even greater problem associated with small allotments is the absence of any forage reserve. For the few ranchers who make their entire living from small allotments, even a minor reduction in livestock numbers could be sufficient to plunge them into insolvency. For one small operator in the Gila National Forest, the economic reality of small allotments is clear: "We can't afford to change our numbers very much year to year." [32] A public-land rancher in southeastern Oregon gives a similar account in a 1988 issue of the *Western Livestock Journal:*

> The price of this ranch . . . was based on the fact that it would run 230 head of cows. That means we paid for the right to graze on BLM administered range land and without it we cannot pay for the ranch and without it our ranch is worth a small fraction of what we paid for it. We have no room for a margin of error in ranch management. Two months early gathering these cattle [due to drought] means buying additional hay or selling off mother cows. We cannot afford to do either. [33]

The bottom line for this permittee and for others who share dependence on small allotments is that they must graze their land to stay in business. They cannot afford the forage reserve that Joe and Susan Fallini set aside for harsh times, nor can they exercise the luxury of nonuse as Marc Stevens does. If anything, they must overgraze their allotments during periods of drought, when soils and plants are most vulnerable.

Federal managers, overly sensitive to the economic predicament of small livestock operators, often tolerate levels of grazing that would be unacceptable elsewhere. Historically, that has been the case in almost every national forest, from the Santa Fe to the Custer. When Marc Stevens asked why several small allotments in the Custer National Forest enjoyed substantially greater stocking rates than larger ones, he was informed that they needed the economic advantage. The response served to highlight the agency's greater concern for "social democracy" than for the stewardship role of successful ranchers like Marc. Such stockmen were symbols of the monopoly the Forest Service hoped to break.

Pursuing social equity and welfare on the western range has been costly. "However noble the social goals of improving local communities," Rowley writes, "the policy [of small allotments] served in some instances to lay the foundation for conditions of overgrazing." [34] Such a policy has also been costly by creating stumbling blocks to agency management of public lands. Spending dollars and staff time on small allotments makes neither economic nor administrative sense. Both the Forest Service and the BLM are aware of the problem. In the Lincoln National Forest, for example, the ten-year plan is to reduce or eliminate small allotments to achieve more efficient land management. But this solution would merely trade one evil for another. In place of many small allotments, the Forest Service is proposing a few community allotments—a solution that historically has done more environmental harm than good.[35]

Community allotments are common grazing lands permitted to and used by more than one rancher. They are not unique to the Lincoln National Forest but occur in almost every national forest and BLM grazing district. Partial Forest Service allotment counts for several western regions indicate that between 10 and 25 percent of all forest grazing units are communal.[36] Although similar data are lacking for the BLM, the percentage of community allotments on public domain lands probably approximates Forest Service numbers.

The significance of community allotments varies between regions and among national forests and grazing districts. At one extreme is the Coyote District of the Santa Fe National Forest, where nine of eleven allotments are communal, ranging in membership from eight to twenty permittees. The largest, the Youngsville Allotment, is licensed for 746 cattle, with one permittee grazing two hundred head and the remaining nineteen grazing between one and sixty head.[37] At the other extreme is the Prescott National Forest in Arizona, where of the forest's eighty two allotments, only four are community grazed, and those four have only two permittees apiece.[38]

Many community allotments are carryovers from the days of the open range. Newly created national forests and public domain grazing districts merely assimilated communal grazing lands into the regime of public-land management. Multiple ranchers were still allowed to graze the same piece of ground, but the grazing unit was at least protected from the intrusion of alien stock. Increasingly, however, the agencies are looking to community allotments as a solution to the economic and administrative inefficiencies of small allotments.

But there are reasons more important than economy and administration that explain why community allotments are preferred over small allotments. First of all, they make the crucial matter of control much simpler for the Forest Service and the BLM. Vested interests, to the extent that they exist on such allotments, are diffused among many permittees, and no single member can exercise the power and influence traditionally associated with ranchers on individual allotments. Moreover, the probability of the communal unit coalescing into a united front to resist agency management is less likely, given the propensity of its members to fight among themselves. Although grazing associations do exist among communal graziers, those associations are frequently chartered under agency regulations. In the Forest Service, each forest supervisor has enormous discretionary power over community allotment grazing associations. Community allotments are also self-policing, at least in matters of authorized livestock numbers. Members, jealous of their allotted stock, become watchdogs over the numbers of livestock run by others. Members who take more than their share of forage are perceived as stealing what might otherwise be available to the group as a whole.

These few advantages may make the land manager's job easier, but they do not make up for the environmental ills that accompany most community allotments. Cultural traditions and social welfare aside, communal grazing entails many of the same environmental problems and stewardship disincentives that come with small allotments. By trading one for the other or by treating the former with preference, the agencies are simply continuing the most pernicious features of the open range. People and nature on the western range remain the victims of an untamed commons.

Communal grazing in itself is not the villain. There is no internal logic, as suggested by Garrett Hardin, that drives a grazing commons to environmental ruin. The failure of the commons, and that of community allotments in particular, is attributable to the displacement of control, not the lack of property ownership. Remember that the tragedy of the western commons arose from institutional barriers that prevented the residents of the western range from coming to terms with the land and its environment. Power resided not in the hands of people most immediate to the land but in layers of bureaucracy distanced from the land.

Montana state grazing districts exemplify modern commons that work. Comprised of private and public lands, each district is democratically run. Power to make essential grazing decisions lies at the local level, among the men and women who use the land and who suffer the consequences and reap the benefits of their management. Members of each district also have vested interests in their communal lands, making possible prudent stewardship goals that can be shared and judicious grazing practices that can be commonly applied.[39]

Communal grazing elsewhere on the western range has not been as successful, either socially or environmentally. With few exceptions, community allotments have perpetuated poor-condition rangelands, depriving them of the modicum of care and stewardship that some individual allotments have offered. Even national grassland grazing associations, once the shining example of local democracy at work, have succumbed to the abuses and flaws of the federal commons. As with community allotments in general, the focus of power has shifted from the membership to the agencies in charge. Bereft of the means to self-regulate and unable to capture the benefits of good management for the common good, communal grazing units fulfill Hardin's prophecy—not because they are compelled by the logic of the commons but because the logic of the commons is forced on them by public land law and policy.

In the Custer National Forest, where Marc Stevens ranches, 706 allotments account for almost 8 percent of all Forest Service grazing permits. The majority of these allotments are permitted to individual stockmen and operated on a basis equivalent to that of the Circle Bar. But 23 percent of the Custer's allotments are communal, supporting on average five permittees each.[40] Marc and his children participate in several community allotments, though not as an integral part of the Circle Bar operation. For Marc, the single community allotment he uses is peripheral to his main operation. For one of his children, however, it is the economic mainstay. In both cases, community allotments have been disappointing.

Voluntary grazing nonuse is the centerpiece of stewardship on the Circle Bar, but that practice is not possible on the community allotments. Taking 20 percent nonuse on an allotment where Marc controls only 10 percent of the stock amounts to a paltry 2 percent, so the costs of taking nonuse far outweigh the benefits. If others joined him, it might be different, but most members lack the outside grazing resources of the Circle Bar—resources vital to the practice of conservative grazing. Even worse, voluntary nonuse by one member may encourage other permittees to increase their stocking accordingly—wiping out the slight advantage offered by one caring rancher.

There are other problems with communal grazing lands. Marc would like to apply the kinds of management he has developed on the Circle Bar, but disagreement among allotment members makes grazing innovation difficult. Also, members sometimes refuse to pull their own weight, preferring instead to let others do the work and make the financial investments. One member of Marc's allotment refused to maintain a spring, claiming that his thirty head did not justify the time and money that would have to be invested. He knew that failure to perform the work might lead to a stocking reduction for all members, but he also knew that whereas he would have to pay the full cost of repairing the spring, he would have to bear only a minute portion of any adjustment in numbers.

For most permittees on community allotments—including Marc and his children—there are no incentives to care for the land. The result is mediocrity and, even worse, deterioration. On Otter Creek, the grazing lands in the poorest condition are more often than not those that are communally grazed. This is not surprising. The connection to the land that made Marc Stevens and Levi Howes care about the Circle Bar is simply absent on community allotments.

Marc is not alone in his experiences. In Brown's Park in northwestern Colorado, the Dickinson family has ranched BLM lands for four generations, stretching back to Charlie Spark's departure from North Carolina and his arrival in Rock Springs, Wyoming, in 1885. T. Wright Dickinson, Charlie's great-grandson, shares management of the ranch with his father and two sisters.[41] Much of the ranch is permitted in the form of individual BLM allotments. For T. Wright, however, the portion of the ranch that lies in community allotments is what sticks out when conversation turns to the trials and tribulations of public-land grazing.

Good stewardship has always meant leaving abundant forage reserves for the dry years. By taking nonuse as needed and by evenly and lightly grazing both private and public lands, T. Wright has been able to attain that goal—at least on the BLM allotments that are exclusively assigned to his family. On those allotments, the family has paid for all the waters and fences needed to ensure the proper level of stewardship. But the story is different on the community allotments that the Dickinsons share with other permittees. Forage reserves are nonexistent, nonuse is rare, and rancher investments are minimal.

Nowhere is the problem more evident than on BLM lands assigned to the Rock Springs Grazing Association in southwestern Wyoming. Encompassing almost two million acres and supporting some sixty thousand sheep and six thousand cattle, the association epitomizes the problems of communal grazing. Private investments are lacking, federal subsidies abound, and forage reserves are minimal to nonexistent. But the greatest problem is what T. Wright Dickinson terms the mentality of the member ranchers—or what Garrett Hardin would portray as the compelling logic of the commons.

Despite moderate to light stocking rates set by the BLM, the community allotment is victim to the worst ravages of the tragedy of the commons. Both cattlemen and sheepmen, eager to use the greenest and most abundant forage, concentrate on the best ranges within the allotment. Each spring, they head to those sites, hoping to arrive before all others, calculating all the while the benefits of first come, first served. When they do arrive, they allow their livestock to graze the forage to dust, knowing that if they do not, someone else will. As a result, the most productive grasslands of the allotment are pulverized by hungry stock and exploited by stockmen attending to their self-interests. Although the allotment *on average* is moderately grazed—a feather in the cap of the BLM and plausible proof of the viability of community allotments—the land is not better off, even with the federal subsidies that fuel the association's grazing appetite. The vicious cycle of degradation continues.

RISE OF THE WELFARE RANCHER AND THE TRIUMPH OF MEDIOCRITY

Conservation reform settled on the western range with the best of intentions. It envisioned a healthy and productive West, one where people would harness their energies to the betterment of both themselves and nature. Yet a century's worth of outcomes has not lived up to the expectations of that progressive vision. The promise of enlightened stewardship has soured with the rise of the welfare rancher, and the hope of scientific land management has dimmed with the triumph of mediocrity.

In many ways, the rise of the welfare rancher is the most regrettable outcome. People whose values are rooted in the land and whose regard for independence and self-sufficiency is legendary have betrayed both by becoming wards of the state. There are, of course, notable exceptions. Ranchers like Bard Heaton, Joe and Susan Fallini, Dwayne and Donna Slaathaug, and Marc Stevens exemplify a public-land tradition that endures—a belief in individual accountability and a commitment to personal stewardship. They are the few permittees who live, rather than merely preach, an ethic of caring and responsibility.

Sadly, most permittees have chosen a different path, one cleared of the obligations of stewardship by the grace of federal subsidies. And often, that choice has been driven by the demands of survival, not preference. Getting by in an environment layered with disincentives and cluttered with innumerable obstacles has meant accommodation and compromise for some. Other ranchers, particularly those whose interests have never been in the long-term well-being of their federal allotments, have welcomed their roles as welfare ranchers. In both cases, the rise of the welfare rancher has occurred simultaneously with the demise of stewardship.

The origins of subsidies for public-land ranchers can be traced back to the beginnings of scientific land management. The Civilian Conservation Corps built fences and corrals and developed springs and earthen reservoirs throughout the West, to the benefit of thousands of public-land ranchers. And animal damage control, a coordinated federal and state program for killing unwanted predators, saved ranchers lost livestock at taxpayers' expense. Wolves were exterminated and coyotes, cougars, bobcats, and bears ruthlessly pursued with aerial gunships, packs of dogs, poisons, and millions of rounds of ammunition. Today, the combined state and federal cost of killing one coyote for the sake of saving a handful of lambs can cost as much as $12,000.[42]

A consistently below-market value grazing fee is the most prominent subsidy tied to public-land ranching. Total direct costs of the combined Forest Service and BLM grazing program in 1983, for example, exceeded grazing fee receipts by $41 million.[43] The same discrepancy continues today. But taxpayer subsidization of public-land grazing through low fees is not new; it began with the creation of the Forest Service and continues at ever-increasing levels. As a result, calls for higher grazing fees are being made with more urgency. Fiscal conservatives eager to find solutions to the federal deficit, and environmentalists eager to curb the abuses of public-land grazing, have joined in common cause to raise public-land grazing fees to the equivalence of private-land lease rates.

Land agencies have also joined in the chorus for higher fees, but their motives have not been to eliminate a subsidy. Additional grazing fees translate into more range betterment funds—the monies that the Forest Service and the BLM use to maintain and improve public grazing lands.

The agencies give up a subsidy of no benefit to them (low fees) for a subsidy that can enhance their range programs (range betterment dollars). And for ranchers, the loss of the grazing fee subsidy is at least partially offset by vastly increased range improvement investments—subsidies provided at taxpayers' expense.

The prospect that higher fees may expand range improvement aid is most relevant to the rise of the welfare rancher. Subsidies in the form of low grazing fees, animal damage control, and one-shot federal conservation projects have made the business of public-land ranching easier—though at considerable public cost. They have not, however, relieved ranchers of the responsibility to steward the lands they use or to stand accountable for their use of the land. But the subsidies that pay for the maintenance and improvement of federal lands are another matter. They not only make the business of public-land ranching easier but also free ranchers of the need to care for the land and dilute their accountability for its condition.

Public-land laws and policies in recent decades have created the ideal environment for the rise of the welfare rancher and the demise of stewardship. In the name of bureaucratic autonomy and control, the role of public-land ranchers has been steadily narrowed to abusers of the federal range and recipients of federal handouts. And options that might have encouraged permittee stewardship have been discarded by a landscape vision more intent on extending its influence than fulfilling its original promise.

Bureaucratic commitment to welfare ranching has shielded the land from alternative uses and protected stockmen from competition from other land users. By paying ranchers to stay in business and by prohibiting them from using the plants, streams, and soils of federal rangelands for any licensed use other than raising stock, the Forest Service and the BLM have shackled the western range to the past. The agencies have granted a land-use monopoly to a small segment of American society and, in so doing, have made conflict and politics the deciding factors in the fate of the western range.

To hold on to that monopoly in the face of mounting environmental protest, ranchers have changed their attitudes toward government subsidies. Motivated by desperation as well as pragmatic calculation, they now support Forest Service and BLM calls for increased federal range improvement spending. Hanging in the balance is their livelihood, the small piece of paper that declares their right to graze the land and signifies their only interest in it. Increasingly, they have taken a defensive position as they justify themselves to a world that is largely indifferent to their fate.

Their backs against the wall, stockmen lash out at the rising public sentiment in favor of alternative uses of federal lands. Unable to accommodate popular demand for fisheries, recreation, and wildlife, ranchers resort to the tools of politics and the tired and worn arguments of multiple use to perpetuate land uses that only federal bureaucracies seem to favor. Public law and agency policy make it clear that if they wish to stay on the land, then they must graze it. They must play the role of welfare rancher because they have no option.

Playing the role of welfare rancher has not been difficult in the environment of progressive conservation. In the name of economic stability and social assistance, both the Forest Service and the BLM have invested taxpayers' dollars in massive programs aimed at keeping ranchers and their communities alive and well. Well-funded Forest Service range rehabilitation programs in the 1950s and 1960s pumped dollars and forage into communities dependent on federal rangelands. And agency concern for small ranchers and the cultural traditions they symbolize has entailed significant expenditures in forests like the Santa Fe. In every instance, Rowley writes, the danger of inducing permittee dependence on government subsidies has been tempered by fear that "the economic stability of the grazing community would be threatened if these subsidies or services were suddenly withdrawn by a change in government policies."[44]

The Vale Rangeland Rehabilitation Program in southeastern Oregon provides a perfect example of how BLM programs have contributed to the rise of the welfare rancher.[45] Prior to 1963, rangelands in the Vale District were drastically overgrazed, with livestock numbers exceeding carrying capacity by an estimated 40 percent. Making matters worse, the majority of Vale allotments were not only small but also communal. Those factors, plus the historical overobligation of grazing rights and the vested interests they created, made Vale permittees reluctant either to invest in range improvements or to adjust livestock numbers. By 1963, less than one 1 percent of the Vale area had received any range improvements and voluntary grazing nonuse was far below the national average. Not surprisingly, conflict and strife between permittees jealously holding on to grazing numbers and BLM staff attempting to enforce reductions dominated the years immediately before the project's implementation.

Bob Skinner, a rancher in the Vale area, looks back with regret at the episodes of rangeland abuse that brought Vale rangelands to their deteriorated state.[46] He is ashamed that local ranchers did not reverse the overgrazing and heal the degraded lands. But they were unwilling to invest in communal allotments and were often financially unable to spend more money because of the small size of their herds. Their only option was to fight to maintain livestock numbers, even though they all knew that too much stock was already present. And so, when they were faced with the prospect of impending livestock reductions, permittees joined with politicians and the BLM to lobby Congress for what became the 1963 Vale Rangeland Rehabilitation Program. Over a ten-year period, the federal program paid for widespread plowing, reseeding, and spraying of overgrazed rangelands. Fences were built and livestock waters developed. By 1986, almost $20 million had been spent on a program that required half a million dollars per year for maintenance to benefit only 183 permittees.

Range conditions improved somewhat, particularly during the first years of the program, but by 1986 significant areas of treated rangeland were being reinvaded by sagebrush.[47] Only the 10 percent of Vale rangeland reseeded into crested wheatgrass appeared to be marginally holding its own. Of forty-two pastures studied in 1986 and reported in a 1988 evaluation of the Vale program, twenty-seven were declining and only fourteen appeared to have improved. Even more discouraging, there was "no clear relationship between numbers of most [wildlife] species and the Vale Program."[48] Soil erosion also remained a critical problem, and only riparian areas that had been fenced off from livestock appeared to have improved.

From its inception, the Vale program was a welfare project. A community of ranchers who had abused rangelands for thirty years was awarded with a massive infusion of federal funds. Less costly options, such as the elimination of community allotments, reductions in total livestock numbers, and the merging of remaining small allotments into expanded individual units, were bypassed in the name of political expediency.[49] Certainly, those options would have displaced many ranchers; however, for a fraction of the program's total cost, displaced ranchers could have been bought out with federal funds and allowed to buy other ranches or seek alternative employment. Rangelands would still have improved, local communities would have attained balance with the land's carrying capacity, and taxpayers would have been saved the burden of a long-term subsidy program. Only the BLM would have failed to benefit. The Vale program has been repeated in various forms, in varying degrees, on almost all BLM and Forest Service lands. In the late 1970s, the BLM undertook a multimillion-dollar project to develop water pipelines on the Rio Puerco Resource Area in central New Mexico.[50] Made up of communal and small allotments, the resource area had been overgrazed both before and after the Taylor Grazing Act was passed, resulting in depletion of vegetation and serious soil erosion. Moreover, the allotments lacked the base waters that were required by law before permittees could graze public domain lands. The BLM's project was aimed at giving ranchers those base waters and providing the range improvements that were properly the responsibility of the permittee. Today, range conditions are still depleted, and members of community allotments are refusing to maintain the water system paid for with tax dollars.

Experimental stewardship programs (ESPs) undertaken jointly by the BLM and the Forest Service are further examples of the rise of welfare ranching. Set up by the Public Rangelands Improvement Act of 1978, ESPs were intended to provide "incentives to, or rewards for, the holders of grazing permits and leases whose stewardship results in an improvement of the range condition of lands under permit or lease." They were also designed to include a broad array of interest groups in the decision-making process. By making individuals other than ranchers a part of allotment planning, lawmakers hoped to reduce multiple use conflicts and strengthen communications between public-land users and land managers. The result, however, has been to discourage permittee stewardship.

On one of the larger ESPs, the Modoc-Washoe in northwestern Nevada and northeastern California, a 1988 GAO study reported overall investment had increased due to government support but permittee investment was "either questionable or unsupported."[51] Much the same was reported for all other ESPs, where permittees' shares of public-land investments were actually lower than they were for non-ESP lands. Moreover, recent BLM surveys indicate that there have been no significant changes in range conditions on the Modoc-Washoe since the program began.[52] Static conditions also prevail on other ESPs.

Joe Harris, a longtime rancher on the Modoc-Washoe, attributes the lackluster performance of ESPs to two factors.[53] First, ESPs were the only alternative many ranchers had to massive livestock reductions. Joining

ESPs was a matter of expediency in which survival and subsidy took precedence over improvement of degraded range. Second, communal grazing, at least on the Modoc-Washoe, reduced the incentives of ranchers to invest and forced them to the lowest common denominator of management—the level set by the least cooperative and least caring member of the allotment.

ESPs have simply ignored the underlying problems of public-land grazing. They take the route of subsidization rather than the course of policy reform to keep livestock grazing healthy and alive on the western range. As a result, the stewardship program has saved local ranchers from livestock reductions by installing range improvements at the public's expense. Jean Schadler, a spokeswomen for the Modoc-Washoe ranchers, is careful to point out that the stewardship program should not be evaluated solely in terms of its benefits to the land. What matters, she insists, is that ESPs have rescued local communities from economic hardship and saved them from social decay.[54] What she does not mention is that they have also benefited local Forest Service and BLM range programs. ESPs have brought increased funding to agency coffers.

Forest Service and BLM support for ESPs, however, is not based on dollars alone. Both agencies see advantages in the multiple use committees that make the management decisions for participating allotments. Those committees, it is claimed, have improved communications among competing user groups and have made it easier for them to agree on multiple use goals. In this sense, ESPs are similar to the Forest Service's integrated resource management planning and the BLM's cooperative resource management planning. All three rely on broad-based public participation to arrive at planning decisions that meet multiple uses and multiple needs, but their common effect is to dilute the accountability of public-land ranchers.

Instead of making graziers responsible for land maintenance and improvement, all three processes spread responsibility among diverse interest groups. Ranchers are once again relieved of the need to care for and steward their permitted lands. They can maintain their livestock numbers without having to pay the full costs of doing so, and they bear no responsibility for mistakes. And if management mistakes are made, permittees need not worry. Others divvy up accountability until it vanishes into thin air, leaving the final tab to be paid by the American taxpayer. In this way, the place of the welfare rancher on the federal range is secured by a system more intent on quelling multiple use conflict than on promoting caring and stewardship.

For the Forest Service and the BLM, welfare ranchers are an asset. They have given the agencies a handle on control. Stockmen who must depend on federal subsidies to maintain their authorized numbers are far more likely to do the agencies' bidding. As noted in the GAO's 1988 report on ESPs, "the program did result in improved communication and cooperation between agencies' range managers and permittees in several geographic areas where hostile reactions previously existed." [55]

Heavily subsidized ranchers may be the blessing of federal land agencies, but they are the bane of public grazing lands. They add to the crisis of accountability that has undermined the health of the western range since its opening to settlement in 1862. And the public-land policies that bail them out have subjected the western range to a most insidious process of natural selection. Ranchers who care are dissuaded from good stewardship, and ranchers who do not care are subsidized for their indifference. Without a word of alarm or regret, the ranks of the former are depleted and the numbers of the latter are swollen. Mediocrity is the final evolutionary product.

Nearly a century has elapsed since the first optimistic stirrings of conservation reform. Yet the progressive vision of a healthier, more vibrant landscape remains as elusive as ever. Rangelands are still depleted, and the promise of scientific land management is far from fruition. The goal of the National Environmental Policy Act of 1969—"to create and maintain conditions under which man and nature can exist in productive harmony . . . "—has not been met in the hundred-year reign of a second landscape vision.

CHAPTER TEN

Cleansing the Land

T. *Wright Dickinson and Ken Spann have three things in common. Both are fourth-generation Colorado ranchers, both care deeply for their lands and their way of life, and both devote almost all their time to the business of ranching. The similarities end there. T. Wright ranches BLM land in Brown's Park in the sparsely populated northwestern corner of Colorado.[1] Ken grazes cattle four months each year in the high country of the Gunnison National Forest and winters them for eight months on his private lands in the valley between Crested Butte and Gunnison.[2] Tourists pass his rangelands every day on their way to the towering mountains that surround the two west-central Colorado towns.*

More than geography, though, separates the two ranchers. Isolated from the main battle lines of public-land conflict and the major thoroughfares of public travel, T. Wright Dickinson works far from the mainstream of public-land ranching. Decades of change, so discouraging to most permittees, have not noticeably diminished his attachment to place or lessened his sense of control on the federal range. T. Wright's family, by virtue of location and a benign local BLM office, has been shielded from the worst of public-land law, policy, and bureaucracy. Caring for public lands has been an easy choice for the Dickinsons because they are optimistic about their future.

Ken Spann's permitted lands offer no such hope. Unlike T. Wright, Ken relies on public grazing lands for only a fraction of his forage needs. The heart of his ranch lies in the irrigated pastures and grassy meadows that his family has owned for a century. Those lands share the fertile valley bottom between Crested Butte and Gunnison with the pastures and meadows of ten other ranches. Although Ken's future is rooted in private land, his forest allotments are vital during summer, when valley fields are rested or set aside for growing hay. For Ken, however, federal grazing is not the simple matter of good management and caring stewardship that it is for T. Wright. A maze of public-land laws and agency rules has mired the business of ranching in a morass of technocratic and legalistic barriers, making Ken's place and his children's future in the Gunnison National Forest ever so tenuous.

Ken must also contend with a new vision of the western range—a vision that seeks to free the land of livestock and cleanse it of man's historical presence. Although that vision offers no immediate threat to grazing in the Gunnison National Forest, it compounds the layers of disincentives Ken now faces with the fear of exclusion from the forest. As a result, he is no longer willing to spend his dollars or apply innovative management on lands over which he has no control. He will graze the Gunnison for as long as he can, but he is prepared to retreat to the valley when laws, policies, and bureaucracy become too much to bear. There, he can attend to the rural vision that underlies his conservation ethic.

Yet it is that vision and ethic that make Ken's displacement from forestlands so tragic and potentially so costly. One has only to visit his valley ranch to witness what caring stewardship can do. His meadows, grazed only in moderation, are rich in biological diversity. Along with ten other ranches, his lands provide 52 percent of big game winter range in the mountain-valley ecosystem that stretches from Crested Butte to Gunnison. Ken understands how important his lands are to wildlife, but he also knows how vital they are to those who live in the valley and to those who only visit. For that reason, he and his neighbors have written a code of ethics for recreational use of valley and mountain lands. He has also spent hours with hunters, skiers, hikers, and wildlife enthusiasts talking about recreational use and the pursuit of environmental quality.

Most of all, he has taken care to preserve his lands. The recreational and environmental value of the Gunnison-Crested Butte corridor does not lie solely in the majesty of its fourteen-thousand-foot peaks. The uniqueness of the landscape resides in the striking contrasts between lifeless granite peaks, forested slopes, and picturesque valley meadows. In that setting, people and nature can come together in a fashion that is aesthetically pleasing and ecologically promising. That fact has deeply influenced Ken, reinforcing his commitment to stay on the land and resist those who want to turn his meadows into vacation subdivisions. Residents of the valley, from Crested Butte to Gunnison, share that vision.

The Forest Service does not appear to share the vision, however. Certainly, the agency is concerned about many of the same things. A game management area has been set up in the Gunnison National Forest to provide habitat for elk and deer, and recreation is a major priority in forest plans. Still, the Forest Service sees no necessary link between long-term residents like Ken and the continuing health of forest ecosystems. What counts is not who uses the land but the power of the agency to manage how it is used.

But without Ken and his neighbors, the mountain and valley ecosystem will be less sustainable as ranchers are limited to bottomlands, as livestock and wildlife compete for diminished winter forage, and as summer homes encroach on valley meadows. An even more profound effect will come from bureaucratic boundaries setting granite peaks and forested slopes apart from the meadows and communities below. The many visions of caring and stewardship that have made ranching an integral part of the Gunnison-Crested Butte ecosystem will never reach beyond the valley floor. Different, or even better, ways of caring for public lands will languish for want of opportunity or incentive—victims of a new and more righteous conservation.

RUMBLINGS OF DISSENT

Pastoralism is an ancient and enduring way of life. Yet of all its varied forms, it is hard to imagine one more ill suited to the land and its human element than the American system of public-land grazing. Even more difficult to imagine is how and why such a system could perpetuate itself on the western range for almost a century. That it has done so, even in the aftermath of the National Environmental Policy Act, is remarkable. Decades of change simply have not altered the basic features of progressive conservation or influenced the course of its unconstrained vision. Sadly, its promise of a more productive and healthier federal range remains as distant and elusive today as it was a century ago.

How and why such a system could continue for so long and with so little public outcry is perplexing. Quite possibly, the explanation is a matter of advantage and convenience. Both land agencies and ranchers are self-interested, and reforms that might have speeded up range recovery were not to the advantage of either. The Forest Service and the BLM preferred to continue the status quo, even if it meant piling layers of disincentives and subsidies onto an economically marginal use of federal rangelands. Ranchers did not resist. In the fickle and tenuous environment of public-land policy, ranchers found it more convenient to put up with the flaws of public-land management than to risk basic reforms. As dominant players in the fate of the western range, agencies and permittees have managed to preserve the fabric of public-land grazing with remarkable constancy.

Beneath the veneer of complacency, however, have been rumblings of dissent, the earliest of which came from John Muir. He shared with Gifford Pinchot, his contemporary, a disgust over mismanagement of western forests, warning that they were "desperately near being like smashed eggs and spilt milk." [3] He spared no words in vilifying western stockmen, particularly sheepherders, whose "hoofed locusts" swarmed over the high Sierra and Cascade ranges, carrying "desolation with them." [4] But he went a step further and challenged the central tenet of progressive conservation, the belief that nature's purpose was to fulfill human needs. "Why," Muir demanded, "ought man to value himself as more than an infinitely small composing unit of the one great unit of creation?" [5] Nature, the living fabric of creation, had value independent of human measure and purpose beyond society's storehouse of natural resources. If anything, unspoiled nature was mankind's refuge from the discomforts of civilization.

Not surprisingly, Muir was at odds with progressive conservation and its agenda of rational and efficient exploitation of natural resources. And he was not alone. The Sierra Club, which he founded in 1892, and a growing number of conservationists and professional ecologists joined him in denouncing Pinchot's utilitarian conservation ideology. At first, they focused much of their anger and passion on the progressive movement's early commitment to predator control. But the event that set Muir and his followers furthest apart from progressive conservation was the damming of the Hetch Hetchy Valley in Yosemite National Park in 1914.

The purpose of the Hetch Hetchy reservoir was to quench what was becoming an insatiable thirst among California's burgeoning urban population and booming agriculture. Its effect was to pitch Muir's vision of preservation and protection of nature against Pinchot's vision of extraction and development of natural resources. "These temple destroyers, devotees of ravaging commercialism," Muir lamented, "seem to have a perfect contempt for Nature, and instead of lifting their eyes to the God of the Mountains, lift them to the Almighty Dollar." [6] Pinchot's response was far less impassioned: "As to my attitude regarding the proposed use of Hetch Hetchy by the city of San Francisco . . . I am fully persuaded that . . . the injury . . . by substituting a lake for the present swampy floor of the valley . . . is altogether unimportant compared with the benefits to be derived from its use as a reservoir."[7] These two visions of nature sounded the broad theme of environmental reform that would engulf the western range and challenge the ethical propriety and ecological wisdom of grazing sheep and cattle in an arid land.

The dissent sounded by Muir and his supporters was only the first of many challenges to progressive conservation. In the years since Hetch Hetchy, Muir's opposition to Pinchot's vision has resurfaced in many forms and through many voices. Only recently, however, has the dissent become a dominant theme in public-policy debate. Since Earth Day in 1970, almost all facets of federal management of public lands and resources have been assailed in the pages of a growing environmental literature. Alston Chase's *Playing God in Yellowstone*, Marc Reisner's *Cadillac Desert*, and Randal O'Toole's *Reforming the Forest Service* make it clear that the tenets of Pinchot and the vision of progressive conservation no longer enjoy broad-based support.

Public-land grazing has been particularly buffeted by escalating dissent. Analysts ranging from William Voigt, Jr., in *Public Grazing Lands*, to Denzel and Nancy Ferguson, in *Sacred Cows at the Public Trough,* have mounted angry and at times vicious attacks on the practice and outcome of grazing livestock on federal lands. Edward Abbey, in "Even the Bad Guys Wear White Hats," and Lynn Jacobs, in *Free Our Public Lands!,* have been no less sparing. Their sentiment, echoed in a November 1989 *Forest Watch* article, is clearly antiranching: "The public interest . . . would be better served if our public lands were withdrawn from livestock grazing and primarily devoted to preservation of wildlife habitat, water quality and ecological integrity."[8]

Grass-roots organizations, such as Earth First!, have cut fences and disrupted ranching operations to make sure that federal rangelands are "Cattle Free by '93" or that there is "No Moo by '92."[9] And movements such as deep ecology have attacked the hands-on management of land agencies as ecologically disastrous and ethically unacceptable. Their preference is to return to the tradition of hands-off management—Muir's righteous management—that dominated the western range prior to the arrival of European settlers and the scourge of their alien livestock.

Most environmental critique, however, has focused on more immediate concerns. The Sierra Club, the Audubon Society, the Natural Resources Defense Council, and the National Wildlife Federation have taken the Forest Service and the BLM to task for failing to do their mandated jobs. They claim that public grazing lands have fallen short of the biological mark set by decades of progressive conservation. They have also shaken the complacency of land agencies and permittees and cast doubt on the tools and ideas underlying the system of permitted grazing and the science of public-land management. Most of all, a youthful environmental movement has extended the rumblings of dissent beyond the plight of the western range to the politics of its use and control.

A century of progressive management, critics charge, has not altered the historical hold of the ranching community over the western range. Livestock still dominates and overgrazes the public landscape, and permittees still exercise more influence over land management than their numbers warrant. Whether large or small operators, caring stewards or not, public-land ranchers are seen as exploiters of the land and as antagonistic competitors for control of the federal range. The twenty-seven thousand stockmen licensed to graze public lands are nagging reminders of democracy promised but denied.

It is the democratic failure of past visions as much as the environmental plight of public lands that now energizes the glimmerings of a third vision on the western horizon. The outlines of that third landscape vision are clear. The vast open spaces of the western range—the grazing lands betrayed by both ranchers and land agencies—are being seen as hallowed ground. These lands are being viewed as the potential citadels of a new national commons, a land devoted to *all* the people. A blending of agrarian and progressive traditions, it is the environmental vision.

BREAKING NEW GROUND

The environmental vision rose to political prominence only in the aftermath of World War II, but its ideas and values are not new. They are part of an environmental tradition that stretches back to the mid-nineteenth century and the writings of Henry David Thoreau and George Marsh. But the proper moment for the environmental vision to surface came, as it did for agrarianism and progressive conservation, naturally and in tempo with the rhythms of change in America.

Passage from agrarian to progressive visions had taken place in the broad context of a revolution in social conditions and cultural mores. As urban values and industry eclipsed rural values and agriculture, the western range, which had been the domain of self-reliant farmers, became the resource depository of a growing nation. But the transition from one vision to another did not visibly alter the way most Americans thought about the arid West. Except for a handful of western residents and dedicated conservationists and an expanding land management bureaucracy, it remained an inhospitable landscape, a desolate barrier standing between the populated Atlantic and Pacific coasts. With few exceptions, the vast public rangelands lying within its boundaries were the lands that nobody wanted.

Popular attitudes toward federal lands changed little with the rise of progressive conservation. If anything, the West receded in the American mind as industrialization and waves of European immigration brought far-reaching social and cultural changes to an increasingly urbanized country. Even the coming of the automobile and the brief interlude of peace and prosperity in the 1920s did not reverse widespread indifference to public lands. Recreation was not a viable option in a region where roads were unimproved, towns were few and far between, and service facilities for travelers were almost nonexistent.

The prosperity of the post–World War II years changed all of that. Rising incomes and more leisure time, along with an expanding network of western highways and service centers, opened the western range to more Americans than ever before. Some sought new beginnings in the vibrant urban centers of the West; many others went as tourists. Significantly, Americans traveling to the West after 1950 arrived with different perceptions and expectations of public lands. For them, the western range was less formidable and far less threatening than it had been for the first wave of western migration. Public lands were no longer the lands that nobody wanted. They had become lands to be used by all Americans in their pursuit of happiness.

By the 1980s, there could be no doubt that the purpose of public lands had moved far beyond the confines of traditional users and commodity production. Millions of Americans were spending almost three billion hours per year seeking pleasure and adventure on Forest Service and BLM lands, and the public's demand for recreation showed no signs of letting up.[10]

In this setting of relative affluence and leisure, rumblings of dissent coalesced into an environmental agenda, a landscape vision impatient with the conservation record of the past and eager to break new ground in the cause of public-land protection. The vision is an amalgam of past visions. Agrarian traditions are alive in the vision's devotion to preserving federal lands for a common, democratic purpose. But only part of the Jeffersonian legacy lives on. Homes and workplaces, the pillars of Jefferson's virtuous republic, are nowhere to be found on a western landscape sculpted by an environmental vision. Also absent is local rule, the opportunity for people to practice face-to-face democracy.

Not surprisingly, advocates of the environmental vision embrace Gifford Pinchot's mistrust of the unfettered individualism linked to Jefferson's agrarian virtues and share in the ethical presumption that its excesses—the excesses of public-land ranchers—laid waste to the western range. The ranchers' historical control of millions of acres of federal range, in their view, has undermined the democratic purpose of America's vast landed estate and deprived citizens of their rightful claim to a share of its seemingly unlimited bounty. Correction of the ecological abuse brought on by overzealous individualism and a paucity of control and regulation is a common goal linking the environmental and progressive visions. By virtue of the unconstrained quality of their ideologies and the enormous expanse over which they hope to rule, the environmental and progressive visions also look to identical means to achieve their ends. Enlightened government, rather than the uncontrollable rule of Jefferson's "natural aristocracy," is the common path followed by each in its pursuit of reform and protection of the western range.

Apart from these basic similarities, the two visions part ways in matters of scientific land management and the sanctity of expertise. For advocates of the environmental vision, the science of grazing management is a dismal failure, the engineering of multiple uses a reckless juggling act, and the practice of both a lame excuse for continuing an activity that is ecologically unwise and environmentally harmful. Advocates of the environmental vision also assail the elitism that has historically permeated Forest Service and BLM management. Two decades of protest by environmentalists and a series of federal statutes, beginning with NEPA, have forced land agencies to expand the business of managing public lands beyond the tight circle of managers and traditional users. The success of various environmental groups in gaining standing in public-lands litigation has also contributed to the opening of the decision-making process to a number of previously excluded parties. Landmark cases, such as the Natural Resources Defense Council's 1974 challenge to the Department of the Interior's choice of "programmatic" grazing environmental impact statements over "site-specific" ones, have assured critics of progressive conservation a hearing in the courts as well as in the offices of the Forest Service and the BLM.

Unclaimed by legitimate interests and abused by special interests, the public grazing lands have become the special ward of a movement and ideology intent on fulfilling a democratic promise. Only an agenda provided by an environmental vision, it is assumed, will revive and renew lands orphaned and left to the caprice of western stockmen and malleable land agencies. And only by rededicating those lands to collective ownership will the protection and preservation of the federal range be ensured.

Collective ownership, one of two central themes of the environmental vision, has a long and hallowed tradition in American conservation. For many, the vast expanses of the western range assume a special cultural meaning, one echoed in Woody Guthrie's moving refrain, "This land is your land." Elizabeth Junkin, in *Lands of Brighter Destiny*, argues that the meaning of public lands is intensely personal. There is, she infers, "something within us, as Americans, that needs to know that there is publicly-owned land." [11] Others concur, pointing out that the use and management of public lands instill a strong sense of collective participation.

Common ownership, and the collective participation it nurtures, resolves what many believe to be a flaw in the structure of American society. Public lands overcome the nation's tendency toward social atomism by closing the gap between collective and private values. Joseph Sax, in a 1984 essay that supports retention of public lands, notes that "to retain public lands only where they now exist—principally in the West—and to leave the rest of the country in private ownership is not as 'inconsistent' as it may seem at first glance. It is control in favor of civic values." Civic values, he adds, are enforceable only "through the decision-making apparatus of the state." The goals of "wilderness preservation, wildlife habitat, and 'open' public recreation" can be attained only on a landscape where collective values—the values voiced by democratic government—hold sway over private interests. [12]

John Muir advocated much the same in his passionate writings on the condition of American forests. "Only what belongs to all alike is reserved," he wrote, "and every acre that is left should be held together under the federal government as a basis for a general policy of administration for the public good." [13] Nearly half a century later, Bernard De Voto expressed similar sentiments from his "easy chair" on the pages of *Harper's Magazine*. It was clear to him, as it had been to Muir, that collective ownership of the federal range was a precondition for the reconstruction of the West. Yet beneath the conservation concerns of both men was a more fundamental assumption: the shared belief that public lands are an essential part of the American experience and identity.

The cumulative effect of a legacy of collective ownership and participation has been the revitalization of the western commons in the agenda of the environmental vision. "The strength that allowed the environmental movement to stop, stall, or reverse the Reagan Revolution," notes Ed Marston, publisher of *High Country News*,

> comes from its roots. In the West, those roots are in the public land—in our land. In the case of these Western lands, the metaphor conveyed by Garret Hardin's essay, The Tragedy of the Commons, should be replaced by a new metaphor, The Glory of the Commons. [14]

Renewed faith in the western commons and belief in its workability do not signify a nostalgic return or tribute to the days of the open range. The commons envisioned by many environmentalists is one in which livestock and stockmen are less visible and their impact is greatly diminished. More impassioned environmentalists have followed Edward Abbey's lead, demanding that public-land ranchers "get their cows off our property." [15] But the rank and file have framed their demands in the broader context of making public lands serve *all* the American people. Bernard Shanks, in *This Land Is Your Land*, restates those demands in a simple declaration: "The [public] lands need a manifesto for the future. They should be managed so all citizens can use them democratically as a national heritage and trust." [16]

Shank's call for a manifesto has not gone unheeded. In his 1986 address before the annual convention of the Sierra Club, Bruce Babbitt, then governor of Arizona, provided the clearest statement yet of the emerging environmental vision:

> We . . . need a new Western land ethic for non-wilderness. The old concept of multiple use no longer fits the reality of the new West. It

must be replaced by a concept of public use. From this day on, we must recognize the new reality that the highest and best, most productive use of Western public land will usually be for public purposes—watershed, wildlife and recreation.

The time is at hand to go beyond multiple use. Mining entry must be regulated, timber cutting must be honestly subordinated to watershed and wildlife values, and grazing must be subordinated to regeneration and restoration of grasslands. Many of the Forest Service and BLM plans . . . ignore the primacy of public values. It is now time to replace neutral concepts of multiple use with a statutory mandate that public lands are to be administered primarily for public purposes.[17]

Babbitt's emphasis on public purposes other than making a living underscores the second theme of the environmental vision—the spiritualization of the federal range. Western rangelands, once residences for settlers and stockmen and later a national reservoir of natural resources, are in transition from being physical landscapes to becoming depositories of religious values. Elevated to mythic proportions to meet the spiritual demands of an environmental movement wary of the excesses of an urban, industrial America, public lands have become as much symbol as substance.

Roderick Nash, in *Wilderness and the American Mind*, stresses the religious meaning of public lands to generations of Americans. Their advocacy, he notes, is filled with the passion of religion and surfaces in such statements as "My God is in the wilderness. . . . My Church is the church of the forest."[18] Like "wilderness cathedrals," public lands are envisioned increasingly as sanctuaries of the spirit—sacred places in which nature is freed of the materialistic vision of Jefferson and the mechanistic vision of Pinchot.[19] And their defenders, those who are giving the final touches to the agenda and ideology of the environmental vision, are, in Joseph Sax's judgment, moralists who, "right or wrong, persuasive or not, . . . [know] something about what other people *ought* to want [emphasis mine]." They are, he writes in his gracefully worded *Mountains Without Handrails*, "secular prophets, preaching a message of salvation."[20] Their message is one of protection and preservation.

PROPHETS OF PURIFICATION

Disillusionment is the contagion that today compels the environmental vision toward a new ideal of how humans should relate to the land. A century of living, working, and consuming on the western range has left a legacy of weeded landscapes, eroding hillsides, and muddied streams. For environmentalists, the results are discouraging. They cast serious doubt on people's ability to live in harmony and peace with the environment, and they explain, in part, the spiritualization of America's public lands. Lands reaffirmed in collective ownership, and looked to for their inspirational value, allow no provision for people as residents or consumers—nor do they suffer the predictable consequences. Sacred landscapes permit only visitors, and even then only visitors who tread carefully and softly.

Put into the context of the western range, this means that people may come to the environmental commons so long as they leave no more than footprints and take no more than snapshots. Zoos, museums, and natural sanctuaries have long operated on such a premise. But on the public lands, that premise entails much more. It projects people as a foreign and unwelcome element in the many ecosystems of the federal range and recognizes their proper habitat and niche to be only in the communities and workplaces of urban America. The natural world is to be protected from human intrusion and harm.

Belief that humans are intrinsically harmful to nature is not new. Its roots are firmly established in the history of American conservation. George Marsh, writing one hundred years in advance of the environmental movement, left no doubts about where his sentiments lay:

> Nature, left undisturbed, so fashions her territory as to give it almost unchanging permanence of form, outline, and proportion . . . . The earth was not, in its natural condition, completely adapted to the use of man, but only to the sustenance of wild animals and wild vegetation . . . . [As a consequence], man is everywhere a disturbing agent. Wherever he plants his foot, the harmonies of nature are turned to discords.[21]

John Muir was no less hesitant in expressing his views. He had witnessed firsthand the devastation brought to western forests and mountains in the wake of wave after wave of settlement. Homesteaders, in Muir's view, were "pious destroyers [who] waged interminable forest wars . . . spreading ruthless devastation."[22] Marsh's observation and Muir's impassioned insistence that man was an intruder in the natural world conform well with the assumptions of the environmental vision. "Our species," declares Paul Watson, cofounder of Greenpeace, "[is] the AIDS of the Earth: we are rapidly eroding the immune systems of the Earth . . . destroying [her] ability to cleanse herself."[23] Contemporary man, the source of war and famine, stands accused of being a cancer on the natural world.

Ecological principles have given scientific credence to environmental accusations and aspirations, making protection and preservation of nature an issue of necessity rather than simply one of civic values and spiritual renewal. Indeed, the very foundation of American ecology rests on the assumption of man as an alien presence in the natural evolution of western rangelands. Frederic Clements, a pioneer in American ecology, set the tone and pace of western ecological studies with the publication of *Plant Succession: An Analysis of the Development of Vegetation* in 1916. His seminal work on plants and plant communities made it clear that the natural history of vegetation was distinct from the social and political history of mankind. Humans not only lacked a role in the evolution of vegetation, but their very presence could also disrupt or prevent the natural movement, or succession, of vegetation toward its destined end point: the monoclimax.

Distinct plant communities—the collage of grasses, wildflowers, shrubs, and trees growing on a particular landscape—were, in Clements's view, like organisms at different stages of development. At any point in time, a unique assemblage of plants might occupy a given site, indicating the organism's stage of development. But a plant community's true nature could be known only in its development through time, as it evolved into its final collage of persisting plants. As with the butterfly emerging from the cocoon, the terminal, or climax, plant community was the end product of an inevitable evolutionary process.

The monoclimax was the destined and natural vegetative cover, or plant formation, of each of the several terrestrial biomes that divided the United States. The tallgrass prairies and desert grasslands that existed prior to white settlement, for example, were the true plant formations of the western range. They embodied the biological potential of the land and stood for the ecological destiny that nature intended for arid landscapes. Whatever prevented or impaired their expression was ecologically wrong,

183

whatever hastened their evolution was necessary, and whatever preserved their physical form was ecologically correct. "It was clear to Clements, as it had been to others," writes Donald Worster in *Nature's Economy*, "that the white man was not part of [the western range]: he came as a disrupter, an alien, an exploiter." [24]

Clements's ecology has played, and continues to play, a prominent role in the natural history of the western range. His climax theory, Worster notes, is "a yardstick by which man's intrusion into nature could be measured." [25] In fact, both the Forest Service and the BLM use his ecology to assess the health of the land and to design management intended to restore climax plant communities. But Clements's vision also offers a portrait of nature as it *should* be: a guide to the land's potential, a glimpse of what the western range once looked like, and a sobering reminder of the sad consequences of man's intrusions. And it helps explain the urgency of the environmental commons. Only through collective ownership, and only on landscapes insulated from human intervention, can succession unfold on the western range and nature attain its right and proper climax.

The importance of these assumptions to the environmental vision cannot be overstated. By elevating succession to the level of biological necessity and making climax the measure of the land's health and integrity, Clements's ecology has remained as relevant today as it was in 1916. It has altered the very nature of the public-land debate, moving it from the plain of conflicting interest groups to the battlefield of ecological right and wrong. It has infused the environmental cause with moral certainty, masking intolerance with the respectability of science and the aura of righteousness. And for those whose lineage lies closest to the tradition of John Muir, the battle has taken on the trappings of Armageddon. Civic and spiritual values, what democracy should and must be about, are pitted against the tired and worn values held by the likes of intransigent western stockmen.

When put into the context of Aldo Leopold's land ethic, the moral implications of Clements's ecology become crystal clear. "A thing is right," Leopold tells us, "when it tends to preserve the integrity, stability, and beauty of the biotic community. It is wrong when it tends otherwise." [26] If by "right" one means those "things" that contribute to the physical survival and clinical health of a piece of land and its life, then ecological good may assume any number of shapes and forms. They may range from proper farming practices and viable farms to advanced horticultural practices and thriving city parks to good grazing management and sustainable ranches to preservation and pristine wilderness. And the performance of these "things," and the vital signs of the landscapes they affect, can be measured, objectively portrayed, intelligently assessed, and—more often than not—universally agreed upon.

But if one means by "right" those things that contribute to the movement of a piece of land and its life toward Clements's envisioned end point, then there is only one meaning and form of ecological good. It is the climax, the collage of plants and animals that identify a landscape as such, and the "things" that bring it about and preserve its "integrity, stability, and beauty." All other conditions are inferior, and all those things that tend otherwise are wrong. Farms, ranches, city parks, and the "things" that make them sustainable are unnatural and therefore outside the realm of ecological good. Being creations of man rather than the unfoldings of Clementsian nature, they are blemishes upon the earth, contagions from which public lands are to be cleansed, purified, and protected in wilderness.

The stakes being what they are, it does not seem to matter that Clements's ecology is increasingly discredited among European and American ecologists (see chapter 12) or that knowledge of how most climax landscapes should look is as much a matter of conjecture as it is of good science. A paucity of facts on climax plant communities has not stopped the Forest Service and the BLM from managing land for Clements's envisioned end point, nor has it restrained advocates of the environmental vision from seeking what largely exists in the minds of observers and in the isolated diaries of a few early explorers and settlers. As elusive as it is and as ecologically questionable as it now appears to be, Clements's ecology is essential to the vision of protection and preservation—a vision in which humankind is exiled forever from the fragmented remains of Eden on the western range.

Deep ecology is the clearest and most impassioned expression of the new environmental ethic of exile and preservation. Its name, coined by Arne Naess in 1973, describes a "deeper, more spiritual approach to Nature" as "exemplified in the writings of Aldo Leopold and Rachel Carson."[27] It envisions a world in which people and their environments are melded together in the harmony ascribed to primitive man. "For millennia," writes deep ecologist Dolores LaChapelle, "primitives communicated with the earth and all its beings by means of rituals and festivals. . . . It's not that nature refuses to communicate with us [today], but that we no longer have a way to communicate with it." [28]

Building new lines of communication with nature, deep ecologists insist, begins with a conscious changing of human attitudes. People must once again see themselves as one with nature and must adopt humility toward the natural world. They must acknowledge equality between themselves and all other life forms, recognizing that humans have no more intrinsic worth than any other creature. Above all, people must change the values that have made them foes rather than friends of the earth. Changing basic values means abandoning the "dominant worldview" of western society for the kinder worldview of deep ecology. Emphasis on materialism, consumption, and high technology must give way to an appreciation for spiritualism, simplicity, and "nondominating science." Nature should no longer be seen as humanity's warehouse but should be viewed in the light of some greater, more encompassing purpose. Bioregions and minority traditions should supplant the centralized community of nations. [29]

The vision of deep ecology vigorously rejects both the Judeo-Christian ethic and the assumptions of modern humanism. It preaches instead the sacred wholeness of nature. "In order to achieve an enlightened environmental ethics," observes ethicist Harold W. Wood, Jr., "we need what can only be termed a religious experience." [30] That experience can come only from ecology—the "subversive science" that undermines the traditional sciences of biology, chemistry, and physics. Its teachings of interrelatedness clear the air of the rubbish of modern capitalism and the hubris of humanism, making way for a new mysticism.

Deep ecology's mysticism denies the reality of nature as revealed by the tools of traditional science. The natural world, it claims, is knowable only by intuition—the "mystical insight" ascribed to primitives. "Land wisdom," the product of mystical insight, flows naturally from the spiritual union of reverent peoples and sacred land. Its intuitive powers set the tempo and direction of early people's relation to their environment, allowing them to live in presumed harmony with the natural world. Land wisdom, so crucial in the past, is deemed to be even more important by deep ecologists critical of a modern world misled by the ideology of "resource conservation development."

For deep ecologists, that ideology, synonymous with scientific land management, is the scourge of public lands. The hands-on management practiced by the Forest Service and the BLM has wrongly bent nature to mankind's will, exposing western lands to the abuses and insults of cattle and timber harvests. The integrity of nature, symbolized by old-growth forests and remnants of pristine grasslands, has been the victim of human arrogance. A more "righteous management," one founded in intuition and pursuant to the preaching of John Muir, will guide people's relation to and use of nature. Science and technology, deep ecologists warn, is a dangerous substitute for land wisdom.

Despite its rhetoric of natural harmony and its commitment to "decentralized, fully democratic structures," deep ecology is not a break with the past. Like agrarianism and progressive conservation, it is a vision of conquest, intolerance, and unconstrained ambitions. We "must use all political avenues," claim Bill Devall and George Sessions in *Deep Ecology*, ". . . to protect vast expanses of ecologically viable habitat."[31] Deep ecology, and the environmental movement for which it speaks, may envision an altogether new western range, but the means to achieve that end have not changed since the opening of the West to settlement. Only the perceived sacredness of the land and the intensity of idealism aimed at its protection have altered with time. The structures of progressive management—the mechanisms of control and regulation—remain unchallenged and intact.

Coercion in service to nature, Muir's "one soldier in the woods armed with authority and a gun," is the right and proper answer to those whose visions collide with the tenets of Clements, the ethics of Leopold, and the righteousness of environmental prophets. The state may be imperfect, concedes Joseph Sax, but it is "the inevitable price of representing the interests of the political community"[32]—or, for that matter, the interests that "other people *ought* to want."[33] "Preservationists," Sax favorably notes, "do not merely aspire to persuade individuals how to conduct their personal lives . . . they have directed their prescriptions to the government."[34]

Environmental and progressive visions are merging at the peculiar junction of Clementsian ecology and reliance on state coercion. Nature left to itself, free to evolve without intrusion from man, is capturing the imagination of environmentalists and the management prescriptions of land agencies. Natural regulation is gaining credence among a new generation of land managers—a cadre of scientists, conservationists, and administrators more impressed with the environmental visions of Muir, Clements, and Leopold than with the agrarian ideals of Jefferson and the technocratic designs of Pinchot.

CLOSING EDEN'S DOOR

Protecting nature from people is an idea that has come of age in an environment in which futility and failure overshadow enthusiasm and success in the management of public lands. This is particularly true for federal rangelands, where more than a century of livestock grazing has left a legacy of impoverished landscapes and a tradition of social strife and conflict. By almost any indicator, the human presence on the western range has been less than beneficial. And this continues to be true even under the watchful eyes of land agencies.

It is not surprising, then, that options to traditional uses and management of public-land resources have become so prominent in the environmental agenda. A crisis of faith has shaken confidence in the hands-on management of the Forest Service and the BLM. It has convinced some people that no level of management or amount of investment can compensate for the losses that attend such activities as livestock grazing. It has forced the conclusion that unmanaged public lands, when freed of consumptive uses, will be better off than lands whose resources are both managed and extracted. And it has given merit to an ecology in which nature is managed best when the meddling of humans is minimized.

No human management is the best management—the natural regulation that allowed pristine grasslands to evolve and to sustain themselves on the western range. Natural regulation is the righteous management of John Muir, the historical management of Clements's unfolding climax communities, and the preferred management of an environmental vision committed to protection and preservation. But on the western range, natural regulation is embryonic. Its merits are being debated with passion and intensity on grasslands that are still grazed by cattle and on forests that are still logged. Only on public lands where multiple use has never taken hold, or where its principle is constrained by law and regulation, are the tenets of righteous management coming of age.

Lands of the National Park Service are a case in point. A number of national parks have taken the lead in adopting policies of no management or minimal intrusion in the workings of natural processes. For Devall and

Sessions, this entails a "significant move in the direction of implementing deep ecology and land ethic principles."[35] They point to the example of the Redwood National Park and highlight the commitment of the park's managers not to circumvent "the long, slow, inexorable processes of Nature" in rectifying past watershed damage with the shortsighted meddling of "technological ingenuity."[36] But hands-off management has also been tried and tested on more familiar territory.

In 1963, the Advisory Board on Wildlife Management, commissioned by Secretary of the Interior Stewart Udall and chaired by A. Starker Leopold, the son of Aldo Leopold, issued what is now known as the Leopold Report. Its major recommendation was to maintain or re-create "biotic associations" within each park "as nearly as possible in the condition that prevailed when the area was first visited by white man." This would require that "observable artificiality in any form must be minimized and obscured in every possible way." In so doing, "a reasonable illusion of primitive America could be re-created, using the utmost in skill, judgement and ecological sensitivity."[37]

The report's full impact became evident as its recommendations were forged into management policy in Yellowstone National Park. Garbage dumps that had provided grizzly bears with food since the park's founding in 1872 were closed or bear-proofed. Elk populations, lacking any natural predator other than man, were left alone to self-regulate. The assumption was that grizzly bears would become wild once again and elk numbers would match the land's carrying capacity as available forage set the natural limits to population increase.

Nature would prove the efficacy of righteous management and verify the assumptions of an equally righteous environmental vision. Yet as Alston Chase has reported in *Playing God in Yellowstone,* natural regulation and management have not been kind to the land. Grizzly bear populations teeter on the brink of extinction in Yellowstone, and elk numbers far exceed the carrying capacity of the land. Rangelands are overgrazed as surely as they were on the open range. The 1988 fires have given temporary reprieve to the troubled Yellowstone ecosystem by invigorating grasslands and reestablishing groves of aspen and stands of willow, so crucial to wildlife. But the underlying problem of Yellowstone remains unchanged—the nagging reality that the ecology of the park has been forever changed by the presence of humans.

Parks as unalike as the Chaco Culture National Historic Park (commonly known as Chaco Canyon) in New Mexico and the Rocky Mountain National Park in Colorado bring home the unpleasant message of Yellowstone—the likelihood that protected and preserved lands are not nearly as wild or as natural as they seem. Both parks, despite their long exclusion of people, show signs of environmental deterioration. The grasslands of Chaco Canyon, shielded from cattle and sheep for decades, are decadent and dying. And in the Rocky Mountain National Park, too many elk has left an imprint on natural vegetation as marked as that of too much livestock.

The ecological systems of the two parks have been irreversibly altered by the presence of people. The soils and vegetation of Chaco Canyon were depleted by native peoples long before a park was envisioned, and neither protection nor preservation can restore the park rangelands to a pristine state.[36] The problems of the Rocky Mountain National Park occurred more recently, but they too are the results of human activity. Elk habitat is disappearing as vacation homes encircle the park and as pine forests choke out aspen groves and fill in meadow openings. And because management policy in the park precludes such artificial intrusions as controlled burns and hunting, elk are forced to overgraze the land to survive.[37]

The management practice of benign neglect is not limited to national park boundaries. Public grazing lands, so profoundly altered by settlement and resource depletion, are beginning to feel the impact of a vision intent on erasing people from the ecological picture. Federally designated wilderness is the most obvious example. The Aldo Leopold Wilderness in southwestern New Mexico, for example, is literally suffocating from human intervention even though it has supposedly been protected. Cattle still graze its lands, but the management that might mitigate their environmental impact or the innovative practices that might make them a factor in healing historically overgrazed ranges is almost impossible under wilderness rules that mandate nonintervention. A more serious problem is the long history of fire control that has allowed prime wildlife habitat to be inundated with juniper and pine. Shrouded by their canopies, once vigorous grasslands have become barren, eroding benches and hillsides. As a result, elk and deer are forced to leave their wilderness sanctuary for the "unnatural" public lands that are still logged and mined and the "unnatural" private lands that have been thoroughly tamed.

Even the streams and fisheries in the Aldo Leopold Wilderness have been affected by the legacy of hands-off management. Timber conditions created by the Forest Service's long-standing policy of fire control and Congress's insistence on wilderness nonintervention led to the Divide fire in 1989. Because of the fire, wind and rain moved ash and silt through Deadman Canyon and down into Diamond Creek, muddying the water with lethal pollutants and destroying habitat and individuals of one of the largest remaining populations of endangered Gila trout.[38]

Other wilderness areas show similar signs of a management philosophy unwilling to accept the permanent changes created by man's past intrusions or to shoulder the responsibility those changes entail. In the judgment of the congressional subcommittee that oversees Forest Service wilderness, the national forest wilderness system "is deteriorating."[39] Deterioration, however, is not limited to lands already designated as wilderness. It also threatens lands proposed for wilderness and encumbered by special rules and regulations that discourage caring management.

What has become practice in national parks and wilderness areas is being proposed for massive areas of the larger western range. Frank J. Popper and Deborah E. Popper, professors in the departments of urban studies and geography at Rutgers University, are secular prophets whose writings on the Great Plains project an environmental vision of enormous sweep and unwavering moral certainty. In the December 1987 issue of *Planning* magazine (and later in more popular publications, such as the *Washington Post*), they describe the Great Plains as an inhospitable environment where non-Indians are an alien element, unsuited, unwelcome, and destructive to the environment. "Private interests," they observe, "have overgrazed and overplowed the land and overdrawn the water . . . responding to the usually increasing federal subsidies, they have overused the natural resources the subsidies provided."[40]

Rather than eliminate those subsidies (the relics of a progressive vision), the Poppers offer their own vision of what is right for the eastern edge of the western range. They call for the creation of a "Buffalo Commons" stretching westward from the 98th meridian to the Rocky Mountains.[41] Rural lands, most of which are privately owned, would be nationalized by the federal government, and their residents would be evicted and relocated. In one fell swoop, an additional third of the nation would be added to the public's share of the western range—a vast domain including the better parts of Texas, New Mexico, Oklahoma, Kansas, Colorado, Wyoming, Nebraska, the Dakotas, and Montana. Under the Poppers' plan,

the Buffalo Commons will become the world's largest historic preservation project, the ultimate national park. Most of the Great Plains
will become what all of the United States once was—a vast land
mass, largely empty and *unexploited* [emphasis mine].[42]

But the Poppers' vision does not stop with the making of a revitalized
western commons. "Creating the Buffalo Commons," they acknowledge,
"represents a substantial administrative undertaking . . . [and will require]
a regional agency like the Tennessee Valley Authority or a public-land
agency like the Bureau of Land Management, but with much more sweeping powers."[43] Like the dominant visions of the past, power and control
inevitably become the final means and ends of unconstrained ambitions.
Clements and his ecology, each a product of the Nebraskan Great Plains
and both implicit in the Poppers' ambitious plunge into central planning,
unite progressive and environmental visions in common cause. The man
and his idea spearhead an alliance in which the vision of Pinchot attains
the long-sought goal of absolute control and the vision of Muir attains the
righteous end point of absolute exclusion of man.

Less spectacular visions of environmental protection and preservation,
each tethered in its own way to the cause of central planning, are appearing
with increasing regularity. Righteous management, whether purposeful or
not, is being felt across the landscapes of the western range. Environmental legislation and litigation in the 1970s and 1980s, for example, have
played a crucial role. But environmental gains have come at the expense
of declining rancher investments. A more accessible and democratic commons, one in which private action and caring are discouraged or disal-
lowed, has only made the business of welfare ranchers easier and the life
of concerned ranchers more impossible. In such an environment, positive
management has become less likely and little or no management more
probable.

Caring stewardship has succumbed to righteous forces in many public-
land arenas. Well-intentioned endangered species acts and proposed legislation advancing the crucial issue of biological diversity entail values that
most Americans share. Yet their practical effect has been to distance ordinary people from their environments. Public-land ranchers on the Great
Plains, for example, have traditionally viewed prairie dogs as adversaries,
pests whose holes riddle and deplete productive rangelands. Subsidies provided by federal animal damage control programs and gratuitous research

by land grant universities have made it easy and cheap for ranchers to eradicate vast colonies of prairie dogs. But the war against prairie dogs has escalated to new heights in the shadow of the endangered black-footed ferret. Because the ferret relies on prairie dogs for its diet, stockmen are afraid that what was once a pest will become an excuse for greater agency control of grazing and further reductions in livestock numbers.

Yet for all the anger ranchers feel toward prairie dogs and ferrets, it is doubtful that they will ravage black-footed ferrets as much as the custodians of endangered species and biological diversity have already done. In just a few days in 1985, teams of scientists on a small private ranch in Meeteetse, Wyoming achieved what a hundred years of livestock foraging, trampling, and poisoning had failed to do. Well-intentioned biologists, eager to protect the last known population of ferrets, brought dogs to locate their nests and introduced canine distemper, which whittled the numbers of ferrets down to a handful. Today, only a few mating pairs of black-footed ferrets survive in cages.[44]

Many examples can be given of how laws and policies aimed at preservation and righteous management have pitted stockmen against wildlife, tearing down rather than building an ethic respectful of nature and its creatures. One has only to recall the testimonies of ranchers like Dwayne Slaathaug to appreciate the magnitude of the problem. But the tragedy of caring people needlessly turned against wildlife is only part of the story. The rest of the tale is what happens to the land and its life when people are torn by law from the fabric of nature, when they are exiled from the mixed landscapes that comprise the western range. The residents of the western range who must live that story are responding in the only way they can.

Herb Metzger, the rancher near Flagstaff who wanted to restore forest rangelands, is giving serious thought to selling his public-land ranch and subdividing his private inholdings for vacation homes. The presence of more and more elk, all of which are the property of the state and the product of Forest Service management, is depleting his deeded winter range, leaving little forage for his cattle. It would be fine if Herb could make a living from the elk that come down from the forest to graze his private lands or from the people who hike, fish, and backpack on his permitted lands in the Coconino National Forest. But there are no such things as forest permits for recreation and hunting. The only permit allowed in national forests is the one Herb already has, the license to graze cattle.

And the long-term forest plan has already outlined how grazing will be managed. Its presence and impact will be contained by managers and a management philosophy hostile to ranching and indifferent to private lands. If Herb chooses to keep his public-land ranch, he will be stuck with all of the costs of wildlife and recreation and denied virtually all of the benefits. His only option is to sell.[45]

Closing Eden's door to caring people like Herb Metzger or his neighbor Ken Spann, four hundred miles to the northeast, may make the job of land managers easier, and for some it may cleanse and purify the land. But for the public lands that this vision hopes to protect and preserve, it merely brings us full circle to where we began—to the tragedy of the western commons. It repeats the errors of the past by re-creating a western commons remarkably similar to the open range of the late nineteenth century—a commons in which all Americans are welcomed as visitors but none is encouraged to care for the land and its resources.

COMING FULL CIRCLE

All things considered, little has changed on public grazing lands in the passage of visions from agrarian to progressive to environmental. Public lands continue to be seen and treated exactly as before, as landscapes for the temporary convenience of transient interests rather than as permanent places for residence and work. Only the particulars of their use have changed in the succession of visions. Federal rangelands, once valued as homesteads for Jefferson's noble yeomanry and later as depositories for the nation's natural wealth, are being celebrated and figuratively consumed for recreation and spiritual renewal. What should be vibrant and coherent living spaces remain the fragmented building blocks of ethereal visions. And what could be locally diverse and sovereign communities are national sanctuaries created not by nature but by people.

The laws that forge these sanctuaries do so in the name and spirit of democracy. Yet this democracy is an anomaly, strangely out of step with a western range that once promised independence, local rule, and social equality. It is a democracy of anonymity, in which people are independent of the land, self-rule is a matter of nature minus man, and social equality is the greater equality of the pristine and wild over the civilized and humane. It is a democracy that breeds contempt for those, such as public-land ranchers, whose familiarity with the land comes from residence and work rather than play and worship. It is, for all practical purposes, indistinguishable from the democracy sought by Gifford Pinchot and enshrined in progressive conservation.

The environmental vision is succumbing to the same temptation that tarnished agrarian ideals and inflated progressive expectations. With nature as its prophet and the mountains and prairies as its guides, it strives to impose what is just and right on the lands and people of the western range. But righteous preservation cannot evade some responsibility for the invasions and intrusions that have plagued western lands since the arrival of European settlers. The shared vision of Clements and Muir entails environmental costs and ecological consequences well beyond the intent and design of preservation and protection. Predicting those costs and anticipating their consequences, however, are not the major concerns of environmental activists. All else pales against the ecological travesties of the past.

Looking out onto the western range, environmental visionaries focus attention and blame on public-land ranchers, stockmen of less than good will who stand convicted of abusing and mistreating western rangelands. The Forest Service and the BLM are also accused of negligence, of aiding and abetting ranchers by turning their backs to overgrazing and ignoring the severity of its impact on wildlife, plants, and soil. But bureaucracies failed only for want of will, the visionaries conclude, and federal laws and regulations were evaded only because of inadequate enforcement. Things would have been different if agencies had plied their will and if statutes had been given backbone.

The environmental vision has now had time and opportunity to effect changes in public-land laws and to shatter the complacency of the Forest Service and the BLM. Agency will has been stiffened, and stronger laws have been passed and enforced. As a result, ranchers have less freedom and flexibility than ever before. Their livestock is more closely supervised, administered, and controlled. Yet for all these changes, man and nature on the western range remain at odds. Public-land ranching is still the most conspicuous use of public lands, and resource problems connected with grazing still ignite passion and anger. Stewardship is in disarray, a victim of agencies claiming a lack of money and of ranchers either dissuaded from caring or comfortably insulated from caring by public subsidies. And environmentalists, eager to attain their agenda of re-creation and spiritual renewal, seek to re-create a western commons already tried and tested and found deficient.

Public grazing lands are shrouded in a crisis of accountability. As laws, bureaucracies, and environmental groups work in unison to limit stewardship to a small cadre of experts and righteous managers, a shared democratic vision moves the western range back toward the tragedy of the open range. In a show of supreme irony, history comes full circle to the agrarian vision that first spawned progressive revolt and planted the seeds of environmental dissent.

III

The Promise of
Many Visions

CHAPTER ELEVEN

Limits of the Visionary State

*H*ighway 24 is a two-lane county road that loops southwest past the
Guadalupe Mountains and then turns northeast as it enters and
traverses the much higher and more expansive Sacramento Mountains. The southwestern leg of the route, about forty-five miles in length,
passes through the towns of Dunken and Pinon, New Mexico. Dunken is
the smaller and more northerly of the two, having a population of two people
and one dog, whose duty it is to guard the volunteer fire department. Pinon
is larger, with several residences, a post office, and a general store. Most of
the people who call Dunken and Pinon home live on the rolling plains that
connect the two towns and that separate the Sacramento and Guadalupe
mountain ranges.

Sheep, cattle, people, and mule deer, in that order, are the most visible
residents of the Dunken-Pinon plains. All make their homes among the
grama grass ranges, the brushy arroyos, and the juniper-bedecked hills, and
all are players in a story that is endemic to the western range. Change the
place names and the particulars of plant species and the scene could just as
easily be in eastern Montana as in southeastern New Mexico. Ranchers,
livestock, and deer try to make the best of a situation in which landownership
is fragmented and responsibility is divided.

In the case of Dunken-Pinon, 40 percent of the land is deeded to individuals, 45 percent is entrusted to the BLM, and 15 percent is owned by the New Mexico State Land Office. Altogether, there are nearly a half-million acres of private and public rangelands, all of which are hopelessly intermingled, imposing a crazy-quilt pattern of landownership on every ranch. As a result, public-land ranching is a matter of necessity for the people of Dunken-Pinon.

Complicating the picture are the many lines of authority that divide the Dunken-Pinon plains into as many fragments. Sheep and cattle, the mainstay of most of the families in the area, are managed and supervised by a triad of private landowners, BLM range staff, and the State Land Office. Recreation and wildlife are overseen entirely by federal and state agencies. The BLM is responsible for providing citizens (mostly hunters) with access to public lands and for conserving habitat for wildlife. The New Mexico Game and Fish Department controls hunting—and in Dunken-Pinon, that means deer.

Ranchers and agencies, each with its own agenda and each hoping to take as much from the land as possible, view the Dunken-Pinon plains in the narrowest of terms. Permittees look at the landscape as a place suited only for raising domestic stock. For them, the circumstance of federal grazing permits reduces public recreation to a business liability and wildlife to a cost measured by lost forage. The BLM treats Dunken-Pinon as a multiple use landscape to be exploited for a variety of uses and users. Its experts plan the maximum number of people, livestock, and deer that the area's plants and soil can presumably support. The two state agencies see the land and its wildlife mostly as a source of revenue. The State Land Office leases grazing land to help finance the public school system, and the Game and Fish Department sells hunting permits to fund its annual budget.

Without malice, private and public interests in Dunken-Pinon play out the tragedy of the western commons. All of the players attend to their own needs with little regard for the needs of one another and the land. But the land is not the loser in this story. Plants are relatively vigorous, and soils are largely intact and stable. The victims are the mule deer, which grazed the land when buffalo and antelope ruled the western range.

The problem is that there are too many hunters and, as a consequence, too few deer.[1] It was not always that way, though. During the 1960s and 1970s, deer populations were up, hunters were generally satisfied, and Dunken-Pinon had a reputation for being one of the better hunting areas in southern New Mexico. But the area's reputation became its downfall as it attracted more and more hunters. Today, there are far fewer bucks than in the past, and hunters are more disgruntled than ever before. Something is clearly wrong.

Part of the fault lies with ranching. With fewer sheep and cattle, there might be more food and shelter for the deer. But with the Game and Fish Department selling unlimited permits to hunt the Dunken-Pinon plains and with the BLM building roads and providing public access to more and more acres of federal land, hunters would quickly exhaust any additions to the deer herd.

That is precisely what is happening. The mule deer are being driven to exhaustion because no one has control and no one is in a position to protect them from the commons. The BLM opens federal rangelands to everyone, as its mandate demands. The Game and Fish Department sells more and more permits to keep the flow of revenues in line with a growing budget. Hunters buy permits, drive on the BLM's roads, and shoot the deer. And stockmen scheme how best to lock up their permitted federal lands and insulate their operations from the excesses of multiple use and the revenue-enhancing activities of wildlife managers.

As a result, does produce fewer fawns, some of which are born perilously close to winter due to unnaturally long mating seasons (the result of too few bucks). The fawns that are born late either die or become stunted as cold and hunger take their toll. Male fawns who survive the first winter are stalked before maturity by disgruntled hunters willing to shoot anything. All that remains of a magnificent mule deer herd are a few scraggly bucks and an overabundance of aging does—the final gasp of a dying population and the lingering reminder of the beneficence of the environmental welfare state.

THE ENVIRONMENTAL WELFARE STATE

Landscape visions on the western range share utopian beginnings. Agrarian democracy promised the establishment of a virtuous and noble yeomanry republic. Men and women who tilled the soil would forge from America's wilderness a secular paradise, a "Citty upon a Hill" where democracy and independence would be the perpetual harvest of Jefferson's natural aristocracy. Progressive conservation was no less utopian. America's best and brightest men and women would bring a rebirth of democracy to a nation blemished by greed and self-interest. They would bring order and efficiency to federal lands wracked by disorder and plagued by waste. Pinchot's elite would provide the moral fiber to build a new city upon a hill, one in which the earth and its natural wealth would be the property of all and the common means to attain political equality and social justice.

Utopian ideals are now infusing a nascent environmental vision with energy and passion as increasing numbers of people look to the western range for meaning and values that are conspicuously absent in a society absorbed in production and consumption. Protected and preserved lands are the nation's spiritual sanctuaries—the last outposts of nature unspoiled by humans. When the earth's human population has been trimmed to a mere one-hundred million, these protected and preserved lands will be the seeds for new social and political beginnings and the catalyst for the final city upon a hill. Political boundaries will give way to the natural boundaries of bioregions. Men and women will practice industry and devise technologies suitable to the ecological needs of earth and its living diversity. Small, scattered, sustainable communities will rekindle the harmony that once existed between native peoples and their environments, and true participatory democracy will be established.

It will be a world, writes Murray Bookchin, in which natural evolution will end in the "humanization of nature" and the "naturalization of humanity." At that point, the ecology of freedom—the title of his book—will reconcile man with nature, freeing both from the tyranny of domination and restoring each to some semblance of ecological health and well-being. "We can try to reclaim our legitimacy . . . in the natural world," Bookchin concludes, by becoming "the rationality that abets natural diversity and integrates the workings of nature with an effectiveness, certainty, and directedness that is essentially incomplete in nonhuman nature."[2]

Bookchin's future world is the "ecotopia" envisioned by poet Gary Snyder in his essay "Four Changes"—a work hailed as a "deep ecological manifesto" by Bill Devall and George Sessions in *Deep Ecology*. Snyder offers a vision of people and the land in which "man is but a part of the fabric of life," in which "balance, harmony, [and] growth . . . is mutual growth with redwood and quail," and in which "true affluence is not needing anything." He advises:

> We have it within our powers not only to change our "selves" but to change our culture. If man is to remain on earth he must transform the five-millennia long urbanizing civilization tradition into a new ecologically-sensitive harmony-oriented wild-minded scientific/ spiritual culture . . . nothing short of total transformation will do much good.[3]

Utopian ideals, however, have fallen considerably short of expectations when translated into public-land policy and practice. The agrarian vision, infused with Jeffersonian principles, did not enshrine democracy on the western range or sustain thriving, independent farms on arid, windswept landscapes. The best intentions of progressive conservationists did not reinstate democracy, mend broken dreams, or rehabilitate public lands. And the impassioned idealism of Muir's righteous management has not altered the course and predicament of the nation's federal estate.

As young as the environmental vision is, its record of conservation and stewardship has been dismal. In an effort to mold and shape federal lands into a democratic and spiritual haven, the environmental vision has unwittingly supported and perpetuated the worst of the western commons. It has enshrined the environmental policies and ecological follies of the open range of the late 1800s in a cathedral built from the living soil of western rangelands, sculpted by federal statutes and judicial decisions, and held together by layers of bureaucracy. America's public lands are coming to an evolutionary end point, a terminus where people and nature are further apart than ever before and disharmony is the disquieting reality.

Simply stated, righteous management is concluding what the visions of Jefferson and Pinchot began: the making of the environmental welfare state. What started in the modest Lockean spirit of bringing "empty" western lands and landless immigrants together under the rubric of private property has evolved into something altogether different. Government has made the bold leap from being a neutral arbiter and facilitator between citizens and their lands to becoming an advocate and guardian of visions that presume to know what is right and best for people and nature on the western range. In the process, government has elevated its role to that of the visionary state—a sovereign entity empowered to make particular visions the official creed of government, just as Catholicism in the Middle Ages was made the official theology of much of Europe.

An overpowering arrogance underlies faith in the visionary state on the western range. It assumes the infinite plasticity of man and nature—the ability and propriety of encompassing visions to change the social and natural world to fit the whims and desires of the righteous. It encourages a godlike stance, in which mere mortals aspire to the omniscience of ecologist-kings. And on the western range, it has encouraged progressive and environmental reformers to attempt the superhuman task of orchestrating the future of America's forests and grasslands to meet the material and spiritual needs of society. Yet with central planning so discredited in the comparatively simple realm of national economies, it is perplexing that ecologically minded people would want to apply the same tools to an infinitely more complex nature.

Certainly, part of the explanation lies in an unwavering belief that the visionary state bears little or no blame for the fury and abuse that have plagued federal rangelands for one hundred and thirty years. Progressive and environmental spokespersons either ignore the culpability of the state or attribute its shortcomings to outside causes. In most cases, lawmakers and executive policymakers are blamed for failing to grant adequate power and sufficient control to land agencies. George Coggins, in his five part series of "The Law of Public Rangeland Management," published in *Environmental Law* (Spring 1982 to Spring 1984), argues just that. He points to the BLM's poor record of land management and suggests that it is correctable if the agency is restructured along the lines of the Forest Service. Giving the agency more authority and more money, he believes, will cure its historical inadequacies.

Coggins assumes that the simple exercise of power and control can heal overgrazed lands and make men and women act with greater environmental care, if not conscience. Much the same reasoning drove agrarian proponents to maintain the open range at gunpoint. Only the might of the state, they believed, could prevent stockmen from undermining democracy in the West. Indeed, concern for democracy propelled progressive conservation to weaken the historical ties of stockmen to federal lands and, today, explains the bitter animosity of environmentalists toward public-land ranchers. But sheer power and unlimited control, for whatever ideological cause or reason, has proven environmentally disastrous.

This should not be surprising. Force and coercion are poor substitutes for a land ethic and even poorer incentives for motivating people to care for their environment or to invest their energies in its conservation and enhancement. One has only to look at the landscapes of the western range to appreciate the limitations of the environmental welfare state. Yet for some inexplicable reason, force remains the dominant management strategy on America's public grazing lands. Unfortunately, force and coercion have a life of their own: They are virtually uncontrollable. Rules and regulations governing public grazing lands have grown by quantum leaps as one landscape vision has succeeded another and as attempts to curb private interests have intensified.

Private interests, of course, remain at the center of debate and controversy as environmentalists raise the specter of cattlemen raping public lands. But their concern leads to the same tired and worn logic. Calls for reform emphasize only the need for more comprehensive laws and more stringent rules and regulations, all backed up with more vigorous enforcement by the Forest Service and the BLM. Empowering land agencies and diminishing the place and role of public-land ranchers is offered as the final solution to past grazing abuses.

Ridding federal rangelands of public-land grazing, however, misses the point just as surely as layers of bureaucracy have failed to address the essential problems of the western range. Nowhere in the scenarios of the three landscape visions is serious consideration given to the liability of government. By focusing narrowly on the *symptoms* of ailing rangelands— uncaring ranchers, excessive livestock, disturbed landscapes, and lifeless streams—advocates of each vision have treated the symptoms of the ailment rather than its causes. The enormous sums of taxpayers' dollars spent on the BLM's Vale project, for example, never addressed a flawed permit system, overadjudication of livestock numbers, perpetuation of common grazing, and too many ranchers for too little land. Instead, ranchers were bought off with subsidies and degraded rangelands were temporarily covered up with crested wheatgrass and a well-orchestrated public relations campaign.

Abused landscapes like that in Vale, Oregon, reveal the ultimate irony of federal rangelands. Past failures in public-land policy have strengthened rather than weakened the bond between dominant visions and the power of the state. The more the state has faltered in its stewardship of the western range, the more Pinchot's elite and Muir's righteous have called for its expansion and empowerment. By a logic explicable only in the context of intolerant visions, repeated failures have reinforced rather than corrected the malfunctioning of the environmental welfare state. Common sense tells us that this should not be, that it is pathological when any institution thrives by making more rather than fewer mistakes.

An ecologically sound and complete understanding of the western range begins and ends with the role and function of the state and its land agencies. It is not enough to conclude, as Leopold did, that government is adept at handling "all necessary jobs that private landowners fail to perform."[4] Rather, one must look at "governmental conservation," just as Leopold did in his more critical moments, as a "mastodon" that succumbs to its own unwieldy dimensions.[5] Ecologist Ramon Margalef wisely noted in his *Perspectives in Ecological Theory* that "it is impossible in these times to develop a *natural* ecology, one that ignores the impact of man."[6] On federal rangelands, understanding that impact means appreciating the far-reaching consequences of the environmental welfare state.

As the lands of the western range testify, the legacy of the environmental welfare state entails unintended consequences. The laws and policies designed to preserve the West for small farmers brought overgrazing instead of democracy. The experts and bureaucracies dedicated to rational land-use planning brought the demise of stewardship rather than the triumph of efficiency. And the coming of environmentalism has brought more of the same. The National Forest Management Act of 1976, for example, placed limits on the size of clear-cuts in national forests, a major victory for environmentalists. Unfortunately, limitations on clear-cut size led the Forest Service to escalate its road-building program to gain access to the smaller cuts. And more roads meant accelerated erosion and increased disruption of wildlife habitat, effectively nullifying a large part of the environmental victory. Similarly, environmentalists' calls for higher grazing fees—clearly justified, given the current below-cost grazing fee—may actually entrench the historical position of livestock grazing on public lands. Higher fees, when funneled into range improvement funds as mandated by law, will mean more welfare for ranchers and larger operating budgets for the Forest Service and the BLM.

Unintended consequences are the rule rather than the exception on the western range. The most impassioned visions and the best-conceived state intrusions have failed in their objectives with startling consistency. Western landscapes that thrived for millennia in the absence of Pinchot's elite and Muir's righteous are today deluged by environmental problems. And those problems show no signs of abating, despite the vigorous efforts of an ever-expanding environmental welfare state. Why and where the visionary state went astray is the essential question. Its answer is to be found in the ecology of landscape visions, among the crucial factors of resilience, information, and diversity.

USING AND ABUSING THE LAND

Ecological systems, ranging from the extremes of intensively managed livestock pastures to pristine high-mountain meadows, obey the same physical and biological laws. Life in each begins with energy—whether in the crude form of light or in the refined essence of information. How those systems utilize that energy or information determines their resilience and survivability in the face of change. Although many factors contribute to resilience and survival, none appears more important than diversity.[7] Multiple management strategies on domestic grazing lands, for example, can be as important to ecological health as the full contingent of member species is to a tufted hair grass meadow in the high Colorado subalpine region. Variety in management approaches, like diversity in plants and wildlife, contributes to stability. It insulates environments from disturbances that might otherwise be biologically devastating. Above all, it offers options—new ways to deal with problems when old ways have proven to be flawed or deficient.

But diversity on the western range was never the objective of the environmental welfare state, and as events attest, it has not been the outcome. In the service of single visions, the state has meticulously applied itself to dictating the fate of public lands. It has used its power to mold the western range in the forms demanded by three ideological regimes: agrarian, progressive, and environmental. Those regimes have relied on singular approaches—what can be termed management monocultures—to realize their distinctive landscape goals. Because of that, the variety of uses and management that might have been possible on the western range has been lessened just as the diversity of the land has been diminished.

As the narratives and stories in past chapters suggest, management monocultures on the western range have been as pernicious as human-caused monocultures have been in other realms. In the view of Richard Stroup and John Baden, authors of *Natural Resources: Bureaucratic Myths and Environmental Management*, monocultures are "notoriously fragile and short-lived":

> Although there are questions about this view, uniformity in human society is likely to limit the possibilities for adaptation to change . . . . Just as a biological monoculture may be less likely than a biologically diverse community to withstand environmental shocks, a monotechnological society is certainly more prone to serious danger from external shocks.[8]

Instability is the hallmark of most monocultures and is the single most crucial factor in the dominance of the visionary state on the western range.

To this day, policy and management of public lands have been unable to adjust to the environmental circumstances of the West or to accommodate the changing needs of diverse rangelands, a multiplicity of resident life (human and nonhuman), and a wide range of public interests. Old ideas and tired strategies based on the assumptions of power and control continue to litter the landscapes of the western range and to block the flow of innovative ideas and more promising approaches to conservation and stewardship. As a result, the public range is in ecological turmoil, its biology turned topsy-turvy by good intentions gone astray and its social features left in disarray from the meddling of arrogant visionaries.

There is, however, an even more pervasive and disturbing threat to public lands. That threat lies in the sheer immensity of the federal domain, where the benevolent hand of the environmental welfare state is virtually unrestrained. It touches almost every corner of the western range, imposing a human-designed monoculture of unprecedented proportions. When mistakes are made or when well-intentioned laws and policies bring unintended consequences, as they have with alarming frequency on public grazing lands, the environmental and ecological consequences are virtually unlimited in scope and intensity.

Imagine, for example, what might have happened if 160-acre homesteads had been the voluntary preference of a handful of settlers rather than the policy of an entire nation. Those foolish enough to limit their homesteads to that size would have quickly learned that 160-acre plots of arid land were ill suited for cultivation and inadequate for livestock raising. They would have been forced to choose between either farming or grazing their small holdings to death, or acquiring additional lands. Had they chosen the former, they would have quickly gone out of business. Had they chosen the latter, they would have survived and possibly flourished. In either case, *there would have been no open range to be overgrazed and abused.*

Under these circumstances, settlers would have had to claim and protect enough land to support their families or else face the prospect of failure. To have relied on the unclaimed and unprotected lands of the open range would have been a temporary solution at best, lasting no longer than the arrival of the next wave of settlement. Faced with such prospects, most settlers—even the most foolish—would have adapted their visions and their industry to environmental reality. Freed from the politics of a national vision, they would have been able to respond quickly and efficiently to the cues of nature. Instead of tragedy for the western range, there would

have been tragedy only for those who fought rather than heeded the lessons of the land—a more forgiving tragedy, one limited in both time and
space. All in all, there would have been fewer acres of the western range
overgrazed, fewer tons of soil lost to erosion, less wildlife displaced, and
fewer lives broken.

The same reasoning can be applied to the visions of Pinchot and Muir.
Things might be different on today's western range had progressive and
environmental ideals been tried outside the protective custody of the environmental welfare state. Livestock grazing in the West would be free of
subsidies and the twisted incentives of grazing permits and multiple use.
More important, there would be more space and opportunity for recreation and wildlife—provided in part by the very people who today envision
only cattle and sheep on western lands. And the prognosis for restoration
of diversity and ecological health would be enhanced. A greater diversity
in ideas and visions would prevent policy and management from being
entrapped by excessively narrow, parochial beliefs. It would prevent the
calamity that Alston Chase feared for America's national parks:

> This close relationship [between policymakers and environmental
> groups] threatens the integrity and independence of the Park Service
> and the environmental community and may undermine efforts at
> wildlife preservation throughout the national park system. Having
> gained enormous influence within the Park Service environmental-
> ists risk closing questions of wildlife management to legitimate de-
> bate. By winning the political battles of the '60s, they may lose the
> war to save wildlife in the '80s.[9]

Scenarios of what might have been, or might still be, are meaningless
in the context of today's intolerant visions. For better or worse, blinders
of ideology are steering the environmental welfare state on an unwavering
and arrogant course, one that is insensitive to all but the most catastrophic
events and oblivious to alternative ways and ideas. Indeed, it was visionary
arrogance that drove the Forest Service to defend outmoded ideas on fire
control and prevention. So enthralled was the agency with rescuing timber
and homes from fiery conflagration that it failed to see the environmental
harm of what it was doing. By imposing its single-minded policy indis-
criminately over the vast expanse of western timberlands, it brought the
expected harvest of an imposed monoculture—a harvest to be repeated
with deliberate design on the grazing lands of the federal range.

But that harvest of visionary management is not contained by the boundaries of public lands. In devising and implementing programs for the national forests and the public domain, the Forest Service and the BLM have unwittingly shifted environmental costs onto private lands and generated waves of unintended consequences. They have missed the vital link existing between private and public lands on the western range.

Places like Otter Creek and the Gunnison–Crested Butte valley are reminders of the costs and consequences of ignoring that vital link. They are monuments to the ecological folly of drawing artificial boundaries across western landscapes and testaments to the limits of the environmental welfare state. They highlight the futility of human arrogance, whether in the form of progressive conservation or righteous management, and point to the burdensome liability that monocultures inevitably bring to man and nature. Most of all, they are examples of what happens when people's ties to the land are defined more by the politics of visions than by the practical necessities of living and working. Conflict and struggle supplant caring and cooperation, waylaying the best of intentions and wasting the limited resources that people have to defend and steward the lands in which their lives are so deeply entrenched.

Clearly, there can be no satisfactory resolution to the problems of public grazing lands until the western commons is adequately reformed or transformed. Elimination of livestock from public lands, the objective of many environmental groups, is one possibility. But ending public-land ranching cannot, by itself, resolve the worst features of the western commons. To address adequately the ecological need for diversity, accountability, and responsibility on public lands, one must begin at the level of landscape visions. One must decide whether intolerance is a strategy worthy of utopian aspirations. Above all, one must reconsider the role of the environmental welfare state. Only when visionaries accept the limitations that come with tolerance and agree to forgo the temptations of the environmental welfare state will there be a lasting solution to the western commons.

MAN AND NATURE ON THE WESTERN RANGE

Every landscape, be it a high-prairie grassland or a deciduous eastern forest, makes up a viable ecological space—a space in which people and nature can devise and evolve any number of sustainable living and working relationships. For example, a tallgrass prairie may be a picture of ecological health to those who value the wild and untrammeled. But for those with different visions, a healthy prairie is also one that is grazed by livestock, plowed for commercial crops, or developed into cities. Although such options may not be as desirable as the original wilderness, all of them have the potential of being within the landscape's viable ecological space. As long as people are responsive to their physical surroundings and adjust their lives to its cues and needs, human-forged landscapes can flourish. But if people do not respond to the cues and needs of their surroundings— if they overgraze the land, improperly till the soil, or discharge harmful effluents—then they step outside the bounds of the prairie's viable ecological space. Their landscape visions stop being ecologically sound and become environmentally destructive.

These are the limits of landscape visions, the parameters within which they are ecologically viable and beyond which they are not. As creations of the human spirit, they are neither right nor wrong, neither true nor false. Only opinion and nature in their proper realms can separate the desirable and viable visions from the ugly and unworkable ones. On the public lands, where intolerance has replaced opinion and arrogance has supplanted nature, that separation is evident. The limits of landscape visions have not been heeded, and the people and lands of the western range have paid the social and environmental costs.

What has happened on the western range is tragic, and it forces us to reconsider the lingering question first posed in chapter 1: What role has a personal land ethic played in the natural history of public grazing lands? By most accounts, the destruction and waste of federal rangelands came about because of the conspicuous absence of a land ethic among western stockmen. Whatever truth lies in this assumption, however, it is only partial. Although public-land ranchers are undeniably responsible for their role in the tragedy of the western range, it is incorrect to single them out as the principal source of environmental harm and havoc. To assign them primary moral responsibility for all that has gone astray on those lands is to ignore the lessons of the federal range.

Agents more powerful and vocal than western stockmen shaped the natural history of the western range. Intolerant visions swept across arid landscapes independently of the ethics of individual ranchers, transforming the land and affecting its people for the worst. And the authority and power of the state have been ever present, giving overwhelming physical form to what otherwise might have been the hapless and harmless motions of visionary zeal. It is simply not enough to explain the natural history of the western range in terms of a nonexistent or poorly expressed personal land ethic. Etched on the western landscape is evidence of a greater ecological cause, a more encompassing explanation for all that has transpired during one hundred and thirty years of livestock grazing on public lands.

The environmental welfare state is the factor most responsible for the biological and social problems of the western range. Through the expansion of federal control over arid rangelands, the diversity of the land and its people has been diminished and the resilience and potential of once viable ecological systems have been undermined. A continual shifting of power from local landscapes and local residents to bureaucratic institutions has eroded the ecological integrity of the public's vast landed estate, leaving its bounty as unprotected plunder for warring factions of special interests. It has made the western range vulnerable to the shortcomings of laws and policies conceived beyond its borders and susceptible to the ongoing waste and depredation of an uncontrolled commons.

But there is more to the fate of man and nature on the western range than overgrazed rangelands and the reign of environmental mediocrity. The relationship of people to the land's arid environment has been redefined to that of either resource consumer or spiritual participant in an envisioned commons. Through a relentless realignment of power and control, the western range has become the province of institutions rather than individuals and communities. The result is alienation. Discrete and local community has succumbed to the imagined national community of public-land users and public-land agencies—the community to which progressive democracy was dedicated. As Aldo Leopold wrote in his essay on the land ethic, "Your true modern is separated from the land by many middlemen, and by innumerable physical gadgets. He has no vital relation to it." [10]

The vital relation that occupied Leopold was the role and place of people in the land community, their membership and participation in the discrete environments that make up their homes and workplaces. Only men and women who were fully integrated into their surrounding environments could evolve the requisite sense of ethical responsibility toward the land and its life; only they could arrive at what Leopold termed the land ethic.

When viewed in the context of his axiom of ecological right and wrong,

Leopold's land ethic takes on special significance for public lands. It is, by Leopold's account, the most critical factor in preserving "the integrity, stability, and beauty of the biotic community." Those things that contribute to its making are necessarily good and proper; those things that tend otherwise are wrong. The middlemen who stand between people and their environments and the gadgets that weaken and dissolve the vital relation fall in the second category. Today, the most visible middleman on the western range is the visionary state, and the most intrusive gadgets are the mechanisms of landscape visions—the tools and practices of both scientific and righteous land management.

Separated from the western range by imposing bureaucracies, people are taught that they have no rightful place in pristine nature, that they are by their own nature destructive, and that whatever relation they evolve with the public range must be at arm's length. They are disenfranchised from the natural world. Men and women may view the wonders of the western range from afar, and they may even extract some of its products under the watchful eye of technocrats. But under no circumstance may they become a permanent part of its land community. The vital relation that consumed Leopold's life—the realization of a land ethic—is denied to them in the name of democracy, environmentalism, and progressive conservation.

A lasting solution to the ecological problems of the western range must begin by changing the direction of federal-land use and management. It is simply not enough to add layers of new bureaucracy upon old and disproven layers—to try to wipe clean a record of land management blemished by one hundred and thirty years of repeated failure and unprecedented environmental harm. And even if the Forest Service and the BLM could be reformed, that would not heal the unnatural divisions that impassioned visions and imperial laws and policies have left between people and nature on the western range. As John Passmore notes in *Man's Responsibility for Nature*, "we do not regard an ecological problem as satisfactorily solved merely because someone has thought up a device which would produce the desired results with a minimum of consequential disadvantages." [11]

Whether one likes it or not, scientific land management and righteous land management are only devices. Their successful use by a reformed bureaucracy might permit experts to engineer solutions to some of the biological problems plaguing public lands. But even if that were possible—which is unlikely, given the ecological track record of the environmental welfare state—we would be no nearer to narrowing the gap between people and nature that has been created by excessive legalism and bureaucracy. Men and women would be no closer to having a place and role in the diverse land communities of America's public lands. Despite the best of intentions, Leopold's land ethic would remain captive to state institutions—a permanent hostage of arrogant and overly ambitious landscape visions.

Resolving the predicament of the western range must begin with new approaches, using strategies that forgo the promise and allure of single visions and that avoid the ecological follies and limitations of the visionary state. Those solutions reside in the potentials of a free society. There, diverse ideals and innovative ideas will thrive or perish on their own merits, without the aid and assistance of the environmental welfare state. And the mandate of the National Environmental Policy Act will find fertile ground and flourish. *Man and nature can*—and will—*exist in productive harmony.*

CHAPTER TWELVE

A Market of Landscape Visions

*W*hen Dayton Hyde first came to Chiloquin, Oregon, his private and permitted rangelands were dry expanses of pine trees and shrubby bitterbrush.[1] Except for scattered grassy parks and a few small sagebrush openings, the landscape extended in all directions as forest. But Dayton had a personal landscape vision, a vision with enforceable limits that began and ended on his small forested ranch in southwestern Oregon. He believed that ranchers had an obligation to care for their lands—particularly their private lands, the ones over which they had greatest control. That was why he started Operation Stronghold, a voluntary landowner's alliance devoted to using private property for wildlife conservation. It was for a similar reason that he began the Institute of Range and the American Mustang (IRAM). Today, he is using IRAM to set up voluntary private reserves for wild horses in South Dakota.

Landscape visions are like charity, though: They are best begun and observed at home. For Dayton Hyde, the power and allure of his vision lie not in the four hundred members and several million acres of Operation Stronghold or in the good intentions of IRAM but in the beautiful, sculpted landscapes that his ethic of caring has brought to his small ranch.

One of those landscapes is a marshland. Dayton turned the dry valley *bottom lying below his headquarters into a mosaic of clear streams, open pools, sedge and willow bogs, and lush meadows. He marshaled and stewarded the feeble headwaters of the Williamson River with holding ponds, water diversions, and proper grazing management. His efforts paid off in many ways. His family enjoyed a healthier and richer environment, fishermen angled for prize trout on formerly barren land, and plant and wildlife species thrived and flourished.*

Cattle are part of Dayton's vision. He uses them to enhance the diversity of the marsh, grazing them carefully so that they do not disturb nesting birds or upset fish spawning grounds. Yet if livestock were not so vital to the health of the marsh, he might do just as well without them—at least dollarwise. During the summer, five fishermen per week pay more than $100 per day apiece for lodging and angling. And during the winter, the large number of mule deer and elk that rely on his marsh for water and food attract paying hunters. As it turns out, a judicious mix of recreation, wildlife, and cattle allows Dayton and his family to make their living off the land without overgrazing its plants, eroding its soils, or exhausting its other renewable resources. In fact, it enables them to give more to the land than they have taken.

They would like to give even more. Not long ago, Dayton asked the Forest Service for permission to reduce stocking on public lands adjacent to his marsh. He believed that deer and elk could graze and maintain the marsh just as well as livestock. To offset lost revenue, he offered to pay the same grazing bill as before, even though he would no longer be running as many cows. The Forest Service denied his request, telling him that his grazing permit was for cattle, not wildlife.

As important as the marsh is to Dayton, the pride and joy of his wildlife vision is a second landscape—a small lake that he carved out of the Oregon wilds. At most ten miles from his headquarters, it is a sanctuary where he can wile away hours writing naturalist and wildlife books and pass balmy afternoons running and hunting with the timber wolf he raised from a pup. It is also a special refuge for fish, birds, and mammals. On one of many boulders around the lake, Dayton and I sat and watched the wildlife, listened to the wolf's howl, and talked about the quarter-mile stretch of man-made water below us.

Before the lake existed, the land was well drained and densely timbered in pine. Wildlife was hardly visible and far from diverse. But Dayton arrived with his vision and built a dam to hold water. Over the years, he watched as the lake filled, plant life changed, and wildlife appeared in greater numbers and species. He was especially pleased with the varieties of bird life that found homes on his newly made refuge. His first counts had shown only eight species. But after the lake was filled, he counted eighty three species of birds, including the American bald eagle.

When the Forest Service learned that the lake had attracted bald eagles, it closed a road that Dayton had long used to maintain the perimeter fence protecting his private refuge. The agency did not want him driving on the road because the noise might disturb nesting eagles. He was angered. He was the one who had brought the bald eagle to the Winema National Forest by spending $200,000 to build the lake. Why should he be viewed as a potential intruder?

Dayton was able to resolve part of the problem by swapping a portion of his marshland for Forest Service property adjacent to the lake. The new land made it easier for him to maintain fences, control access, and preserve the ecological integrity of the refuge. But he was saddened when he returned to the portion of the marshland that now belonged to the Forest Service and found it despoiled. Gone were the profusion of fish, the dense grasses, and the rich variety of mammals and birds.

Other disappointments have since marred what should have been an unblemished triumph of human will. Well-intentioned environmental zoning codes passed by the people of Oregon are making it difficult for Dayton to do as he wishes with his private sanctuary. Although he built the lake with his own money and labor, state planners are authorized to tell him what he can and cannot do with it. For example, Dayton would like to build a few fishing cabins on the far side of the lake to help cover the costs of maintaining its water level and conserving its wildlife. But doing that may not be possible, given Oregon's strict environmental regulations. The only option that state law allows him is to breach the dam and return the lake bed to its forested and relatively lifeless past.

Dayton is also disappointed that the Forest Service will not allow him to try his vision on public lands. He would like to heal eroding meadows and improve wildlife habitat by building a series of ponds and diversion lines to spread water evenly over the landscape. But he cannot. The best he can do is sit on the boulder next to me and ponder the options left him by state planners and land managers. We hear the unsettling howl of the lake's solitary wolf. Two endangered species make their stand: one a symbol of a world past, the other an agent of a world that might be—a world where visions are free and the likes of Dayton Hyde are tolerated.

ECOLOGY, MARKETS, AND LANDSCAPE VISIONS

Freeing the western range from the tyranny of single visions and the misrule of the visionary state begins with seeing and appreciating that nature is more complex and dynamic than intolerant visions have allowed. It starts by envisioning the western range apart from the narrow constraints well-intentioned people have set and by entertaining possibilities beyond cultivated fields, engineered landscapes, and sacred places. And it means facing the shortcomings of agrarian, progressive, and environmental visions and understanding why they failed in their quest to capture and remold landscapes into a single, unchanging form.

Among those ideologies, the one that most threatens the relation of man and nature on the western range is the presumption that the land has a life and destiny independent of people and their communities. Today, that ideology lives in the lingering legacy of Clements's ecology. It colors progressive and environmental perceptions of the western range, pointing to an absolute standard for measuring the health and well-being of the land. And that single image of how the land once was, and should be again, tightens the regulatory grasp of the environmental welfare state and heightens the zeal of righteous managers. Yet beneath the certainty of visionary rhetoric, there is another reality—one that challenges the unnatural division of people and nature on the western range.

Three-quarters of a century of science has all but demolished Clements's vision of a deterministic world, where man is more intruder than welcomed member. A tradition of ecology anchored in the writings of H. A. Gleason and Robert Whittaker and continued at the cutting edge of patch dynamics theory paints a portrait of an altogether different world—a natural world characterized more by indeterminacy and disturbance than by climax and predictability.[2] Clements's vision, it is argued, fails to account for the role of chance and accident in the sculpting of nature and its vegetation. And plant communities, far from being organisms evolving toward a preordained end point, are simply collages, collections, and patches of individual species as they occur along multiple environmental gradients.

Moreover, continuous change is the rule for plant communities. Shifting patterns of species within discrete patches of vegetation are the transient faces that landscapes assume in their ever-changing nature. Far from being the negative factor that Clements blamed for undermining vegetation structure and stability, disturbance is the essential feature of healthy and sound ecological systems. From this perspective, Clements's ecology is obsolete. As James Gleick notes in *Chaos,* "those looking to science for a general understanding of nature's habitats will be better served by the laws of chaos."[3] Those laws teach the indeterminacy of nature—a revelation, Gleick observes, that forced ecologist William Schaffer to reconsider his basic assumptions on ecology:

[He] found himself realizing that ecology based on a sense of equilibrium seems doomed to fail. The traditional models are betrayed by their linear bias. Nature is more complicated. Instead he sees chaos, "both exhilarating and a bit threatening." Chaos may undermine ecology's most enduring assumptions . . . [but] "what passes for fundamental concepts in ecology is as a mist before the fury of the storm—in this case, a full, nonlinear storm."[4]

A "nonlinear storm" is already besieging those who have dared to assert and impose what is right and proper on the western range. By pinning their landscape ideals and hopes to the static, illusory world of Clements, land agencies and righteous managers have taken a path as far astray from ecological good as the course followed by the cattlemen who overgrazed and abused federal rangelands. Visions of engineered landscapes and sacred places have deluded progressive and environmental thinkers into believing that nature can be mastered and set on a straight and narrow course as dictated by the will of the state. Such inflexible visions, unfortunately, have steered well-intentioned people away from the standard and test of ecological right and wrong set by Aldo Leopold.

Whatever defects mar visionary portraits of the public lands, they are exacerbated by an underlying mistrust of people in general, a belief that men and women are disrupters of nature and interlopers on the western range. Only the environmental welfare state, staffed with right-thinking and properly caring people, can mitigate the worst effects of human presence and isolate public lands from the contagion they threaten.

Viewing people in such light, though, merely reinforces the reign of intolerant visions and the rule of the visionary state. To challenge the supremacy of both, we must discard simple formulas that describe humans as virulent agents eating away at the immense biological diversity and ecological health of western rangelands. In making that challenge, of course, we cannot overlook the environmental damage caused by modern man's assault on nature, nor can we forget that the biological richness of the earth has been diminished by human action. But it would be wrong to assume that people are bad or that man cannot live in harmony with nature.

People are an inescapable and necessary part of their environments.

They are not, as Clements regretfully told us, intruders on virgin grasslands; they are not, as experts inform us, special interest constituencies who are properly managed and supervised by mammoth bureaucracies; and they are not, as Muir would have us believe, nondescript hordes of destroyers ravaging western forests. The role people play extends far beyond the handful of institutions that make up the environmental welfare state and the chosen few who staff the ranks of those holding encompassing visions.

Landscape ecology, a youthful discipline born in European rather than American ecology, has theory and evidence enough to substantiate the pivotal role of man in nature.[5] The intricate patterns of vegetation—both civilized and wild—that clothe the earth's diverse terrains are as much the outcomes of historical human action as they are the products of climate, soils, species dispersal, genetic drift, and local topography. Landscape ecology accepts men and women as legitimate members of the natural world. Climax communities, in the sense perceived by Clements, are nonexistent. Possibility, rather than inevitability, characterizes the protean land communities of landscape ecology.

Ecological systems, like those on the western range, are envisioned by most ecologists as hierarchies of organization, starting with single organisms and extending onward through the levels of populations, communities, and ecosystems. For landscape ecologists, including such prominent American ecologists as Eugene and Howard Odum, the hierarchy culminates at what is termed the ninth level of integration—at the realm of landscapes and the total human ecosystem. It is there that people are included in the ecological picture, completing what in nature entails a viable and functioning human ecosystem. "By human ecosystem," writes ecologist Frank Egler,

> we certainly do not mean a virgin, climax, primeval wilderness, which man has utilized, exploited, raped or ruined and which would return to its "balance of nature" if only man would "preserve" it. This is the archaic view of those scientists who are pegged at the Eighth (Ecosystem) Level, and have hit their intellectual ceiling. On the contrary, the idea of the Total Human Ecosystem [THE] is that *man-and-his-total-environment* form one single whole in nature that can be, should be and will be studied in its totality.[6]

Merely asserting that man is an integral part of the natural world, of course, does not resolve the issue of whether his contributions and potential are weighed more heavily toward environmental destruction than toward benevolence. By some standards, human intervention in nature is necessarily bad; it can only blemish the harmony and perfection inherent in a pristine world. John Muir is an excellent example of this sentiment. He saw only the harmful and contaminating presence of man in the forests, mountains, and prairies that were once pristine and unpolluted. Muir made it clear that people add nothing to the complexity and beauty of nature; they only detract from its wonders. Such an assumption, so prevalent in the landscape visions that have dominated law and policy on public lands, is shortsighted and prejudicial. For all the environmental harm that men and women have brought to western rangelands, for all the varied and rich life that stockmen have left trampled and severely grazed in the wake of too many cattle and sheep, the human factor is nonetheless a crucial element in the overall diversity and ecological potential of federal rangelands.

This last point may be best understood by looking beyond the boundaries of the western range. For example, Raymond Coppinger and Charles Smith—both evolutionary ecologists—conclude in "The Domestication of Evolution" that man's modification of the natural world has enhanced the survivability of the human species and its domesticated plants and animals.[7] They acknowledge that ecological systems are becoming simplified at an alarming rate—that species are disappearing and landscapes are becoming impoverished. Much of that loss, they concede, is the consequence of more solar energy, more open spaces, and more nutrients being dedicated to feeding and housing an ever-growing human population. This imminent loss of diversity should, by all accounts, threaten, not enhance, human survival.

Certainly, diversity is vital.[8] It is the lifeblood of natural and social systems—an insurance policy of sorts that allows human and nonhuman life to weather the constant storm of environmental change. It is the network through which energy and information flow to animate life, and at the same time, it is the source of the energy and information needed to maintain life. Every species, subspecies, and individual, including the immense variety of environments in which they thrive and flourish, is part of both the fabric and the process of diversity. Each and every one of these elements of diversity is linked to the survival and stability of both wild and civilized places. If diversity is understood in this manner, as the process whereby life sustains itself rather than simply the many forms that it assumes, then we can begin to understand the anomaly described by Coppinger and Smith.

Despite the accelerating rate of species extinction and the accompanying biological simplification of the global environment, humans have the potential to enhance diversity by creating and processing information—that is, by their ability to propagate through culture, community, science, and art a diversity upon which people and nature can thrive and coexist in harmony. Through such diversity, it is even conceivable that species extinction may be slowed or reversed. As long as humans are able to exercise their special informational skills and respond to their environments creatively and with dispatch, flourishing and viable landscapes are possible and probable. Clearly, of the many roles that people fill in the global ecosystem, that of communicator may be most crucial to the continuance of life.

Ideas and information, then, constitute the power and potential of human diversity—an ecological, as opposed to biological, diversity in which a single species by virtue of creativity is able to play a disproportionate and, with good fortune, a more benevolent role in the health and wellbeing of the earth. It may not be too farfetched to suggest that the human mind mimics the ecological role and function of a single species, or that the collectivity of minds is in many ways analogous to the diversity that comes with genetic variability and multiple species. The only difference between human and nonhuman diversity is choice. Only man has the option to act for better or worse, to turn his skills toward enriching or impoverishing his life and the lives of other species.

Most people would agree that given the option of choice, humans have an obligation to turn their creativity toward salvaging the elements of biological diversity that are currently threatened. And few would question that the overall quality of life, in both material and aesthetic terms, would be enhanced by preserving species and protecting environmental diversity. At the same time, it must be understood that rescuing the wild and pristine does not mean removing man and his creative influence from the natural world. Human diversity, as translated into innovative ideas and responsive information, is the key to viable and desirable landscapes on a planet so overwhelmingly populated by people. It is also the pivotal ecological factor in determining people's ability to live in peace and harmony among themselves and with nature.

Returning to the western range from our overview of global diversity and global ecosystems, it is clear that the problems of the federal estate are similar to those of more distant places. Diversity is endangered, and its restoration is crucial. What is needed to heal overgrazed lands and to enrich western landscapes is a market of landscape visions—an atmosphere of political and environmental tolerance in which individuals and groups are free to pursue their dreams and ambitions without the benefit of political force or the largesse of federal subsidy. In such an environment, the diversity that comes with many minds and as many visions will be unleashed, innovative ideas can be pursued, and new approaches and strategies for the use, conservation, and preservation of wild and tamed lands can be tried and tested.

Such a market will bring visions down to earth, making them answerable to the land, to the wildlife, and to the social communities that invariably bear many of the costs and benefits of environmental abuse and benevolence. The question is how to arrive at a market of landscape visions, how to unleash the power of diversity and the promise of many visions on the lands of the federal range.

DIVERSITY, PROCESS, AND ENVIRONMENTAL GAIN

A market of landscape visions is not something tangible, like the market for automobiles or the thousands of flea markets that spring up every weekend across the country. It is not the millions of monetary transactions that shuffle resources, products, and people around the nation with dispatch. A market of landscape visions describes a political and social environment in which basic beliefs and underlying ideologies are left to the discretion of the individual and his community.

Choice and voluntarism are the key components of a market of landscape visions, just as they are the attributes of a free-market economy. But between the two market types, there is a crucial difference in the emphasis placed on choice and voluntarism. The markets that concern economists have traditionally focused on products and services for people. Although such markets can and do affect the environment (quite often for the worse), they are not designed to address issues relating to environmental health and ecological well-being. Moreover, they are often departures from the free-market ideal, being regulated by laws and policies aimed at

223

specific national goals. To the extent that choice and voluntarism are valued and relied upon, it is because they enhance society, not because they enrich nature.

The new resource economics (NRE), however, argues that traditional markets can serve the needs of the environment when government regulation is minimal and when property rights are identifiable, enforceable, and transferable. Under those conditions, it insists, incentives will exist to channel human action in more environmentally desirable directions. People will be more responsible toward the land because they will bear the financial risks of bad management and assume the potential benefits of superior management. Adam Smith's "invisible hand" will make choice and voluntarism the unwitting handmaidens of ecological good.

A growing body of evidence suggests that the NRE is right, that markets work for the environment when people are accountable and when human action is guided by choice and voluntarism. A market of landscape visions starts with those assumptions but goes one step further. It harnesses choice and voluntarism directly to the fate of the environment and its ecology. What counts is that people have the *opportunity* to ply their dreams where it matters most, on the land. Better incentives to deal kindly with nature are simply inadequate to correct all the problems that plague the federal estate. They might motivate ranchers to graze their lands more carefully; they might encourage agencies to be more cost-effective; and they might inspire other land users to be more conscientious of the lands they rely on for recreation. But incentives alone would not unleash the potential that inevitably comes with having many landscape visions. To crack the political hegemony that rules the federal range, more than incentives is needed. The answer is diversity.

Diversity is the product of a market of landscape visions. Many minds and many visions generate the wealth of information needed to help keep environments healthy and ecological systems viable. And as long as those minds and visions operate by choice and through voluntary means, the market of landscape visions can become a proving ground. Like the services and products in traditional markets, which come and go according to how well they satisfy consumers, landscape visions will rise and fall to the extent that they meet the environmental and ecological demands of the land. There will be no need for taxpayer bailouts. Unworkable visions—like subsidized grazing and price-supported agriculture—will cease to exist. Rushing in to fill the vacuum left by failed visions will be those that are gentler to the land and more responsive to the needs of people.

In a very real sense, ecology and economics converge in the marketplace of landscape visions. The biological world of nature and the social universe of people meld together in the arena of many competing visions. And it is only proper that they should. Healthy landscapes and free markets are two sides of the same coin; one is the biological and the other is the human face of self-regulating ecological systems. Moreover, a concern for efficiency and conservation is central to both the economic and the ecological perspectives and establishes common ground between the two. Energy and information, whether in the currency of dollars, ideas, species, or sunlight, are stewarded by man and nature alike. Biological and economic systems must make do as best they can with the limited resources they have or face decline and death.

Ecology and economics (at least free-market economics) share an even greater affinity in diversity.[9] The economic power of free markets, like the ecological strength of natural communities, comes from the profusion of diversity that emanates from both. Just as a diverse economy insulates a city or region from the full brunt of economic shock, so also does a diversity of species and habitats insulate landscapes from the full biological turmoil of environmental change. More important, diversity creates options. Consumers in free markets, when faced with a shortage of some vital product, are almost always able to find satisfactory substitutes. Likewise, deer or elk, when faced with the loss of favored forage due to disease or insects, are able to find substitute feed.

The allure of a market of landscape visions is that it unites the common features of ecology and economics under a single metaphoric roof. Landscape visions that are unfettered by state regulation and not shielded from the lessons of nature by subsidies and political intrusions will almost always offer more to man and nature than will single, encompassing visions. The presence of many visions is, in fact, as crucial to the health and soundness of the environment as are the nonhuman factors of soil, water, plants, and animals. Above all, a diversity of visions provides a modicum of assurance that human needs can be met while the integrity of the natural world is maintained or enhanced. A market of landscape visions, like the final stage of ecological integration at the level of the total human environment, is the interface between people and the land. There, man and nature work out their relations, for better or worse.

On the western range, those relations have been destructive. The evidence is overwhelming that the single visions that have imposed the policy hegemony of the environmental welfare state have been unworkable and ecologically flawed. There is, it would seem, no other direction to go but toward free and unfettered landscape visions—toward the marketplace, in which each individual and community decides how best to live with the land and nature becomes the final arbiter of ecological right and wrong. Such a direction leads to what Robert Nozick, in *Anarchy, State and Utopia*, calls "a framework for utopia." [10] But to arrive at that point, where freedom and openness guide human action, conditions must be met.

For citizens and their communities to become fountainheads of diversity on public lands, power and control must be devolved. In the past, federal policy and land bureaucracy have encroached on local sovereignty and have negated whatever contributions the diversity of many minds and visions has had to offer. Laws, regulations, and policies requiring public input into Forest Service and BLM planning have forced land agencies to listen, but they have not made citizens and their communities masters in their own lands. The ecological possibility of many minds—the promise and potential of their creativity, culture, and visions—has been lost for want of the means of implementation: power and control.

Power and control translate potential human diversity into maximum ecological benefit when visions can be tried on landscapes where individuals and their communities are both responsible and accountable for what they do. This is the essence of a market of landscape visions. It does not mean that lands must be owned in the traditional sense or that property rights must be vested in the hands of single individuals. It requires only that people have secure control over the landscapes on which their visions are to be tested and that such control be attained by peaceful rather than forceful means.

Other conditions must also be met to ensure the workings of a market of landscape visions. In particular, the information that is vital to making visions work must be abundant, accessible, and sought after. Abundance of information, of course, is a natural outcome of a community of many minds and many visions. Opening the western range to more players than a handful of bureaucracies and a few powerful lobbying groups should expand ideas and information manyfold over what exists today. But making information accessible and sought after is another matter. In part, it

comes with the expansion of opportunity and the inclusion of more players. Yet what facilitates it most is the removal of obstacles. Markets of
information—or of visions—must be freed of the distortions that subsidies and political intrusions inevitably bring. People will be more likely to
seek out superior information, and should have greater success in obtaining it, when spared the disincentives of federal handouts and freed of the
bureaucratic middlemen who stand between themselves and their land. If
these guidelines—decentralization of power, establishment of local control, and expansion of accessible information—are followed, the shortcomings and failures of intolerant visions will, at the very least, be side-
stepped. At the most, those guidelines will help bring out the best of
human nature, nurturing peace and harmony between people and the lands
of the federal range.

The Forest Service and the BLM are obstacles to a market of landscape
visions. They are the technologies of an age of arrogance, when elitism
ruled the politics of public lands. And they are obsolete. Freeman Dyson,
in his collection of essays titled *Infinite in All Directions*, offers a description
of technological evolution that fits today's land agencies remarkably well.
"During its phase of rapid growth and spectacular success," he notes, a
technology "is usually small, quick and agile." As it ages, "it becomes
settled and conservative, prevented by the inertia of size from reacting
quickly to sudden shocks." Finally, Dyson writes, "when a technology has
grown so big and sluggish that it can no longer bend with the winds of
change, it is ripe for extinction."[11] The Forest Service and the BLM are
technologies that no longer bend with the wind.

Today, the Forest Service and the BLM are entangled in a web of laws,
policies, and administrative requirements. Their time and budgets are
spent increasingly on internal affairs and the *procedures* of land management. Layers of bureaucracy compounded with layers of competing interest groups have made land stewardship a small item on the agenda of
public-land management. Aldo Leopold's fear that government conservation might share the fate of the mastodon is coming true. Land agencies
are succumbing to the mass of their bureaucracies and the limits of their
visions.

It is time to recognize that nature on the western range is too complex
to be orchestrated by mammoth agencies or a handful of special interest
groups. It is time to move beyond Pinchot's elite and Muir's righteous. By
replacing the disproven technologies of centralized planning with a market

of landscape visions, federal lands will reap the economic and ecological benefits of a free society and gain from the diversity of many minds and many visions.

Expanding the number of active players on the deserts, grasslands, and forests of the western range will do three things. First, it will buffer the environment against ill-advised visions. Human actions that are detrimental to the land will be limited in space and time. Fewer acres will be disturbed for much shorter periods of time. There will no longer be environmental mistakes on the scale of the homestead acts and federal grazing policies. Second, the possibility that highly desirable landscapes will be preserved or re-created will increase as more minds and visions find and try environmentally superior ideas. Third, the dreams and ambitions of all Americans will have more elbow room. There will be ample opportunities—landscape opportunities—for people to seek and fulfill their visions of how best to live on the western range.

To appreciate the significance of landscape opportunities, picture the "viable ecological space" of chapter 11 as the area bounded by an imaginary cube. Within the cube are any number of smaller spaces corresponding to the array of landscape possibilities in which people and nature can coexist in long-term harmony. These "subsets of the ecological space" may include such varied examples as an industrial or metropolitan complex, a wildlife preserve, or a well-managed farm. What is common to each of these landscape possibilities is that they can be sustained indefinitely. They are viable because they are self-supporting, and they are stable because they exist within the limits and constraints of their respective environments. Public-land grazing has never met any of these criteria—nor have the other activities on federal lands.

The point is that realistic landscape opportunities are finite, occurring within real but largely unexplored and untapped ecological spaces. The single visions that have dominated the western range have consistently fallen outside those spaces. They have been able to continue for so long only because taxpayers have paid the bill—and because the political clout needed to change public-land management has been divided and diluted by the maneuvering of land agencies and the bickering of special interest groups.

There is, unfortunately, no guarantee that a market of landscape visions will generate opportunities that fall consistently within the ecological cube. But there is certainty on three counts. The first is that visions that seek impossible landscapes are doomed to failure. Bereft of the forced generosity of American taxpayers and the politics of special interest groups, they must sink or swim. Second, a market of landscape visions virtually ensures that more rather than fewer of the cube's viable landscapes will be explored and tapped by those who wish to mix their labor and love with the land. Enough visions will find a place to flourish within the imaginary cube that the western range will at last meet the expectations of all Americans, not merely a privileged few. Opportunity will replace bureaucratic fiat, and diversity will supplant the visionary state.

Third, and most significant, a market of landscape visions will enlist all Americans in the destiny of their western lands. Today, a handful of trained experts and impassioned special interests exercise unchallenged dominion over one-third of the nation's land. Tomorrow, a market of landscape visions could open the western range to the historically disenfranchised. More people than ever would become part of the future of the nation's landed wealth. And even more people, through the invisible hand of the marketplace, would make their opinions heard. Visionaries and their visions, when focused on federal lands, would have to pay attention to more than the many messages of nature; they would have to listen and attend to the many voices of the American people.

Public-land ranchers would be less likely to overgraze their lands, or even to graze them at all, if the cues of the marketplace carried greater persuasion than the logic of the permit system or the dictates of bureaucracies. Stockmen would be able to see that their meadows and streams had value other than as feed for sheep and water for cattle. They would be able to respond to the wishes of the American public by doing things prohibited to them for over a century. And even if they did not, others with greater insight and ambition would. Under a market of landscape visions, the federal range would no longer be the protected province of ranchers and their livestock. Indeed, every acre of the Forest Service and the BLM estate would be freed from the multiple use mandates that have empowered special interest groups for decades to log, mine, ranch, and four-wheel drive the nation's forests and rangelands into environmental depletion. There would be abundant room for other visions, ensuring that Americans would get what they increasingly want: open space, recreation, wildlife, and escape. People would gain, wildlife would benefit, and the land would blossom in almost infinite diversity.

Arising from the market of landscape visions is one truth: that ecological good as defined by Leopold's axiom is virtually indeterminate. There is no final answer on what is environmentally and ecologically proper. Within the bounds of the imaginary ecological cube or on the surface of healthy and thriving landscapes, what constitutes ecological good is as much a matter of opinion as it is a subject of science. If a landscape is viable—if a vision "tends to preserve the integrity, stability, and beauty of the biotic community"—then it is, by Leopold's test, right. On the western range, this means that multiple possibilities rather than single solutions will determine the destiny of the land and its people.

One crucially important sidelight to this "truth" of indeterminacy is that the form or structure of visions and the landscapes they forge is less important than the way in which they are realized. In other words, what matters is not the constellation of visions and the multiple landscapes that ultimately find sanctuary on federal lands. What counts is how people pursue their visions and, most important, how responsive their visions are to the ecological demands of the land and its varied life.

Process, in the final analysis, is what a market of landscape visions is all about. It entails hardly an iota of ideology except the simple dictum that the affairs of man and nature are best left to their own devices, free from the political intrusions that have for so long forced them down unwelcome and shortsighted paths. The trace of ideology that colors the market process does not, and cannot, dictate what should or should not be done with the lands of the western range. A market of landscape visions and its ounce of ideology merely provide the environment of tolerance and freedom in which visions can be mixed with the land. But mostly, they form the tribunal where visions are judged against reality and where visionaries are held accountable to society and nature. The many verdicts passed down by this court drive the process of landscape visions inexorably in the direction of diversity.

Yet not even diversity is the ultimate test of a market of landscape visions. The presence of many species and many visions is important, but its importance does not lie in the aesthetic potential diversity offers; it lies in the ecological process it sustains. Everything comes back to process. Diversity is significant not because it offers a finished portrait of how nature should look but because it offers the way and means by which people can live in harmony with the environment. That is the lasting harvest of a market of landscape visions.

DEMOCRATIZATION OF THE
WESTERN RANGE

An infinite number of factors can complicate the task of change and reform. This is particularly true for the western range. In the hundred and
thirty years since the first homestead act, public lands have become encumbered by special interest claims and by injustices that call out for immediate attention. Ranchers and miners who see the federal estate as their
personal domain proclaim their rights to its forage and minerals in the
name of archaic and ecologically unsound laws. Logging communities and
timber mills that have historical ties of dependence to national forests
make compelling moral, if not legal, claims to the timber resources of
public lands. And those Americans who want to use public lands for
something other than minerals, beef, and timber have a long list of griev-
ances. In their minds, they have been denied the legacy of the western
range.

Given the complexity of the legal status of public lands, one must decide
how best to address the region's woes. One solution is to dive headfirst
into the complexity of laws, rights, claims, and injustices that weigh heavily on today's federal range. One could attempt to correct every law, address every grievance, and respect every right and claim. But by the time
such a Herculean task were completed, the solution might well be more
cumbersome than the original problem.

A simpler, cleaner approach is to recognize that what exists is beyond
salvage. Cosmetic changes just will not work. George Coggins's idea of
reforming the BLM by remaking it in the image of the Forest Service
would only intensify the powers of a disproven and failed management
monoculture. Randal O'Toole's proposal to reform the Forest Service by
exposing individual forests to the forces of the marketplace would be only
a half-step toward a market of landscape visions.[12] Bureaucracies would
still be entrenched on soil that is rightfully that of all citizens.

Environmentalist demands that multiple use be overhauled to give more
standing to nontraditional values and uses on federal lands would only
perpetuate more of the same mismanagement. Worst of all, legislative
schemes like the proposed American Heritage Trust Act would pump bil-
lions of federal dollars into expanding the domain of land management
bureaucracies. Not only would more lands be subject to the fate of the
western commons, but people and nature would also be driven further

apart. A land ethic based on living with the land would become that much less likely as layers of bureaucracy erected higher and mightier walls between Americans and their landed birthright.

What is needed on the western range is reform that strikes at the heart of the problem, not at the endless procession of symptoms that have come and gone in the region's tragic history. Meaningful reform must address the environmental harm of the past, promising something more hopeful than mediocrity and offering something better than stale visions and bureaucratic management. Above all, effective reform must address the inequity and injustice that have shrouded the federal range since it was opened to settlement.

Democracy lost is the legacy of past visions. Restoring that legacy is the proper aim of a market of landscape visions. What matters most is that reform tap the democratic sentiment that infuses the federal estate and direct it toward expanding opportunities for all Americans—making certain that this time, all citizens, not merely the wealthiest, most ambitious, best educated, and most righteous, have a role and place in the destiny of the western range. This means that public lands should no longer serve the interests of a few or suffer the consequences of their intolerant visions. It means that many minds and many visions must be given a chance to have their democratic say.

Change for the better is within reach if the fateful step is taken toward real public ownership of the federal estate—toward what amounts to democratization of the western range. Democratization requires creating a level playing field, where visions are free to flourish and citizens are free to pursue them. There are, I imagine, any number of ways to bring democracy to the western range, to reach at last the beginning point of a market of landscape visions. What I propose, however, is simply this: that the public lands managed by the Forest Service and the BLM be given back to the American people.

In 1982, Vernon L. Smith, professor of economics at the University of Arizona, wrote an intriguing article, "On Divestiture and the Creation of Property Rights in Public Lands," for the *Cato Journal*.[13] Seven years later, as I traveled through the West, meeting and interviewing the people whose stories make up this book, I met Professor Smith. We discussed a wide range of ideas, but we always came back to his article and how it might be fashioned into a reform proposal in concert with the themes of democracy and the workings of many visions. What we concluded, and what formed in my mind in subsequent months, took me increasingly afield from his original plan. But one crucial feature of that plan stuck with me: that Americans were shareholders in the public lands and that the shares they held were the key to democratizing the western range.

With that thought in mind, I wondered, what if . . . what if those shares were made real and tangible, and what if they could then be used by people to create the environment for a market of landscape visions? The possibilities were exhilarating and endless. Here lay one path to reform, a direction toward an explosion of visions, tolerance, and diversity on the western range. And it was possible. It could be done in such a way that special interest groups, federal agencies, and the silent majority of Americans divorced from the fate of federal lands could benefit. Most of all, it would redress a long history of environmental trespass and provide the possibility of escaping the closing circle of an uncontrolled and uncared-for western commons.

The proposal is simple and straightforward. Over a twenty-year period—the start and finish to be set by statute—the federal government would be required to divest itself of the surface rights to all lands managed by the Forest Service and the BLM. Five of those years would be set aside for laying the groundwork for what would be the most sweeping land reform in American history. The remaining fifteen years would be spent in the actual transfer of federal lands from managing agencies to an array of citizens, citizen groups, and local communities.

For simplicity's sake, federal lands managed by the National Park Service, the U.S. Fish and Wildlife Service, and other, less visible, agencies would be exempt, along with the subsurface estate of minerals and energy managed by the BLM. Parklands and refuges, for example, hold special meaning and significance for many Americans. Their inclusion with Forest Service and BLM lands would cloud the ecological issue of democratization with an excessive emotional outcry. Similarly, the subsurface estate is seen by many as being vital to the nation's well-being. To make it a key part of a plan of divestiture would pit perceived national interests against needed environmental reform.[14]

To calm the fears of those who have already leaped to the conclusion that my proposal is merely a sellout of public lands to people wealthy enough to acquire them, I offer this reassurance. In the scenario to be laid out in the following pages, there would be no sudden blossoming of "For Sale" signs on federal property, no massive subdivision of the western

233

range into private parcels and kingdoms, and no imminent takeover of public lands by foreign investors. Quite the contrary.

Every American holding a social security number at the time the proposal is implemented would receive one hundred shares in America's public lands. American citizens would be the immediate beneficiaries of divestiture. Each would be given a claim to the federal range and would then have the opportunity to determine its fate.

Each shareholder would have three options. The first would be to allow his or her shares to expire by not applying them against parcels of land before the end of the twenty-year period. This is unlikely, given the value that would be attached to them. For it would be shares, not dollars, that would determine how public lands would be democratized and in what ways they would be divested from bureaucracies to citizens. The other two options would require action. Americans would have to either sell their shares to others or apply the shares to the purchase of public lands. *All* Forest Service and BLM lands would, by law, be divested by the end of the twenty-year period. Unused shares would be, at the very least, lost income and, at the most, lost opportunity.

Whichever option people chose, one inviolable rule would hold sway: Only those individuals, groups, or communities (including towns, cities, and counties) holding shares would be allowed to negotiate in the marketplace of Forest Service and BLM lands. National and state governments would be expressly prohibited by law from holding or acquiring shares— or, for that matter, from holding or acquiring interests in shares. Retirement of federal lands would be the business of the American people, not the concern of their distant governments. The only active role to be played by the federal government would be in the transfer and interim management of public lands.

All shares would be electronically credited to individual tax accounts by the Internal Revenue Service. And only the IRS would have the power to move shares between accounts as citizens sold them for cash or exchanged them for land. Moreover, the Forest Service and the BLM would be given the task of surveying and appraising public lands and the public and private improvements existing within their boundaries. These inventory and surveying tasks, along with a one-year interim period for publicizing the divestiture plan and for educating the public on its operation, would last approximately five years. At the end of those five years, shares would be allotted to all citizens and a fifteen-year period would be set aside to transfer public lands from the bureaucratic sector to the public sector.

In addition, the land agencies would be directed to continue managing public lands for as long as they remained under federal control—at most twenty years after the passage of enabling legislation. During that period, there could be a hiring freeze within the Forest Service and the BLM. Staff remaining after the completion of the program could be given the option of early retirement or continued service in some other federal agency.

Citizens having legal claims to public lands and public resources (such as ranchers, loggers, and miners) would be given special consideration only to the extent that their leases, permits, and contracts would be honored during the plan's twenty-year transition period. Moreover, existing laws and policies governing licensed uses of public lands and resources would remain in effect for the duration, enforced by the Forest Service and the BLM.

Public-land ranchers would be allowed to graze livestock at current grazing fees within the existing constraints of public land law and management. Timber sales would be permitted to continue so long as harvests were scheduled within the twenty-year span and so long as standards already set by long-term Forest Service planning documents were followed. Energy and mineral leases would be honored up to the last day of the twentieth year. After that date, companies would have to negotiate with surface owners for the right to continue their below-ground activities. The surface estate would reign supreme. And after twenty years, there would be no more energy and mineral extraction, public-land grazing, or timber harvests on Forest Service and BLM lands. There would be no Forest Service and BLM lands left.

The mechanics of transferring federal lands into the hands of citizens would be handled by the free market. People wishing to acquire particular tracts would have to buy their shares on the stock exchange—again, with the IRS playing the role of middleman. It would not matter which shares they bought, since none of the shares would be tied to specific parcels of land. All that would count would be accumulating enough shares to make successful bids. For stock sellers, the process would be equally straightforward. Their tax accounts would be debited one or more shares and credited with the dollar amount set by that day's market transaction. And only the market value of each person's original shares (if sold) and the profit reaped from buying and selling the shares of others would be tax-able. Tax receipts collected in this way could be earmarked to help pay the costs of the program.

Original shares used to acquire land, or simply allowed to expire, would be tax-exempt. More important, shares donated to nonprofit organiza-tions—such as environmental groups—would be tax deductible. This could be accomplished in one of two ways. The market value of the do-nated shares could be subtracted from taxable net income or, more pref-erably, deducted directly from one's tax liability. In the second case, tax credits could be provided to citizens whose income was below taxable levels. The obvious benefit of doing this would be that citizens who might otherwise be reluctant to donate their shares to community or nonprofit organizations would have the option of doing so without bearing what could be a significant financial loss.

The transfer of discrete parcels of land could be handled in any number of ways. Buyers could initiate the process or agencies could proceed in some systematic manner consistent with keeping costs down while meet-ing the fifteen-year deadline that would follow interim surveys, appraisals, and publicity. In any event, minimum land areas would have to be set for disposal to ensure that administrative expenses did not get out of hand and to avoid divvying up the federal range into ecologically unsound parcels—as was done initially with the homestead acts.

Grazing allotments, some combination of them, or basic administrative units like Forest Service ranger districts and BLM resource areas might be used as the basis for identifying such land parcels. Because they already exist and because their boundaries often follow natural breaks in the land-scape, their use would be convenient and ecologically sound. Only in the instance of small, isolated parcels of federal land might minimum size re-quirements be waived. Already, such scattered islands of the public estate have economic importance and ecological significance only to the extent that they are part of more substantial surrounding private or nonfederal holdings. It would be only natural for them to become permanent parts of those holdings.

Once a land area were identified and marked for transfer, notice of its impending sale would be published in the *Federal Register*. Local realtors and banks would work with the two land agencies by helping with sur-veys, inventories, and appraisals; by providing basic banking and real es-tate services to prospective buyers; and by handling the details of land auctions. Moreover, the public-land surveys, inventories, and appraisals made by local business and government officials could be used to set an initial monetary value on lands proposed for transfer or simply to provide information to potential bidders.

The marketplace would determine the final price of the land. At a pre-determined time, buyers would convene, either physically or through the wonders of electronics. The market, not the government, would set the monetary value of shares and determine by open and competitive bidding whose landscape visions would prevail. And through such means as prudent people—shareholders holding on to their shares in anticipation of higher prices—and futures or options markets, shares would be distributed relatively evenly across the program horizon of fifteen years. The natural workings of a market of landscape visions would ensure that every acre of Forest Service and BLM land would be transferred into the hands of citizens as mandated by federal statute.

All bidders would be treated equally—there would be no right of first refusal. The only advantage some individuals or groups might have would lie in physical assets they owned or controlled on specific parcels of federal land. Public-land ranchers, for example, would receive credit for the discounted value of privately owned improvements such as fences and pipelines and for water rights filed with and recognized by the appropriate state authorities.[15] During the bidding process, of course, they would have to follow the same rules as everyone else. To control their historical grazing lands, they would have to outbid their competitors. If they succeeded, the value of their physical improvements and water rights would be tallied in the net shares debited from their IRS account. If they failed, they would be compensated for property lost.

Surface owners would have the right to enjoin federal lessees from extracting minerals and energy lying below their newly acquired lands following the plan's twenty-year transition period. A skeleton BLM staff would remain to administer the subsurface estate and to facilitate negotiations among landowners, miners, and energy developers. But there is no reason why the subsurface estate could not be dealt with in a manner similar to that for surface lands. Once democratization of the surface estate were complete, it would be only reasonable to proceed with divestiture of the rights that lie below. By that time, concerns of national interest might have given way to realization that free people and free markets *are* the country's best interest.

There is no way to tell what the landscapes of the federal range might look like at the end of the twenty-year program. But one thing is certain: All Americans would have had an *equal opportunity* to benefit from lands that are, by law and tradition, their birthright. Even those who might choose not to mix their visions with the land—to apply their shares to concrete parcels of the western range—would at least have been given the chance. And they would, in any case, enjoy the monetary dividend of having been a partner and shareholder in the federal estate. Indeed, families who sell their shares could expect a modest windfall of hundreds to thousands of dollars.

For those who decide to do something with their shares other than cash them in, the possibilities would be unlimited. Stockmen would have the option to purchase their ranches, and ownership would mean that they alone would be accountable and responsible for stewarding and protecting their lands. It would give them the opportunity to try different approaches to management and to explore new uses of their rangelands. They would be able to make a living off their ranches in ways that could be more beneficial to society and more gentle to plants and animals. Most important, the day of the welfare rancher would be over.

There would no longer be government subsidies to bail out uncaring or careless people whose primary concern lies with how much they can take from the land. Indeed, only stockmen committed to good stewardship would find a lasting home on a decentralized western range. And men and women from many different walks of life would have the chance to do something other than raise livestock on arid lands. In many cases, the values to be captured from public lands—such as traditional ways of living and the aesthetics of wild places—would not give the kinds of monetary return that profit-conscious investors seek. For that reason, ample enough opportunity would exist for people like Dayton Hyde to muster their resources and to create landscapes for wildlife, fisheries, and recreation.

Much of the federal range would become the domain of associations and communities. Single individuals or large for-profit corporations would simply lack the resources or the business interest to acquire many of the most desirable public lands—the landscapes holding the greatest promise for recreation, wildlife, and wilderness and the least potential for profitable logging and grazing. Moreover, even if those lands held economically valuable forage and timber resources (minerals and energy resources are excluded from the initial phase of divestiture), and even if individuals and corporations could raise substantial capital, there would still be no guarantee that they could obtain shares at reasonable prices. Just as wealthy individuals and corporations have not monopolized private lands in the United States in the past, it is just as likely that they would not strive to monopolize divested public lands in the future. In contrast, associations and communities would be able to tap the enormous wealth of shares held by their members and apply them toward commonly held goals. By the sheer weight of membership alone, they would be the biggest winners in the reshuffling of federal lands from bureaucracies to the American people.

Environmentalists—ranging from conservationists to wildlife enthusiasts to wilderness preservationists—would have the opportunity of a lifetime. Their organizations would be free to solicit tax-deductible shares from members and from other citizens supporting their visions of stewardship and protection. They could harness that public support to the cause of environmental good—all made possible because people's shares, not dollars, would control the destiny of the western range. They would be able to focus their efforts and shares where they might be most effective, in the acquisition of wilderness and in the making of wildlife sanctuaries. And the results would be a vision of environmental good defined by them, not by bureaucracy and special interest politics. They would be responsible and accountable for the land, bearing the costs of their errors and reaping the benefits of their successes.

Voluntary associations of citizens would also enjoy unparalleled opportunity on the western range. Sportsmen's clubs and bird-watchers' societies would be able to control landscapes crucial to their interests and their visions. They could establish public corporations in which members who donated shares of stock would be the true owners of the land. Even local communities would find new and exciting options. Towns and counties might solicit shares from their citizens or offer local tax credits in exchange for shares to acquire valuable parklands, to provide a diversity of recreation, or to establish greenbelts and wildlife preserves. And for the multitude of groups and organizations that seek a place and role on the western range, there would be a ready pool of former Forest Service and BLM employees to help them manage and protect their newfound lands.

Ranchers wishing to hold on to their historical grazing lands but lacking sufficient shares might benefit from the awakening of public interest in public lands. For example, they could negotiate conservation easements with local citizens or representatives of larger environmental groups. In this way, all parties could pool their shares to the mutual benefit of each. Ranchers would be able to continue their life-style, and environmentalists would have the satisfaction of knowing that streams, wildlife, and unique landscapes would be protected forever.

Oil and timber companies might enter into similar alliances with citizen organizations and environmental groups. They could combine their shares with those of other interests to buy surface lands with the mutual understanding that resources could be extracted only so long as the ecological needs of the land were met. In some instances, restrictive covenants might be set by the legislation enabling divestiture and placed on lands having unique ecological value. Old-growth forests in the Northwest, habitat for the northern spotted owl, are good examples. Loggers and environmentalists alike would be free to make their competitive bids. The winners would have to abide by congressional deed restrictions, harnessing their visions to the needs of ancient trees and endangered owls. Timber could be cut and recreation developed so long as the overall ecological integrity of the forests remained intact.

Emerging from the market of landscape visions would be a pattern of landownership and control limited only by the imagination and energy of many minds and many visions. Private property would undoubtedly remain a major component on the western range, complementing the already substantial private holdings now in existence. And ranching and logging would still be part of the region's culture and natural history—though this time, they would be practiced in a manner more attentive to the needs of the environment and more in tune with the ecology of the land. But there would be a new wrinkle to the land, its people, and their collective future.

Across the width and breadth of what was once the federal range, an infinite array of decentralized "little commons" would spring forth. These would be lands collectively held and enjoyed by groups of various sizes and diverse interests. They would differ from the western commons of the past in one crucial feature. Their memberships would be able to protect them, wielding effective control over their use and ensuring that the right people would be accountable for their well-being. A commons that people could be part of and take pride in would at last take shape on the vast deserts, prairies, and timbered mountain ranges that lie west of the 100th meridian. Democratization would end the tragedy of the commons and open the land to its unexplored possibilities.

Unfortunately, the decision of whether or not democratization will be tried will be made in the arena of politics, not on the even playing field of a market of landscape visions. But if the plan should come to pass, the western range would at long last be freed of the rule of single visions and opened to the promise of many minds. The reign of special interests, whether livestock, timber or environmental, would be over. The destiny of the western range would be in the hands of many, not few—and it would, more often than not, entail a partnership among friends and neighbors and between communities and associations.

Divesting bureaucracy of its landed estate, however, is only the starting point for realizing the ecological and environmental potential of a market of landscape visions. The potential that comes with human diversity would evolve with time and patience, as the new custodians of the western range plied their visions, corrected their errors, and strove with single-mindedness toward environmental excellence. Lands and people historically divided by unsound laws, distant bureaucracies, and damaging multiple use policies would be reconciled in a crescendo of environmental energy and in a contagious outbreak of democratic enthusiasm. Landscapes of diversity would replace the ailing landscapes of the Forest Service and the BLM. And people and nature could find healthier and more harmonious ways to coexist on the western range.

The politics of conflict and the policies of mediocrity would give way to the peaceful process of the marketplace and the workings of tolerance and diversity. Land reform on an unprecedented scale could finally achieve what Jefferson envisioned but the state never allowed. The second American Revolution would complete what the first sought but could not attain: a virtuous republic of independent, caring, and responsible stewards of the western range.

CONCLUSION

The Ecology
of Freedom

*I*t was my second trip to the valley of Otter Creek. The first
had come almost four months earlier, at the beginning of
summer, when hay fields were still green and uncut and the
surrounding mountains were just coming to life. Now it was early
October. The hay had been cut and stacked, and the hills showed the
signs and colors of late fall. Soon the season's first snowstorm would
arrive, bringing to the land and people of Otter Creek a blast of
Arctic air and the quieting touch of winter.

It was appropriate that I should end my journey at the same place
where it began. In the interval between this visit and the evening
spent on Levi's ridge with Marc Stevens and his son, I had traveled
thousands of miles and spoken to dozens of families. Yet every range
I crossed, every story I recorded, and every conflict I witnessed
brought me back in mind and spirit to this place along the banks of
Otter Creek in the heart of the Custer National Forest.

My visit passed more quickly than I wished, but it was time to
return home and start putting words to the emotions I felt and giving
meaning to the stories I had heard. An hour before daybreak I
awoke, packed, and rested long enough to have a few words with

Marc and a parting cup of coffee. I began the final leg of my journey in the darkness of early morning.

Marc watched and waved as I pulled away from his house and headed down the dirt road past his son's trailer and around the small hill where the remains of Levi Howes's fort stood. All that was visible at that hour was the road, illuminated by my headlights. The valley and its mountains were still hidden in darkness. Staring into the moonless night, my eyes followed the winding road intently as my mind wandered up to Levi's ridge and across the valley of Otter Creek to the grasslands of the Dakotas, the high Rockies of Colorado, and the deserts of Utah and Nevada.

History, places, and people flashed through my mind in rapid succession. I saw in the early morning darkness the good and bad that I had encountered in my long travels and many visits. I recalled my first thoughts on Levi's ridge and the realization that the land and people of Otter Creek were tragically divided by unnatural boundaries segregating valleys from mountains and by laws and institutions pitting residents against wildlife and bureaucracies against both. I was reminded of the decent, conscientious people who had given me hope that a more promising future might await the lands of the western range. My spirits soared with names like Heaton, Fallini, Dickinson, Slaathaug, Hyde, Stephenson, and Spann and then sank as I realized the barriers they and others like them faced in trying to be responsible, caring stewards.

What bothered me most was the enormous waste—not just of physical resources but also of people and wildlife. More than a century of public-land grazing had proven devastating to arid rangelands and costly to the human and nonhuman life that called those lands home. Leopold's sovereign land communities were in confusion and disarray on western landscapes, victims of environmentally unsound laws and ecologically unwise bureaucracies. The good intentions of the National Environmental Policy Act—to create and maintain conditions under which man and nature can exist in productive harmony—amounted to words with little substance. On Otter Creek, every new Forest Service planning document and each additional statute and regulation made caring more difficult for Marc Stevens and good stewardship less likely for neighbors who did not share his personal ethic. By almost every indicator, all was *not* well on the western range.

When I was several miles down the highway, still well within the confines of the valley of Otter Creek, the first light of dawn broke through the rounded summits of the surrounding mountains. There was just enough light to make out a hay field to the right and a large herd of grazing mule deer. I slowed down to watch. Without warning, three large bucks sprang in front of my headlights. One remained in place, frozen by the confusion of the moment. I stopped and exchanged glances for what seemed an eternity with one of the largest and best-antlered mule deer I had ever seen. Like the people who had sheltered and fed me the night before, the buck was part of the land community of Otter Creek. His home lay in the valley as well as in the mountains. He neither recognized nor respected the political boundaries so important to land planners and wildlife managers.

The deer's natural grace and untamed strength fitted in nicely with my understanding of Leopold's dictum of ecological right and wrong. Certainly, the animal was part of the constellation of factors that "preserve the integrity, stability, and beauty of the biotic community." If he was part of that constellation, I wondered, why were not people? Why were people at odds with the valley of Otter Creek or, for that matter, at odds with the mountains, plains, and deserts that lay far beyond? Where was the land ethic that ensured harmony among the earth, the grass, the wildlife, and the ranchers?

If I understood Leopold correctly, a land ethic rested on the premise that the individual is a member of a community of interdependent parts—a social community that includes soils, bodies of water, plants, and animals. Viewed as pieces of a larger puzzle, these interdependent parts make up the land in the fullest sense. People's land ethics are simply the outcome of their belonging to and participating in a land community—the natural act of finding a place within its borders to live and work and the obligation to play a responsible and caring role in its daily life.

This was, I was certain, the origin and meaning of Leopold's vital relation—the ecological link that bonded people to their environments, making them aware of the land's needs and willing to pursue its best interests. Without that vital relation—without people assuming a responsible and participatory role in their land communities—a land ethic was impossible. With it—with people involved in their local environments and dependent on the well-being of those environments—a land ethic was possible and a healthier, more diverse western range likely.

Glancing at the frightened deer before me and conscious of the valley, mountains, and residences about me, I felt that I understood at least part of the problem of the land ethic. The land community of Otter Creek was not whole and sovereign; the vital relation was shattered and missing. Valley meadows and mountain grasslands, resident wildlife and local people, were divided and set against one another by a long tradition of well-intentioned visions and by the unrelenting tempests of political struggle. In the more than one hundred years since Otter Creek had been settled, public-land law and policy had done their best to prevent community from evolving and self-rule from being practiced. And the land and people had suffered tremendously. "One of the curious evidences that conservation programs are losing their grip," Aldo Leopold wrote, "is that they have seldom resorted to self-government as a cure for land abuse. . . . [We] have not tried democracy as a possible answer to our problems."[1] How painfully true his analysis was for Otter Creek and the rangelands that extended for thousands of miles beyond its borders.

Without a land community based on self-government, how could there be an ethic of caring? How could people muster the desire and energy to be active and concerned stewards when distant bureaucracies assumed their roles and when laws and policies effectively isolated them from meaningful contact with the land and its life? The answer was obvious on both counts: There could be no ethic of caring without self-government; there could be no stewardship in a vacuum of power and control.

Having recently read Charles Murray's *In Pursuit: Of Happiness and Good Government*, I recalled the fear he expressed that the vital "tendrils of community"—families, neighborhoods, churches, and voluntary associations—were being steadily displaced by intrusive laws and distant governments. Social community in America, Murray warned, was in danger because its duties and responsibilities were being undercut and assumed by third parties. "Take away the functions, and you take away the community," he warned.[2] The problem was not complicated. Its cause was the same as the one eroding the land community of Otter Creek and dividing the land and people of Gunnison-Crested Butte five hundred miles to the south: centralization of functions that should not be centralized.

The three deer moved swiftly and gracefully up the low hill to my left, toward Levi's more distant ridge. The morning light was brighter now, and the features of the hay fields below and the hillsides above were clearer. The land of Otter Creek was good in many ways, indicative of the men and women who lived and worked on it. Marc and his family, in particular, were persuasive reminders that there were people who could and would live with the land as caring and responsible citizens if only they were given the opportunity.

I realized that across the width and breadth of Otter Creek not all residents, if offered the chance, would strive for excellence in the same way or to the same extent as the Stevenses. There was risk in many visions, just as there was risk in freedom. It meant giving full rein to people whose stewardship was untested and whose land ethics were unknown. It meant giving up the predictability and security of bureaucracies and their management, however bland the two might be, for the uncertainty and unpredictability that naturally comes with freedom and diversity. I was struck by one thought, though, as the last of the mule deer topped the crest and moved down the other side. Nature entailed risk, and the very nature of diversity was risk.

Diversity and risk, however, were only part of the equation I was beginning to unravel. Anterior to both was tolerance, the state of mind that made diversity acceptable and risk unavoidable. Tolerance, I knew, was necessary if dreamers like Levi Howes and Dayton Hyde were ever to have the opportunity to test their notions and stretch their ambitions to the limits of their personal visions. A healthier western range meant that people would have to be free to envision what its landscapes should look like and would have to have the power to make those landscapes come true.

Thoughts of tolerance captivated me, keeping my mind on Levi's ridge and my vehicle on the same spot where the buck had paused and sent my imagination wandering. It seemed so natural to envision a western range freed of all the limits and historical baggage that came with intolerant visions and the well-intentioned policies and programs of the Forest Service and the BLM. After all, those two agencies were merely human artifacts—creations envisioned and molded by the minds and hands of just a few people. Why should they be considered any more sacred or held in any greater esteem than the visions of Bard Heaton and Donna Slaathaug or the visions of millions of other Americans?

Dawn had come fully to Otter Creek as I headed down the paved road toward home. The features of the valley and the mountains were sharp and clear in the fresh morning air, and my eyes hungrily searched for details that would freshen my mind in later months as I tried to recall the emotions and thoughts of this day. Gone were the misgivings that had lingered in my mind from the first evening on Levi's ridge until this morning's departure from the Circle Bar in the predawn solitude. Somehow the surprise and exhilaration of seeing the three bucks in the early glow of daybreak had turned my mind toward the future. I now felt optimism and hope as I began to perceive the first glimmerings of an ecology of freedom.

I could now see the greater significance of Otter Creek and of the many distant places that had been but brief interludes along a journey now concluding. An ecology of freedom meant restoration of Leopold's vital relation; it meant granting people and their visions the power to control their own destinies, the ability to seek landscapes that are intensely personal and that only nature can rule as being ecologically fit or not. And it would begin with a market of landscape visions—a political climate in which no single vision could emerge victorious on the merit of force alone. That market, and its underlying ecology, would allow no option in the matter of tolerance: Visions would have to compete democratically in the marketplace of ideas and beliefs.

An ecology of freedom would also mean that Murray's tendrils of social community would have muscle and purpose. The land community would be rescued from the airy realm of utopian musings and brought down to earth in the practical affairs of people and their environments. Power and control in the land community would be withdrawn from the visionary state and returned to where they have rightfully belonged from the start— in the hearts, minds, and hands of visionary individuals and their communities. There would no longer be a need to resign oneself and one's conscience to the dictates of land administrators and the recriminations of the righteous. Nature alone would be the arbiter between people and their land communities on the vast landscapes of the western range.

It all made so much sense in the euphoria of an October morning. The basic unit of working democracy was the land community. And enlivening that community—reconnecting the vital relation through a market of landscape visions—was the most basic of political and ecological acts. It meant people taking control of their lives and becoming partners in the affairs of their environments. It meant the politics of decentralism—the raucous debates of a New England town meeting as well as the voluntary negotiations between landowners and concerned neighbors wishing to make the land healthier and more fruitful for both people and wildlife.

An ecology of freedom, as I was coming to understand, also meant that duty came with membership in the land community. There would be no institutional barriers restricting or determining people's relationship to the land and its life. People would be free to act as full and equal members of their local communities. But they would be responsible and accountable for their actions. They would enjoy the benefits of the land community and share in the costs of the land's maintenance. Their relation to the western range would be a function of living and working. The ecology of freedom, so dependent on the workings of accountability and responsibility, would offer hope that people and nature might indeed coexist in harmony—that the lands that nobody wanted would at last be wanted and stewarded by caring and thoughtful people.

I wondered what the western range would be like if there were hundreds of thousands of caretakers like Donna Slaathaug and Ken Spann, people even freer to explore the possibilities of new visions and to bring grace and beauty where stubble and erosion were too often the case. The answer lay behind me in a remote valley in southeastern Montana and before me in a flowering of landscape visions. I could see it in the rich meadows of the valley of Gunnison-Crested Butte, hear it in the songs of a thousand birds nesting in a marsh near Chiloquin, and taste it on a balmy summer evening on a distant ridge above Otter Creek. The images that filled my senses, and the many visions that gave them life, promised no utopia—at least no single vision of a perfect western range. But the more diverse and more caring world they heralded was reachable, given tolerance toward people and goodwill toward the land.

Notes

INTRODUCTION: LEVI'S RIDGE

1. For background information on the CMR, see U.S. Department of the Interior, "Final Environmental Impact Statement for the Management of Charles M. Russell National Wildlife Refuge" (Denver: Government Printing Office, 1986). I supplemented the CMR report with additional sources: CMR wildlife biologist (name withheld by request); Bureau of Land Management wildlife biologist, Judith Resource Area (name withheld by request); Pug Jorgenson, Bureau of Land Management supervisory range conservationist, Judith Resource Area; Don Nelson, resource area manager, Big Dry Resource Area; D. Dean Bibles, director, Oregon State Office, Bureau of Land Management; Allan Savory, founding director, Center for Holistic Resource Management; Robert Ross, retired, Soil Conservation Service, Bozeman, MT; and Dr. John R. Lacey, Montana State University, Bozeman. My sources indicate that livestock reductions on the refuge have adversely affected wildlife, livestock, and range conditions both on and off the CMR. The original intent of the CMR was to provide habitat for sharp-tailed grouse and antelope. But the greatest numbers of grouse and antelope are found on adjacent BLM and private lands, which, because of CMR livestock reductions, must now support more livestock than before. In addition, forage on the underutilized grasslands of the CMR is coarse and relatively unpalatable (made worse by the lack of fire to rejuvenate it). This is forcing elk onto private lands and increasing competition between elk and cattle for food and habitat.

CHAPTER 1: WINDOW TO THE WESTERN RANGE

1. Levi S. Howes, *Montana Territory* (Sheridan, WY: Levi S. Howes, 1927), pp. 30–39.
2. Public Lands Council, "Fact Sheet: The Public Lands Livestock Industry" (Washington, DC: Public Lands Council, National Cattlemen's Association, and National Wool Growers Association, 1988).
3. Public Lands Council, "Fact Sheet."
4. Public Lands Council, "Fact Sheet"; U.S. Department of Agriculture and

Notes

U.S. Department of the Interior, "Grazing Fee Review and Evaluation: A Report from the Secretary of Agriculture and the Secretary of the Interior" (Washington, DC: Government Printing Office, 1986).

5. Marion Clawson and Burnell Held, *The Federal Lands: Their Use and Management* (Baltimore: Resources for the Future, distributed by Johns Hopkins University Press, 1957), pp. 48–50; Marion Clawson, *The Federal Lands Since 1956* (Baltimore: Resources for the Future, distributed by Johns Hopkins University Press, 1967).

6. Phillip O. Foss, *Politics and Grass* (Seattle: University of Washington Press, 1960), p. 197.

7. George P. Marsh, *The Earth as Modified by Human Action* (New York: Scribner, Armstrong & Co., 1874), p. 33.

8. William K. Wyant, *Westward in Eden* (Berkeley: University of California Press, 1982), p. 1.

9. Michael Frome, *The Forest Service* (Boulder, CO: Westview Press, 1984), p. 123.

10. Bernard Shanks, *This Land Is Your Land* (San Francisco: Sierra Club Books, 1984), p. 173.

11. Despite significant declines of wildlife populations throughout the West since settlement, marked recoveries have occurred for some species in recent decades. Among the references I consulted for wildlife statistics, the following were most useful: U.S. Department of the Interior, *Restoring America's Wildlife 1937–1987* (Washington, DC: Government Printing Office, 1987); Olaus J. Murie, *The Elk of North America* (Washington, DC: Wildlife Management Institute, 1966); and James A. Tober, *Who Owns the Wildlife?* (Westport, CT: Greenwood Press, 1981).

12. Clawson, *Federal Lands Since 1956*, pp. 6–7.

13. Livestock is not the only source of western land damage. Plowing of High Plains grasslands during the homestead era was probably more destructive than domestic stock. Over twenty-five million acres were plowed by 1936, many of which were later converted to national grasslands. Since 1936, an additional fifty million acres of rangeland have been plowed and turned into marginal cropland.

14. Frome, *The Forest Service*, pp. 130–131; House Committee on Government Operations, "Federal Grazing Program: All Is Not Well on the Range," 99th Cong., 2d sess., 1986, H. Rept. 99–593, pp. 26–27; U.S. General Accounting Office, "Rangeland Management: More Emphasis Needed on Declining and Overstocked Grazing Allotments" (Washington: DC: Government Printing Office, 1988), pp. 22–24. These condition estimates are imprecise and optimistic. Except for Frome's 10 percent figure for the Southwest (which may be on the low side), the condition percentages for Forest Service and BLM lands are probably too generous.

15. Numerical estimates of range improvement over the past century are imprecise and abstract. A stronger and clearer case for stabilized or improving range is made by three photographic surveys of past and present rangeland conditions: James R. Hastings and Raymond M. Turner, *The Changing Mile* (Tucson: University of Arizona Press, 1980); Kendall L. Johnson, *Rangeland Through Time* (Mis-

cellaneous publication 50, Agricultural Experiment Station, University of Wyoming, April 1987); and Walter S. Phillips, *Vegetational Changes in Northern Great Plains* (Tucson: University of Arizona Press, 1963).

16. S. Johnson, "Federal Grazing Fees Are Too Low," *Denver Post,* 14 March 1987, editorial page.

17. U.S. General Accounting Office, "Rangeland Management," pp. 24–25.

18. Marsh, *The Earth,* pp. 38–39.

19. Aldo Leopold, *A Sand County Almanac* (New York: Oxford University Press, 1979), p. 203.

20. Leopold, *A Sand County Almanac,* p. 214.

21. Leopold, *A Sand County Almanac,* p. 204.

22. Leopold, *A Sand County Almanac,* pp. 224–225.

23. William Voigt, Jr., *Public Grazing Lands* (New Brunswick, NJ: Rutgers University Press, 1976), p. 33.

24. Bernard De Voto, "The West Against Itself," *Harper's Magazine* 194:1160 (January 1947), p. 3.

25. Denzel Ferguson and Nancy Ferguson, *Sacred Cows at the Public Trough* (Bend, OR: Maverick Publications, 1983); Lynn Jacobs, *Free Our Public Lands!* (Tucson, AZ: Lynn Jacobs, 1987). These two works exemplify the degree of anger that motivates some opponents of public-land ranching.

26. Edward Abbey, "Even the Bad Guys Wear White Hats," *Harper's Magazine* 272:51–5 (January 1986), pp. 53–54.

27. John Muir, *Our National Parks* (New York: AMS Press, 1970), p. 361.

28. The following works will provide an introduction to the new resource economics: John Baden and Andrew Dana, "The New Resource Economics: Toward an Ideological Synthesis," Working Paper no. 85–9 (Bozeman, MT: Political Economy Research Center, 1985); Garrett Hardin and John Baden, eds., *Managing the Commons* (San Francisco: W. H. Freeman & Co., 1977); John Baden, ed., *Earth Day Reconsidered* (Washington, DC: The Heritage Foundation, 1980); John Baden and Richard L. Stroup, eds., *Bureaucracy vs. Environment* (Ann Arbor: University of Michigan Press, 1981); Richard L. Stroup and John A. Baden, *Natural Resources: Bureaucratic Myths and Environmental Management* (San Francisco: Pacific Research Institute for Public Policy, 1983); and Terry L. Anderson and Donald R. Leal, *Free Market Environmentalism* (San Francisco: Pacific Research Institute for Public Policy, 1991).

29. John P. Workman, *Range Economics* (New York: Macmillan Publishing Co., 1986), p. 13.

CHAPTER 2: LIKE A CITY UPON A HILL

1. John Winthrop, quoted in Loren Baritz, *City on a Hill: A History of Ideas and Myths in America* (New York: John Wiley & Sons, 1964), p. 3. In trying to capture the essence of landscape visions, I found Winthrop's quote irresistible. It captures, I believe, the religious content and fervor of landscape visions. For that reason, I use it liberally throughout the book.

Notes

2. Alexis de Tocqueville, *Democracy in America*, 2 vols., ed. Phillips Bradley (New York: Alfred A. Knopf, 1945), vol. II, p. 74.

3. Henry David Thoreau, "Walking," *The Works of Thoreau*, ed. Henry Seidel Canby (Boston: Houghton Mifflin Co., 1937), p. 672.

4. Thomas Sowell, *A Conflict of Visions* (New York: William Morrow & Co., 1987).

5. Arthur A. Ekirch, Jr., *Man and Nature in America* (Lincoln: University of Nebraska Press, 1973), p. 68.

6. John Muir, *Our National Parks* (New York: AMS Press, 1970), p. 359.

7. Muir, *Our National Parks*, p. 336; John Muir, quoted in William D. Rowley, *U.S. Forest Service Grazing and Rangelands* (College Station: Texas A & M University Press, 1985), p. 25.

8. John Locke, "Of Property," *Second Treatise of Government*, in *The Works of John Locke* (London: Thomas Tegg 1823; reprint ed., Germany: Scientia Verlag Aalen, 1963), pp. 356–357.

9. Henry Nash Smith, *Virgin Land: The American West as Symbol and Myth* (New York: Vintage Books, 1957), p. 141.

10. Thomas Jefferson, *Notes on the State of Virginia*, quoted in *The Life and Selected Writings of Thomas Jefferson*, ed. Adrienne Koch and William Peden (New York: Random House, 1944), p. 280.

11. Jefferson, *Notes on the State of Virginia*, in Koch and Peden, *Writings of Thomas Jefferson*, p. 280.

CHAPTER 3: VISIONS UPON THE LAND

1. Paul A. Delcourt et al., "Holocene Ethnobotanical and Paleoecological Record of Human Impact on Vegetation in the Little Tennessee River Valley, Tennessee," *Quaternary Research* 25 (1986), pp. 330–349.

2. Chaco Canyon was one of several homes of the Anasazi Indians. After generations of residence in Chaco Canyon, the depletion of water, vegetation, and soils—a depletion caused by their activities—forced them to abandon their cliff dwellings. Today, Chaco Canyon is the site of the Chaco Culture National Historical Park.

3. The details of the Sheldon National Wildlife Refuge were conveyed to me by D. Dean Bibles, director, Oregon State Office, Bureau of Land Management. Mr. Bibles shared the information with me during our two-year joint participation (1988–1990) in the Keystone Policy Dialogue on Biological Diversity on Federal Lands—a conference hosted by the major federal land management agencies. Mr. Bibles's knowledge of the Sheldon refuge comes from the fact that it borders Oregon and affects BLM lands in Oregon—lands for which he has exclusive authority.

4. There is another lesson to be learned from the Sheldon National Wildlife Refuge: Livestock is not necessarily incompatible with wildlife. Certainly, a landscape vision that precludes livestock is as valid as one that includes them. But in selecting the vision of exclusion, we should not rely on the tenuous argument that

livestock and wildlife cannot coexist. In choosing to eliminate livestock from a landscape, it is more honest—and accurate—simply to say that wildlife is more desirable than cattle or sheep.

5. The role and importance of diversity in biological systems is a subject of dispute among ecologists. Questions have been raised regarding the ecological advantage of diversity (Robert M. May, *Stability and Complexity in Model Ecosystems* [Princeton: Princeton University Press, 1974]; John Passmore, *Man's Responsibility for Nature: Ecological Problems and Western Traditions* [New York: Charles Scribner's Sons, 1974]). Despite lingering questions, most ecologists view biological diversity as a positive ecosystem attribute. In regard to the function of diversity in social systems, there appears to be general agreement: It is vital.

6. Robert H. Whittaker, *Communities and Ecosystems* (New York: Macmillan Publishing Co., 1975), pp. 35–36.

7. A detailed account of Forest Service fire policy appears in Ashley L. Schiff, *Fire and Water: Scientific Heresy in the Forest Service* (Cambridge: Harvard University Press, 1962).

8. Schiff, *Fire and Water,* p. 170.

CHAPTER 4: JEFFERSON'S LEGACY

1. Details for this narrative were taken from Levi Howes's autobiography, *Montana Territory* (Sheridan, WY: Levi S. Howes, 1927), and recollections of Marc Stevens.

2. Howes, *Montana Territory,* p. 64.

3. *Yellowstone Journal,* 23 August 1884, cited in Dan Fulton, *Failure on the Plains* (Bozeman: Big Sky Books, Montana State University, 1982), pp. 21–22.

4. Fulton, *Failure on the Plains,* p. 17.

5. Ray Allen Billington, *Westward Expansion,* 3d ed. (New York: Macmillan Publishing Co., 1967), pp. 681–682.

6. Billington, *Westward Expansion,* p. 682.

7. Paul H. Roberts, *Hoof Prints on Forest Ranges* (San Antonio: Naylor Co., 1963), p. 17.

8. Roberts, *Hoof Prints on Forest Ranges,* p. 18.

9. Roberts, *Hoof Prints on Forest Ranges,* p. 11.

10. Roberts, *Hoof Prints on Forest Ranges,* p. 11.

11. Fulton, *Failure on the Plains,* pp. 42–43.

12. House Committee on Public Lands, "To Provide for the Orderly Use, Improvement, and Development of the Public Range: Hearings on H.R. 2835," 73d Cong., 1st sess., 1933, p. 70.

13. Interview with Bard Heaton, public-land rancher, Alton, UT, 13 July 1988.

14. W. C. Barnes and James T. Jardine, "Meat Situation in the U.S. Part II: Livestock Production in the Eleven Far Western Range States," USDA Report no. 110 (Washington, DC: U.S. Department of Agriculture, 1916), p. 16.

15. Albert F. Potter, quoted in William D. Rowley, *U.S. Forest Service Grazing and Rangelands* (College Station: Texas A & M University Press, 1985), p. 21.

16. Albert F. Potter, "The National Forests and the Livestock Industry," in Rowley, *Forest Service Grazing and Rangelands,* p. 16.

17. E. R. Jackman and R. A. Long, *The Oregon Desert* (Caldwell, ID: Caxton Printers, 1964), pp. 139–140.

18. Interview with Clayton Atkins, public-land rancher, St. George, UT, 14 July 1988.

19. Interview with Lloyd Sorenson, public-land rancher, Elko, NV, 15 July 1988.

20. The magnitude of overgrazing on public rangelands is illustrated by past and current stocking rates on the Arizona Strip. At the closing of the open range, federal records indicated that 30,757 cattle, 147,962 sheep, 10,735 goats, and 146 horses grazed the area. But a half-century later, BLM figures showed only 15,000 head of cattle licensed to graze the same area. Despite the reduction in livestock numbers, debate continues on proper stocking for the Arizona Strip. Environmentalists are seeking even lower stocking levels to preserve habitat for the desert tortoise.

21. U.S. Department of Agriculture, Forest Service, "The Western Range," Senate Document no. 199, 74th Cong., 2d sess. (Washington, DC: Government Printing Office, 1936), p. 3.

22. Albert F. Potter, "National Forests and the Livestock Industry," quoted in Rowley, *Forest Service Grazing and Rangelands,* p. 16.

23. Albert F. Potter, quoted in Rowley, *Forest Service Grazing and Rangelands,* pp. 20–21.

24. Garrett Hardin, "The Tragedy of the Commons," *Science* 162 (1968), pp. 1243–1248.

25. Hardin, "Tragedy of the Commons," p. 1245.

26. Hardin, "Tragedy of the Commons," p. 1245.

27. George C. Coggins and Margaret Lindeberg-Johnson, "The Law of Public Rangeland Management II: The Commons and the Taylor Act," *Environmental Law* 13:1 (Fall 1982), p. 23.

28. John Baden, "Property Rights, Cowboys and Bureaucrats: A Modest Proposal," *Earth Day Reconsidered,* ed. John Baden (Washington, DC: The Heritage Foundation, 1980), p. 72.

29. Thomas Jefferson to Peter Carr, 10 August 1787, quoted in *The Life and Selected Writings of Thomas Jefferson,* ed. Adrienne Koch and William Peden (New York: Random House, 1944), p. 431.

30. Thomas Jefferson to John Jay, 23 August 1785, in Koch and Peden, *Writings of Thomas Jefferson,* p. 377.

31. J. Hector St. John (Michel de Crèvecoeur), *Letters from an American Farmer* (New York: E. P. Dutton, 1957), p. 36.

32. Thomas Jefferson to John Jay, 23 August 1785, in Koch and Peden, *Writings of Thomas Jefferson,* p. 377.

33. Thomas Jefferson to James Madison, 28 October 1785, quoted in *A Jefferson Profile,* ed. Saul K. Padover (New York: John Day Co., 1956), p. 37.

34. Horace Greeley, *New York Daily Tribune,* 1 April 1848 and 6 May 1852,

quoted in Roy M. Robbins, *Our Landed Heritage* (Princeton: Princeton University Press, 1942), pp. 106, 108.

35. Walter Prescott Webb, *The Great Plains* (New York: Grosset & Dunlap, 1972), p. 424.

36. *Laramie Sentinel,* 8 January 1887, cited in David M. Emmons, *Garden in the Grasslands* (Lincoln: University of Nebraska Press, 1971), p. 191.

37. U.S. Department of the Interior, "Annual Report of the Secretary" (Washington, DC: U.S. Department of the Interior, 1902), p. 11.

38. Gifford Pinchot, *The Fight for Conservation* (Seattle: University of Washington Press, 1967), p. 11.

39. Silas Bent, Colorado Stock Growers' Association, quoted in Emmons, *Garden in the Grasslands,* p. 190.

40. John Wesley Powell, *Report on the Lands of the Arid Region of the United States* (Cambridge: Harvard University Press, 1962), p. 32.

41. Powell, *Lands of the Arid Region,* p. 32.

42. General Land Office, "Report of the Commissioner" (Washington, DC: Government Printing Office, 1875), pp. 6–9.

43. William Jones, rancher, Eddy County, NM, quoted in Gary D. Libecap, *Locking Up the Range* (Cambridge: Ballinger Publishing Co., 1981), p. 16.

44. *Yellowstone Journal,* 23 August 1884, quoted in Fulton, *Failure on the Plains,* pp. 21–22.

45. "Unlawful Enclosures Act," 48th Cong., 2d sess., 1885. Shortly after passage of the Unlawful Enclosures Act, President Grover Cleveland issued Proclamation No. 3 (7 August 1885). The proclamation prohibited anyone from obstructing free passage on public lands and ordered federal officials to enforce the provisions of the Unlawful Enclosures Act.

46. The origin of these state grazing districts is described in Paul Gates, *History of Public Land Law Development* (Washington, DC: Zenger Publishing Co., 1968), pp. 608–610. Their operation is detailed in Montana Association of State Grazing Districts, *Montana State Grazing Districts Handbook,* 5th rev. ed. (Helena: Montana Department of Natural Resources and Conservation, 1983).

47. F. Berkes et al., "The Benefits of the Commons," *Nature* 340 (13 July 1989), p. 91.

48. E. N. Anderson, "A Malaysian Tragedy of the Commons," *The Question of the Commons,* ed. Bonnie M. McCay and James M. Acheson (Tucson: University of Arizona Press, 1987), p. 334.

49. George C. Coggins, "The Law of Public Rangeland Management I: The Extent and Distribution of Federal Power," *Environmental Law* 12:3 (Spring 1982), pp. 541–542.

CHAPTER 5: PROGRESSIVISM'S RESPONSE

1. This narrative is based on my professional involvement with the I-Bar-X ranch as a range specialist (1985–1989) with the New Mexico Department of Agriculture, New Mexico State University, Las Cruces. Many details of the narrative

Notes

are documented in Karl Hess IV and Skeeter Paul, "The Lincoln Report" (Santa Fe: New Mexico Department of Agriculture and New Mexico Energy, Minerals and Natural Resources Department, 1988), pp. 29, 143–151.

2. Frederick V. Coville, "Forest Growth and Sheep Grazing in the Cascade Mountains of Oregon," U.S. Department of Agriculture, Division of Forestry Bulletin no. 15 (Washington, DC: U.S. Department of Agriculture, 1894), p. 10.

3. Gifford Pinchot, *The Fight for Conservation* (Seattle: University of Washington Press, 1967), pp. 79–80.

4. Gifford Pinchot, *Breaking New Ground* (New York: Harcourt, Brace and Co., 1947), p. 505.

5. Pinchot, *The Fight for Conservation,* p. 77.

6. Pinchot, *The Fight for Conservation,* pp. 95–96.

7. Gifford Pinchot, quoted in William Voigt, Jr., *Public Grazing Lands* (New Brunswick, NJ: Rutgers University Press, 1976), p. 45.

8. Pinchot, *Breaking New Ground,* p. 509.

9. Pinchot, *The Fight for Conservation,* p. 81.

10. Pinchot, *The Fight for Conservation,* p. 81.

11. U.S. Department of Agriculture, Forest Service, "A National Plan for American Forestry," Senate Document no. 12, 73d Cong., 1st sess. (Washington, DC: Government Printing Office, 1933), p. 1589.

12. H. A. Pearson, "Statement by Candidate for Office," *Rangelands* 8:5 (1986), p. 244.

CHAPTER 6: THE GRASSLAND EXPERIMENT

1. U.S. Department of Agriculture, Forest Service, "The National Grasslands of the Rocky Mountain Region" (Washington, DC: Government Printing Office, 1985), p. 12.

2. McKenzie County Homestead Map, Township no. 148N, Range 103W (Watford City, ND: County Records, n.d.).

3. U.S. Department of Agriculture, "The Land Utilization Program 1934 to 1964," Agricultural Economic Report no. 85 (Washington, DC: Government Printing Office,1965), p. vi.

4. "The Bankhead-Jones Farm Tenant Act," Public Law no. 210, 75th Cong., 1st. Sess., 22 July 1937, in *United States Statutes at Large,* v. 50, Part 1, Public Laws (Washington, DC: Government Printing Office, 1937), pp. 552, 525.

5. U.S. Department of Agriculture, "Land Utilization Program," pp. v, 12.

6. Interview with Ingebert G. Fauske, South Dakota appointee to the 1964 Public Land Law Review Commission and national grasslands historian, Wall, SD, 7 July 1988.

7. House Subcommittee on Public Lands, "Management and Disposition of Acquired Lands Under the Bankhead-Jones Act: Hearings" (Washington, DC: Government Printing Office, 26 July 1954), p. 27.

8. Fall River County Warranty Deed Records (Hot Springs, SD: County Records, 1938–1939), Book 19, pp. 24–27, 37–39; Book 56, pp. 56–57, 65–66. David

P. Rudeen, a land exchange and appraisal specialist for the Nebraska National Forest in Hot Springs, South Dakota, directed me to these warranty deeds. He indicated that he had located similar warranty deeds in other counties. He also stated that although the overwhelming majority of land transfers to the federal government during this period were done by direct sales, as many as 5 to 10 percent were probably achieved by condemnation.

9. Ingebert G. Fauske to Mr. and Mrs. Dwayne Slaathaug, 27 January 1987, in Dwayne and Donna Slaathaug, personal papers, Ft. Pierre, SD, p. 4.

10. Slaathaug, personal papers, p. 4.

11. E. H. Aicher and S. M. Linge, "Institutional Adjustments Survey: Land Utilization Project, McKenzie County, North Dakota, LU-ND-1" (Washington, DC: U.S. Department of Agriculture, Soil Conservation Service, Institutional Adjustments Division, SCS Region 7, February 1941), pp. 2–3.

12. Dale Greenwood, personal papers, Watford City, ND (n.d.). Select portions of these papers were provided to me during my interview with Dale Greenwood, president, McKenzie County Grazing Association, Watford City, 30 June 1988.

13. Greenwood, personal papers. The quotation is from a typed transcript of the original brochure.

14. Public Land Law Review Commission, *One Third of the Nation's Land: A Report to the President and to the Congress by the Public Land Law Review Commission* (Washington, DC: Government Printing Office, 1970), p. 180.

15. Joyce M. Byerly, "Permittee Association Cooperative Administration on Forest Service National Grasslands" (Watford City, ND: McKenzie County Grazing Association, n.d.). The first part of this paper provides a brief historical overview of grassland associations. Byerly, secretary-treasurer of the McKenzie County Grazing Association, notes that when control of the grasslands was transferred from the SCS to the Forest Service, "there was dissension among Forest Service personnel about continuing the SCS policy of placing the responsibility for management of Title III (LU) lands . . . in the local organizations of users or converting [them] . . . to National Forest status and be subject to usual regulations and policies." The latter option was chosen, effectively undermining the authority and effectiveness of grassland associations.

16. Greenwood, personal papers.

17. Greenwood, personal papers. Additional information was provided in interviews with Dale Greenwood and Dwayne Slaathaug (Slaathaug, president of the National Grasslands Association and a public-land rancher, was interviewed in Fort Pierre, SD, on 28 June 1988).

18. U.S. Department of Agriculture, "Land Utilization Program," p. vi.

19. U.S. Department of Agriculture, Forest Service, "Grasslands of the Rocky Mountain Region," p. 20.

20. Interview with Dwayne Slaathaug, president, National Grasslands Association, and public-land rancher, Fort Pierre, SD, 28 June 1988.

21. Marie Sandoz, *Old Jules,* quoted in Paul W. Gates, *History of Public Land Law Development* (Washington, DC: Zenger Publishing Co., 1968), p. 498.

22. Eleanor H. Hinman, "History of Farm Land Prices in Eleven Nebraska

Counties, 1873–1933," Research Bulletin no. 72, Experiment Station (Lincoln: University of Nebraska, 1934), p. 22.

23. Harold Hedges, *Economic Aspects of the Cattle Industry of the Nebraska Sand-hills,* quoted in Gates, *Public Land Law Development,* p. 501.

CHAPTER 7: TECHNOCRACY AND EMPIRE

1. Interview with Bard Heaton, public-land rancher, Alton, UT, 13 July 1988.

2. Robert Kharasch, *The Institutional Imperative* (New York: Charterhouse Books, 1973), p. 13.

3. Kharasch, *The Institutional Imperative,* p. 60.

4. Gary D. Libecap, *Locking Up the Range* (Cambridge: Ballinger Publishing Co., 1981); Marion Clawson and Burnell Held, *The Federal Lands: Their Use and Management* (Baltimore: Resources for the Future, distributed by Johns Hopkins University Press, 1957); Marion Clawson, *The Federal Lands Since 1956* (Baltimore: Resources for the Future, distributed by Johns Hopkins University Press, 1967); Senate Committee on Appropriations, "Department of the Interior and Related Agencies Appropriations Bill, 1991," 101st Cong., 2d sess., 1991, S. Rept. 101–534. In addition to these sources, statistics on BLM operations were provided by Robert Nelson, senior economist, Office of Policy Analysis, U.S. Department of the Interior, and Billy Templeton, director, Division of Rangeland Resources, Bureau of Land Management.

5. Obtaining comprehensive range improvement data for the BLM proved difficult. Through the persistence of Jerry Townsend, range staff director, New Mexico State Office, Bureau of Land Management, I was able to obtain raw data for all western states. Those data were analyzed and initially presented in Karl Hess, "Landscape Visions and the Western Land Ethic: The Public Grazing Lands" (Paper presented at Liberty Fund Conference on Liberty and the Land Ethic, Big Sky, MT, 11–14 June 1987), pp. 61–66. It should be noted that the data I used on BLM range improvement expenditures for the period prior to the passage of the Federal Lands Policy Management Act of 1976 excludes special congressional appropriations, most important of which was the appropriation for the Vale Rangeland Rehabilitation Program. As I suggest in chapter 9, the dollars spent on the Vale Program did more to rescue a rural economy than it did to improve rangeland conditions. Consequently, its omission from my data does not significantly affect my conclusion that BLM range improvement efforts and expenditures prior to 1976 were minimal.

6. Thadis Box, Don D. Dwyer, and Frederic H. Wagner, "The Public Range and Its Management: A Report to the President's Council on Environmental Quality" (Washington, DC: Council on Environmental Quality, 19 March 1976), pp. 33–35.

7. U.S. Department of the Interior, Bureau of Land Management, "Effects of Livestock Grazing on Wildlife, Watershed, Recreation, and Other Resource Values in Nevada" (Washington, DC: Government Printing Office, 1975).

8. U.S. Department of the Interior, Bureau of Land Management, Division of

Rangeland Resources, "Range Condition Report Prepared for the Senate Committee on Appropriations" (In-house report to Congress, Washington, DC, 1975).

9. Robert H. Nelson, senior economist, Office of Policy Analysis, U.S. Department of the Interior, "The New Range Wars: Environmentalists versus Cattlemen for the Public Rangelands" (In-house paper, Washington, DC, 1980), p. 39.

10. Nelson, "The New Range Wars," p. 40.

11. Nelson, "The New Range Wars," pp. 40–41.

12. Billy Templeton, director, Division of Rangeland Resources, Bureau of Land Management, personal communication, 1988.

13. U.S. Department of the Interior, Bureau of Land Management, Division of Rangeland Resources, "1984 Range Condition Report" (Washington, DC: Government Printing Office, 1984).

14. Hess, "Landscape Visions," pp. 61–66. See note 5 above.

15. National Governors' Association, "BLM Use of Range Improvement Fund 8100," Report to National Governors' Association Subcommittee on Range Resource Management, Task Force on Technical Aspects of Rangeland Policy, 20 May 1981.

16. U.S. General Accounting Office, "Rangeland Management: More Emphasis Needed on Declining and Overstocked Grazing Allotments" (Washington, DC: Government Printing Office, 1988), pp. 22–25.

17. The 1991 appropriation for the BLM grazing program was $40.1 million. Robert Nelson, senior economist, Office of Policy Analysis, U.S. Department of the Interior, notes in a personal communication (1991) that "the true cost of the grazing program (including overhead, etc.) is vastly greater."

18. Henry Clepper, *Professional Forestry in the United States* (Baltimore: Resources for the Future, distributed by Johns Hopkins University Press, 1971), p. 69.

19. Cited in Clepper, *Professional Forestry,* p. 136. An in-depth discussion of the specter of timber famine can be found in Sherry H. Olson, *The Depletion Myth* (Cambridge: Harvard University Press, 1971).

20. Cited in Clepper, *Professional Forestry,* p. 138.

21. U.S. Department of Agriculture, Forest Service, "A National Plan for American Forestry," Senate Document no. 12, 73d Cong., 1st sess. (Washington, DC: Government Printing Office, 1933), p. v.

22. U.S. Department of Agriculture, Forest Service, "The Western Range," Senate Document no. 199, 74th Cong., 2d sess. (Washington, DC: Government Printing Office, 1936), p. 3.

23. F. E. Mollin, secretary of the American National Livestock Association, cited in William D. Rowley, *U. S. Forest Service Grazing and Rangelands* (College Station: Texas A & M University Press, 1985), p. 157.

24. Cited in Rowley, *Forest Service Grazing and Rangelands,* p. 157.

25. Cited in Rowley, *Forest Service Grazing and Rangelands,* p. 157.

26. U.S. Department of Agriculture, Forest Service, "The Western Range," p. 54.

27. U.S. Department of Agriculture, Forest Service, "The Western Range," pp. 54–55.

28. Rowley, *Forest Service Grazing and Rangelands,* p. 173.

29. H. Rept. 733, 81st Cong., 1st sess., cited in William Voigt, Jr., *Public Grazing Lands* (New Brunswick, NJ: Rutgers University Press, 1976), p. 145.

30. Ronald M. Lanner, "Chained to the Bottom," *Bureaucracy vs. Environment,* ed. John Baden and Richard L. Stroup (Ann Arbor: University of Michigan Press, 1981), p. 156.

31. U.S. Department of Agriculture, Forest Service, "The Western Range," U.S. Department of Agriculture, Forest Service, "Annual Grazing Statistical Report" (Washington, DC: Government Printing Office, 1985). Figures provided by Robert Nelson ("The New Range Wars," p. 20) indicate an even more precipitous fall in national forest livestock numbers: from 11,925,000 AUMs in 1935 to 6,390,000 AUMs in 1972. On BLM ranges, a similar decline occurred: from 33,573,000 AUMs in 1935 to 18,308,000 AUMs in 1972.

32. U.S. Department of Agriculture, Forest Service, "Draft 1990 RPA Program," (Washington, DC: Government Printing Office, June 1989), pp. 4–20.

33. Robert Williamson, Forest Service Range Division, comments to the National Cattlemen's Association, National Grasslands Subcommittee of the Public Lands Committee, Phoenix, AZ, 29 January 1989.

34. There is no single statistic to substantiate this claim, but extrapolation from existing data suggests its validity. The cost of Forest Service range planning alone may exceed the total value of livestock forage on national forests. On BLM lands, where planning costs are approximately equivalent, Robert Nelson ("The New Range Wars," pp. 116–117) found that "the total costs involved in grazing EISs approach the total value of the forage to ranchers for livestock grazing." If we add to these planning costs all annual congressional appropriations for the Forest Service's grazing program (including such special appropriations as the Anderson-Mansfield Act) then the claim is reasonably sound.

35. Cited in U.S. General Accounting Office, "Rangeland Management," p. 24.

36. U.S. General Accounting Office, "Rangeland Management," pp. 23–25.

37. Field observations and data on the Carson National Forest crested wheatgrass plantings were taken (unpublished) during my tenure as a range resource specialist, New Mexico Department of Agriculture, New Mexico State University (1985–1989).

38. U.S. Department of Agriculture, "The Relation of Land Tenure to the Use of the Arid Grazing Lands of the Southwestern States," Agricultural Bulletin no. 1001 (Washington, DC: Government Printing Office, 1922), pp. 56–58.

39. Mike D. Young, "Pastoral Land Tenure Options in Australia," *Australian Rangeland Journal* 7:1 (1985), pp. 43–46; Mike D. Young, *Differences Between States in Arid Land Administration,* Division of Land Resources Management Series no. 4, Commonwealth Scientific and Industrial Research Organization, Australia (1979); Mike D. Young, "The Influence of Farm Size on Vegetation Condition in an Arid Area," *Journal of Environmental Management* 21 (1985), pp. 193–203.

40. National Resources Defense Council v. Hodel, 618 F. Supp. 848 (E.D. Col. 1985), cited in D. Bernard Zaleha, "The Rise and Fall of BLM's 'Cooperative

Management Agreements': A Livestock Management Tool Succumbs to Judicial Scrutiny," *Environmental Law* 17 (1986), p. 147.

41. Zaleha, "BLM's 'Cooperative Management Agreements,'" p. 147.

42. Kirk C. McDaniel and Chris D. Allison, "Will the Real Carrying Capacity Please Stand Up," Range Improvement Task Force Report (Las Cruces: New Mexico State University, Department of Animal and Range Sciences and Cooperative Extension Service, 1985).

CHAPTER 8: THE VISIONARY HARVEST

1. Interview with Joe and Susan Fallini, public-land ranchers, Tonopah, NV, 28 September 1988. In the course of the interview, I attended a meeting between the Fallinis and the BLM. It was at that meeting that I learned of the duplicitous role of the BLM in the Twin Springs horse debacle. The local BLM staff, including Ted Angle, resource area manager for the Tonopah Resource Area, did not challenge any of the details of the Fallinis' story.

2. U.S. Department of the Interior, Bureau of Land Management, "Reveille Allotment (0085) Evaluation Summary," Draft Report no. III, Tonopah Resource Area, 10 August 1988, p. 6.

3. The first appropriation to the BLM for wild horse and burro management was made in 1978. That amount was $4 million. By 1985 it had increased to $17 million, and in 1991 it hovered just above $14 million (falling from the 1985 peak due to initially high adoption rates and the early success of private wild horse sanctuaries). In contrast, appropriations for the entire BLM grazing program for 1978, 1985, and 1991 were $28 million, $31 million, and $40 million, respectively. Because of increasing populations of wild horses on western ranges, failure of private groups to obtain funding for wild horse sanctuaries (e.g., Institute of Range and the American Mustang), declines in wild horse adoption rates, and rigorous litigation by the Animal Protection Institute for wild horse protection, the cost of the BLM's wild horse program will escalate. The 1992 appropriation for wild horse and burro management calls for a $1.5 million increase. This may be just the tip of the iceberg. Currently, the BLM has fifty-two hundred mustangs in its corrals, each costing the taxpayer $1.35 per day for food alone. And the number of horses is increasing.

4. Wesley Calef, *Private Grazing and Public Lands* (Chicago: University of Chicago Press, 1960), p. 69.

5. B. Youngblood and A. B. Cox, "An Economic Study of a Typical Ranching Area on the Edwards Plateau of Texas," Texas Agricultural Experiment Station, Bulletin no. 297 (College Station: Agricultural and Mechanical College of Texas, 1922), pp. 130–131.

6. Youngblood and Cox, "An Economic Study," p. 163.

7. U.S. Department of the Interior, Bureau of Land Management, "Notice of Final Decision: Allotment No. 3056, Grazing Record No. 3199" (U.S. Department of the Interior, Bureau of Land Management, Las Cruces District Office, 17 January 1986), p. 3.

8. Letter to grazing permittees (2230) in the Gila National Forest from Richard L. Jourden, acting forest supervisor, 7 February 1985.

9. U.S. Department of the Interior, Office of the Inspector General, "Review of the Bureau of Land Management's Grazing Management and Range Improvement Programs" (Washington, DC: Government Printing Office, 1986), p. 20.

10. U.S. Department of the Interior, Bureau of Land Management, "Approval of Applications for Nonuse of Grazing Preference," BLM Director, Instruction Memorandum no. 86–623, Washington, DC, 1 August 1986.

11. Nonuse averages are based on nonuse data for the BLM from 1962 to 1984 and for the Forest Service from 1974 to 1985. BLM nonuse data are found in U.S. Department of the Interior, *Public Land Statistics* (Washington, DC: Government Printing Office, 1962–1984). Forest Service nonuse data are found in U.S. Department of Agriculture, "Annual Grazing Statistical Report" (Washington, DC: Government Printing Office, 1974–1985) and U.S. Department of Agriculture, "Report of the Forest Service" (Washington, DC: Government Printing Office, 1977–1984).

12. U.S. General Accounting Office, "Rangeland Management: More Emphasis Needed on Declining and Overstocked Grazing Allotments" (Washington, DC: Government Printing Office, 1988), p. 26.

13. George C. Coggins et al., "The Law of Public Rangeland Management I: The Extent and Distribution of Federal Power," *Environmental Law* 12:3 (Spring 1982), p. 552.

14. Karl Hess IV and Skeeter Paul, "The Lincoln Report" (Santa Fe: New Mexico Department of Agriculture and New Mexico Energy, Minerals and Natural Resources Department, 1988), p. 23.

15. Although no one has done an economic analysis of this point, intuition suggests that it is correct. Given the modest grazing budgets of the two agencies (approximately $78 million in 1991), it is certain that the monetary and opportunity costs generated by tens of thousands of individuals and hundreds of organizations attending public meetings and pursuing litigation is the greater of the two sums.

16. R. W. Behan, "The Real Cost of Planning," *Forest Watch* 10:4 (October 1989), p. 5.

17. Behan, "The Real Cost of Planning," p. 5.

18. In 1991, the predicament of wild horses worsened as thousands of mustangs faced starvation on parched rangelands. Prohibited by law from slaughtering excess wild horses and pressured by humanitarian concerns to save those that are starving, the BLM is now caring for fifty-two hundred mustangs in government corrals at a cost of at least $1.35 per day per animal. The number of mustangs in government corrals can be expected to increase sharply as wild horse adoptions decline and private wild horse sanctuaries close for lack of funding. Articles on the worsening predicament of wild horses have appeared in numerous popular magazines and journals. Typical of this coverage is "Washington Whispers—Wild Horses," *U.S. News & World Report* 3:9 (26 August–2 September 1991), p. 22.

19. While employed as a range resource specialist, New Mexico Department of

Agriculture, New Mexico State University (1985–1989), I was invited by the Forest Service to visit the Erosion Allotment and provide consultation for its management.

20. Interview with Kit and Sherry Laney, public-land ranchers, Diamond Bar Allotment, Gila National Forest, 25 October 1988. In addition to the interview, I worked with both the Laneys and the Forest Service on management for the Diamond Bar during my tenure as range resource specialist, New Mexico Department of Agriculture, New Mexico State University (1985–1989).

21. *BlueRibbon* magazine, membership advertisement for the BlueRibbon Coalition, September 1988, p. A13.

22. Interview with Dr. Alex Thal, professor of public policy and administration, Western New Mexico University, Silver City, 1 November 1988. Dr. Thal has worked extensively on the elk issue at the joint request of the Forest Service and the grazing permittees of the Apache Sitgreaves National Forest. Also see "Elk-Livestock Information Workshop" (Tucson: University of Arizona, College of Agriculture, Cooperative Extension Service, 1 October 1988).

23. Interview with Dayton Hyde, public-land rancher, Chiloquin, OR, 25 June 1988. This incident, along with others, is developed in greater detail in the narrative for chapter 12.

24. In my capacity as range resource specialist, New Mexico Department of Agriculture, New Mexico State University (1985–1989), I was invited by the Forest Service and Sterling Carter to participate in the planning of the Black Range Allotment during the period of 1986–1988.

25. Interview with Dayton Hyde, 25 June 1988. This incident is developed more thoroughly in the narrative for chapter 12.

26. Garrett Hardin, "The Tragedy of the Commons," *Science* 162 (1968), p. 1245.

CHAPTER 9: DEMISE OF STEWARDSHIP

1. I was invited by the Forest Service and Elizardo Vigil to participate in the planning of the Grass Mountain Allotment during the period of 1986–1989. During that time span, I was employed as a range resource specialist at the New Mexico Department of Agriculture, New Mexico State University. After I left my position with the university in the summer of 1989, my involvement in planning for the Grass Mountain Allotment continued on a voluntary and nonpaid basis.

2. Sabine Kremp, "A Perspective on BLM Grazing Policy," *Bureaucracy vs. Environment,* ed. John Baden and Richard L. Stroup (Ann Arbor: University of Michigan Press, 1981), pp. 132, 135.

3. Karl Hess, "Landscape Visions and the Western Land Ethic: The Public Grazing Lands" (Paper presented at Liberty Fund Conference on Liberty and the Land Ethic, Big Sky, MT, 11–14 June 1987), p. 58. Information on the Hormay Grazing System was provided by Jim McCormick, range conservationist, Roswell District, BLM, during my tenure as range resource specialist (1985–1989). Jim McCormick is currently stationed at the BLM's Las Cruces District Office in New Mexico.

4. My job as a range resource specialist provided many opportunities to become intimately acquainted with on-the-ground public-land grazing issues. One such opportunity came when I was invited by the Forest Service and the permittee (Grubbs) to participate in the planning of the Walking X Allotment during the period of 1985–1989.

5. Robert H. Nelson, senior economist, Office of Policy Analysis, U.S. Department of the Interior, "The New Range Wars: Environmentalists versus Cattlemen for the Public Rangelands" (In-house paper, Washington, DC, 1980), p. 28.

6. U.S. General Accounting Office, "Rangeland Management: More Emphasis Needed on Declining and Overstocked Grazing Allotments" (Washington, DC: Government Printing Office, 1988), pp. 40–41.

7. U.S. Department of the Interior, Office of the Inspector General, "Survey of Selected Programs of the New Mexico State Office, Bureau of Land Management," Report no. 91-I-198 (Washington, DC: U.S. Department of the Interior, November 1990), pp. 3–4.

8. Nelson, "The New Range Wars," p. 29.

9. Interview with Robert Alexander, resource area manager, Las Cruces District, BLM, 30 November 1990.

10. U.S. General Accounting Office, "Rangeland Management," pp. 41–42.

11. Karl Hess IV and Skeeter Paul, "The Lincoln Report" (Santa Fe: New Mexico Department of Agriculture and New Mexico Energy, Minerals and Natural Resources Department, 1988), pp. 68–69.

12. U.S. Department of Agriculture and U.S. Department of the Interior, "Grazing Fee Review and Evaluation: A Report from the Secretary of Agriculture and the Secretary of the Interior" (Washington, DC: Government Printing Office, February 1986), p. 7.

13. Interview with Miles and Corby McGinnis, public-land ranchers, Kemmerer, WY, 27 June 1988.

14. Interview with Jim Gould, public-land rancher, Meeteetse, WY, 22 June 1988.

15. Memo from solicitor to assistant secretary of the interior, cited in Gary D. Libecap, *Locking Up the Range* (Cambridge: Ballinger Publishing Co., 1981), p. 60.

16. William Voigt, Jr., *Public Grazing Lands* (New Brunswick, NJ: Rutgers University Press, 1976), p. 136.

17. C. W. Hudson, "Annual Grazing Report," quoted in William D. Rowley, *U.S. Forest Service Grazing and Rangelands* (College Station: Texas A & M University Press, 1985), p. 89.

18. Rowley, *Forest Service Grazing and Rangelands,* p. 89.

19. Hess, "Landscape Visions," pp. 62–65.

20. Phillip O. Foss, *Politics and Grass* (Seattle: University of Washington Press, 1960), p. 104.

21. "The Forage Resource," a public land study for the Public Land Law Review Commission by the University of Idaho and Pacific Consultants, Inc. cited in Nelson, "The New Range Wars," p. 23.

22. Interviews with Clayton and Brent Atkins, public-land ranchers, St. George UT, 13 July 1988 and 27 September 1988.
23. Interview with Herb Metzger, public-land rancher, Flagstaff, AZ, 25 September 1988.
24. Phillip Wells, quoted in Rowley, *Forest Service Grazing and Rangelands,* p. 137.
25. U.S. Department of Agriculture, Forest Service, "Revised Draft Environmental Impact Statement, Santa Fe National Forest Plan" (Washington, DC: Government Printing Office, January 1986), p. 82.
26. U.S. Department of Agriculture, Forest Service, "Santa Fe National Forest Plan," p. 82.
27. U.S. Department of Agriculture and U.S. Department of the Interior, "Grazing Fee Review and Evaluation," p. 4.
28. U.S. Department of Agriculture, "Cost and Return Estimates: Northwestern, Northeastern, Central, and Southwestern New Mexico" (Las Cruces: New Mexico State University, Cooperative Extension Service, 1985).
29. The Public Lands Council, Washington, DC, personal communication, 1988.
30. Clyde Eastman and James R. Gray, *Community Grazing: Practice and Potential in New Mexico* (Albuquerque: University of New Mexico Press, 1987), p. 132.
31. Mike D. Young, "The Influence of Farm Size on Vegetation Condition in an Arid Area," *Journal of Environmental Management* 21 (1985), p. 203.
32. Quote from Bill Grubbs, permittee of the Walking X Allotment, Silver City, NM, May 1989. See note 4 above.
33. Nita Lowry, "BLM, Wilderness Team Boots Livestock," *Western Livestock Journal* 72:44 (5 September 1988).
34. Rowley, *Forest Service Grazing and Rangelands,* p. 94.
35. U.S. Department of Agriculture, Forest Service, "Lincoln National Forest Plan" (Washington, DC: Government Printing Office, September 1986).
36. In the fall of 1988, I requested from each Forest Service regional office allotment statistics on the percentage breakdown of individual versus community allotments, allotment sizes (by AUMs and acreage), and numbers of permittees per community allotment. I received raw data (in the form of computer printouts) for grazing allotments in the Northern, Southwestern, Intermountain, Pacific Northwest, and Rocky Mountain regions.
37. U.S. Department of Agriculture, Forest Service, "Coyote District Grazing Report, Santa Fe National Forest" (Washington, DC: Government Printing Office, April 1986), p. 12.
38. Raw allotment data, Southwestern Region, Forest Service. See note 36 above.
39. Interview with Jerry Jack, executive vice president, Montana Stockgrowers Association, Helena, MT, 1 July 1988; interview with Kim Enkerud, executive assistant, Montana Stockgrowers Association, Helena, MT, 1 July 1988; Montana Association of State Grazing Districts, *Montana State Grazing Districts Handbook,*

5th rev. ed. (Helena: Montana Department of Natural Resources and Conservation, 1983).

40. Raw allotment data, Northern Region, Forest Service. See note 36 above.

41. Interview with T. Wright Dickinson, public-land rancher, Maybell, CO, 4 October 1988.

42. Personal communication, Frank DuBois, secretary-director, New Mexico Department of Agriculture (1989). The New Mexico Department of Agriculture, in conjunction with the U.S. Department of Agriculture, is responsible for predator control in New Mexico. The $12,000 figure is for New Mexico alone.

43. U.S. Department of Agriculture and U.S. Department of the Interior, "Grazing Fee Review and Evaluation," p. 7.

44. Rowley, *Forest Service Grazing and Rangelands,* p. 89.

45. My account of the Vale program is based on multiple sources: interview with Bob Skinner, public-land rancher, Jordan Valley, OR, 26 June 1988; telephone interview with Max Lieurance, BLM district manager for the Vale District (1959–1971) at the time of the Vale program, Ontario, OR, 30 November 1988; Harold Heady and James Bartolome, "The Vale Rangeland Rehabilitation Program: The Desert Repaired in Southeastern Oregon," Resource Bulletin no. PNW-70 (Portland, OR: U.S. Department of Agriculture, Forest Service, Pacific Northwest Research Station, 1977); Harold Heady, ed., "The Vale Rangeland Rehabilitation Program: An Evaluation," Resource Bulletin no. PNW-RB-157 (Portland, OR: U.S. Department of Agriculture, Forest Service, Pacific Northwest Research Station, June 1988). Historical background on the area covered by the Vale program is given in Foss, *Politics and Grass,* chapter 7, "The Battle of Soldier Creek."

46. Interview with Bob Skinner, 26 June 1988. The interpretation of the Vale Program is mine, not Bob Skinner's.

47. James W. Bartolome et al., "Changes in Vegetation," in Heady, "The Vale Rangeland Rehabilitation Program: An Evaluation," pp. 38–46.

48. Barbara H. Allen, "Wildlife, Recreation, and Other Resources," in Heady, "The Vale Rangeland Rehabilitation Program: An Evaluation," p. 68.

49. Max Lieurance, BLM district manager for the Vale District at the time of the Vale program (telephone interview, 30 November 1988), indicated that there was an attempt in the 1940s to convert community allotments to individual allotments. When he assumed control of the Vale District in 1959, he stopped the conversion process in favor of maintaining community allotments. He stated that individual allotments do provide greater stewardship incentives to permittees, but they "restrict BLM management options necessary to improve range conditions." To the extent that individual allotments did restrict BLM management options in the Vale District, they did so because of their small size, not because of their assignment to single permittees.

50. Interview with Herrick E. Hanks, Rio Puerco resource area manager, BLM, Albuquerque, NM, 1989; "Chronology of the Rio Puerco Project Area," Draft Document (Albuquerque: Bureau of Land Management, Rio Puerco Resource

Area, n.d.); Rio Puerco Resource Area files (Las Cruces: New Mexico Department of Agriculture, Division of Agricultural Programs and Resources, 1983–1984).

51. U.S. General Accounting Office, "Rangeland Management," pp. 46–52.

52. Interview with Lee Delaney, BLM resource area manager, Surprise Resource Area (part of the Modoc-Washoe ESP), Cedarville, CA, 29 September 1988; memorandum from Lee Delaney to BLM state director, CA, "GAO Report on Rangeland Management [1988], Specifically Experimental Stewardship," Surprise Resource Area, Cedarville, CA (n.d.); "Modoc/Washoe Experimental Steward-ship Program Annual Report" (Susanville, CA: Bureau of Land Management and Forest Service, 1984).

53. Interview with Joe Harris, public-land rancher, Eagleville, CA, 29 September 1988.

54. Interview with Jean Schadler, public-land rancher and member of Modoc-Washoe ESP steering committee, Adel, OR, 30 September 1988.

55. U.S. General Accounting Office, "Rangeland Management," p. 51.

CHAPTER 10: CLEANSING THE LAND

1. Interview with T. Wright Dickinson, 4 October 1988.

2. Interview with Ken Spann, public-land rancher, Crested Butte, CO, 6 October 1988.

3. John Muir, *Our National Parks* (New York: AMS Press, 1970), p. 362.

4. John Muir, quoted in William D. Rowley, *U.S. Forest Service Grazing and Rangelands* (College Station: Texas A & M University Press, 1985), p. 27.

5. John Muir, quoted in Bill Devall and George Sessions, *Deep Ecology: Living as if Nature Mattered* (Layton, UT: Gibbs Smith, Publisher, 1985), p. 104.

6. John Muir, quoted in Roderick Nash, *Wilderness and the American Mind,* rev. ed. (New Haven, CT: Yale University Press, 1973), p. 161.

7. Gifford Pinchot, quoted in Nash, *Wilderness and the American Mind,* p. 161.

8. George Wuerthner, "Public Lands Grazing—It's Time to Just Say No," *Forest Watch* 10:5 (November 1989), p. 25.

9. The slogans "Cattle Free by '93" and "No Moo by '92" are printed as bumper stickers and appear throughout the West. Earth First! takes credit for their phrasing and plays a major role in their distribution. They also occur as posters or small signs that are strategically placed on public-land ranchers' buildings, fences, and gates. Again, Earth First! takes credit for the imaginative use and placement of these antiranching slogans.

10. *Americans Outdoors: The Legacy, The Challenge,* Report of the President's Commission, with case studies (Washington, DC: Island Press, 1987).

11. Elizabeth Darby Junkin, *Lands of Brighter Destiny: The Public Lands of the American West* (Golden, CO: Fulcrum, 1986), p. 219.

12. Joseph L. Sax, "The Claim for Retention of the Public Lands," *Rethinking the Federal Lands,* ed. Sterling Brubaker (Washington, DC: Resources for the Future, 1984), pp. 144, 147.

13. Muir, *Our National Parks,* p. 361.

14. Ed Marston, "The Glory of the Commons," *High Country News,* 24 November 1986, p. 15.

15. Edward Abbey, "Even the Bad Guys Wear White Hats," *Harper's Magazine* 272:51–55 (January 1986), p. 55.

16. Bernard Shanks, *This Land Is Your Land* (San Francisco: Sierra Club Books, 1984), p. 13.

17. Bruce Babbitt, address to the annual convention of the Sierra Club, cited in Charles F. Wilkinson, "The End of Multiple Use," *High Country News,* 30 March 1987, p. 15.

18. Joseph Knowles, *Alone in the Wilderness,* quoted in Nash, *Wilderness and the American Mind,* p. 157.

19. William C. Dennis, "Wilderness Cathedrals and the Public Good" (Paper presented at conference, Environment, Energy, and Enterprise: Toward a Political Economy of Hope—An Exploration with Journalists, Political Research Center, Bozeman, MT, September 1983).

20. Joseph L. Sax, *Mountains Without Handrails: Reflections on the National Parks* (Ann Arbor: University of Michigan Press, 1980), pp. 59, 104.

21. George P. Marsh, *The Earth as Modified by Human Action* (New York: Scribner, Armstrong & Co., 1874), pp. 26, 34, 36.

22. Muir, *Our National Parks,* p. 336.

23. Captain Paul Watson, "On the Precedence of Natural Law," *Journal of Environmental Law and Litigation* 3 (1988), p. 82. The paper was delivered to the Sixth Western Public Interest Law Conference, University of Oregon School of Law, Eugene, OR, 5 March 1988. "Captain" refers to Watson's founding role in the creation of the Sea Shepherds.

24. Donald Worster, *Nature's Economy: The Roots of Ecology* (New York: Anchor Press, 1979), p. 217.

25. Worster, *Nature's Economy,* p. 234.

26. Aldo Leopold, *A Sand County Almanac* (New York: Oxford University Press, 1979), pp. 224–225.

27. Devall and Sessions, *Deep Ecology,* p. 65.

28. Dolores LaChapelle, *Earth Wisdom,* quoted in Devall and Sessions, *Deep Ecology,* p. 95.

29. Michael Tobias, ed., *Deep Ecology* (San Diego: Avant Books, 1985); Devall and Sessions, *Deep Ecology.* These two works provide a comprehensive insight into the philosophy of deep ecology; they are the primary sources for my discussion.

30. Harold W. Wood, Jr., "Modern Pantheism as an Approach to Environmental Ethics," *Environmental Ethics* 7 (Summer 1985), p. 151.

31. Devall and Sessions, *Deep Ecology,* p. 158.

32. Joseph L. Sax, "The Claim for Retention of the Public Lands," *Rethinking the Federal Lands,* ed. Sterling Brubaker (Washington, DC: Resources for the Future, 1984), p. 144.

33. Joseph L. Sax, *Mountains Without Handrails,* p. 59.

34. Sax, *Mountains Without Handrails,* p. 103.

35. Devall and Sessions, *Deep Ecology,* p. 153.

36. Devall and Sessions, *Deep Ecology,* p. 155.

37. A. S. Leopold et al., "Wildlife Management in the National Parks," cited in Alston Chase, *Playing God in Yellowstone: The Destruction of America's First National Park* (New York: Atlantic Monthly Press, 1986), pp. 33–34.

38. I first learned of the degraded condition of Chaco Canyon while attending an introductory course in holistic resource management (Albuquerque, 1986) taught by Allan Savory, founding director, Center for Holistic Resource Management, Albuquerque, New Mexico. Photographs of vegetation within and outside the park boundaries showed a marked fence line contrast. Within the park, vegetation was sparse and soils were eroding despite decades of protection. Beyond the boundary fence, vegetation was denser and soils were more stable, but the land was not protected. There, on the unprotected side, Indian sheep herds grazed heavily and continuously. Prehistoric peoples had so severely abused Chaco Canyon that its lands, not the adjacent and heavily used Indian lands, were the ones most irreversibly altered by human presence. And ironically, park protection compounded rather than reversed Chaco Canyon's environmental decay. Detailed treatments of Chaco Canyon can be found in Allan Savory's, *Holistic Resource Management* (Washington, DC: Island Press, 1988), pp. 135–138, and in Tom Wolf's "Ancient and Contemporary Environmental Problems at Chaco Canyon National Monument" (Unpublished manuscript, Santa Fe, NM, 1992).

37. Karl Hess, Jr., "Rocky Times in Rocky Mountain National Park," *Liberty* 5:3 (January 1992), pp. 31–37.

38. Interview with Kit and Sherry Laney and past professional experience. See note 20, chapter 8. Mention of the Divide Fire is made in U.S. Department of Agriculture, "Gila National Forest Annual Report, Fiscal Year 1989," U.S. Forest Service, Southwestern Region (Washington, DC: Government Printing Office, 1990). In regard to the Gila Trout, the report notes on page 6 that "setbacks experienced from drought, *wildfire,* and floods will delay initial thoughts this year of reclassifying this endangered species as 'threatened'." [emphasis mine]

39. Congressman Bruce Vento, chairman of the House Subcommittee on National Parks and Public Lands, quoted in *Public Land News* 14:8 (13 April 1989), p. 8. Vento's harsh judgment of national forest wilderness conditions was substantiated by a U.S. General Accounting Office report released later that year. The report concluded that wilderness areas managed by the Forest Service have deteriorated in condition since their designation by Congress. Poor management of national forest wilderness, however, has provided a budgetary bonanza for the Forest Service. From 1988 to 1991, the agency's wilderness management appropriation swelled from $12.6 million to over $20 million.

40. Deborah Epstein Popper and Frank J. Popper, "The Great Plains from Dust to Dust," *Planning* 53:12 (December 1987), p. 16.

41. The first presentation of the "Buffalo Commons" was in Deborah Epstein Popper and Frank J. Popper, "The Great Plains from Dust to Dust," pp. 12–18. Subsequent presentations of the "Buffalo Commons" include Frank J. Popper and Deborah Epstein Popper, "Saving the Plains: The Bison Gambit," *Washington Post*

(6 August 1989), p. B3, and Anne Matthews, "Are the Bison Coming?," *High Country News* 23:23 (16 December 1991), pp. 8–13.

42. Popper and Popper, "The Great Plains," p. 18.

43. Popper and Popper, "The Great Plains," p. 18.

44. The story of the Meeteetse black-footed ferrets is common knowledge and is extremely well documented. It has been told in an array of publications, a sample of which include Michael Pearce, "My Friend the Ferret," *Wall Street Journal* 30:1 (1 October 1986); Ted Williams, "The Final Ferret Fiasco," *Audubon* 88 (May 1986); D. Weinberg, "Decline and Fall of the Black-Footed Ferret," *Natural History* 95 (Fall 1986); and R. Blount, "Yet Another True Story of Mankind," *Atlanta* 259 (April 1987).

45. Interview with Herb Metzger, 25 September 1988.

CHAPTER 11: LIMITS OF THE VISIONARY STATE

1. Karl Hess and Ronald J. White, *Dunken-Pinon Proposed Pilot Hunting Unit* (Dunken, NM: Dunken Wildlife Management Association, June 1990). The Dunken proposal was presented to the New Mexico Game and Fish Department at the December 1990 meeting of the New Mexico Game Commission. The report documents the conditions described in the narrative and presents a pilot plan for restoring health to the Dunken-Pinon mule deer herd. No action has been taken on the proposal by either the Game Commission or the Game and Fish Department.

2. Murray Bookchin, *The Ecology of Freedom* (Palo Alto, CA: Cheshire Books, 1982), pp. 315, 366.

3. Gary Snyder, "Four Changes," *Environmental Handbook,* ed. G. Debell (New York: Ballantine Books, 1970), pp. 323–333.

4. Aldo Leopold, *A Sand County Almanac* (New York: Oxford University Press, 1979), p. 213.

5. Leopold, *A Sand County Almanac,* p. 213.

6. Ramon Margalef, *Perspectives in Ecological Theory* (Chicago: University of Chicago Press, 1968), p. 49.

7. The ecological importance of diversity in natural systems is disputed among some ecologists. Its significance in social systems, however, is almost universally recognized. See note 5, chapter 3.

8. Richard L. Stroup and John A. Baden, *Natural Resources: Bureaucratic Myths and Environmental Management* (San Francisco: Pacific Research Institute for Public Policy, 1983), pp. 58–59.

9. Alston Chase, "Sometimes What Threatens Our Parks Is the Park Service," *Wall Street Journal,* 8 April 1986.

10. Leopold, *A Sand County Almanac,* pp. 223–224.

11. John Passmore, *Man's Responsibility for Nature: Ecological Problems and Western Traditions* (New York: Charles Scribner's Sons, 1974), p. 54. The moral dimension of resolving ecological problems comprises the heart of Passmore's book.

CHAPTER 12: A MARKET OF LANDSCAPE VISIONS

1. Interview with Dayton Hyde, public-land rancher, Chiloquin, OR, 25 June 1988.

2. H. A. Gleason, "The Individualist Concept of the Plant Community," *American Midland Naturalist* 21 (1939), pp. 92–110; Alex S. Watt, "Pattern and Process in the Plant Community," *Journal of Ecology* 35:1, 2 (December 1947), pp. 1–22; R. H. Whittaker, "A Consideration of Climax Theory: The Climax as a Population and Pattern," *Ecological Monographs* 23 (1953), pp. 41–78; S. A. Picket and P. S. White, *The Ecology of Natural Disturbance and Patch Dynamics* (New York: Academic Press, 1985).

3. James Gleick, *Chaos: Making a New Science* (New York: Viking Press, 1987). As James Gleick observes in *Chaos,* a first step in understanding nature's order begins by going beyond the simple linearity of steady state systems (like Clements's monoclimax) to the non-linearity that permeates the patterns of nature (including patch dynamics) and provides the basis for the laws of chaos.

4. Gleick, *Chaos,* p. 315.

5. Zev Naveh and Arthur S. Lieberman, *Landscape Ecology* (New York: Springer-Verlag New York, 1984).

6. Frank Egler, quoted in Naveh and Lieberman, *Landscape Ecology,* p. 74.

7. Raymond P. Coppinger and Charles K. Smith, "The Domestication of Evolution," *Environmental Conservation* 10:4 (1983), pp. 283–292.

8. Although aspects of diversity remain debatable, it is appropriate to view the overall function of diversity in both natural and social ecosystems as vital. See note 5, chapter 3.

9. See the previous note. Although the importance of diversity (in terms of stability and survival) may be more persuasively argued for human systems, the similarities in the functioning of diversity in the social and natural realms are too obvious to ignore.

10. Robert Nozick, *Anarchy, State and Utopia* (New York: Basic Books, 1977), p. 297.

11. Freeman J. Dyson, *Infinite in All Directions* (New York: Harper & Row, Publishers, 1985), p. 181.

12. For O'Toole's proposal, see Randal O'Toole, *Reforming the Forest Service* (Washington, DC: Island Press, 1988).

13. Vernon L. Smith, "On Divestiture and the Creation of Property Rights in Public Lands," *Cato Journal* 2:3 (Winter 1982), pp. 663–685.

14. Separating the surface and subsurface estates in the initial stages of democratization has its advantages and disadvantages. I have discussed only the advantages in the text. The disadvantages are many, however, and should not be overlooked. Separating the two estates would create economic, political, and legal problems: It would add complexity and additional costs to a reform proposal that is otherwise simple and relatively inexpensive. Certainly, combining of the two estates is worth serious consideration should democratization reach the forum of public policy debate. I, for one, would soundly endorse such an approach as long

as it did not endanger what I view as the primary goal of my reform proposal, divestiture of the land surface.

15. Many public-land ranchers will take issue with this portion of my proposal because I do not give allowance for the property interests that ranchers believe they have in federal lands. Although property right claims to public ranges based on permit value, preference rights, and the legal theory of equitable estate may have a historical foundation, I have chosen to ignore them for several reasons. First, the legal issue of private property interests in federal lands is far from substantiated. Indeed, Congress and the courts have repeatedly legislated or ruled against property interest claims in those lands. Second, to incorporate such a legally tenuous claim into my reform proposal would almost certainly doom democratization. And were that to occur, everyone—including public-land ranchers—would lose. Third, the historical subsidization of the public-land ranching industry by below-market grazing fees and taxpayer-financed range improvements seriously compromises whatever property claims most public-land ranchers have to federal lands. Finally, I have serious reservations as to whether preference should be given to any group in such an important matter as land reform. Historical claims aside, the fact is that democratization can work only if all citizens have the opportunity to participate on an equal footing. To give a head start to public-land ranchers by recognizing their tenuous property claims to one-third of the nation's land would make a mockery of democratization. Nevertheless, public-land ranchers' property claims to federal lands remain a political and moral problem that cannot—and should not—be simply swept under the rug. The best defense of those claims will be found in Wayne Hage, *Storm over Rangelands: Private Rights in Federal Lands* (Bellevue, WA: Free Enterprise Press, 1990). A less polemic and much shorter discussion of ranchers' interests in public grazing lands appears in Gary D. Libecap, "Economic Interests of Grazing Permittees," in *Privatizing the Public Lands,* ed. James H. Smits (Washington, DC: Public Lands Council, 1983), pp. 53–58.

CONCLUSION: THE ECOLOGY OF FREEDOM

1. Aldo Leopold, "Land-Use and Democracy," *Audubon* 44 (September 1942), p. 264.

2. Charles Murray, *In Pursuit: Of Happiness and Good Government* (New York: Simon & Schuster, 1988), p. 279.

Index

Abbey, Edward, 19, 175, 180
Advisory Board on Wildlife Management, 189
Aldo Leopold Wilderness, 190–91
Allotment management plans (AMPs), 143–50
Allotments. *See* Allotment management plans; Community allotments; Grazing lands, public
Alton, Utah, 97–99
American Heritage Trust Act, 231
American National Livestock Association, 110
AMPs. *See* Allotment management plans
Anarchy, State and Utopia (Nozick), 226
Anderson, E. N., 71
Anderson, Terry, 21
Anderson-Mansfield Act of 1949, 111
Animal husbandry. *See* Grazing lands, public; Western range
Apache Sitgreaves National Forest, 137
The Arrogance of Humanism (Ehrenfield), 41
Atkins, Brent, 154
Atkins, Clayton, 60, 153–54

Babbitt, Bruce, 180–81
Baden, John, 21, 62–63, 207

Bankhead-Jones Farm Tenant Act of 1987, 86, 88
Behan, R. W., 133–34
Berkes, F., 71
BLM. *See* Bureau of Land Management
BlueRibbon Coalition, 136
Bookchin, Murray, 202
Buffalo Commons, 191–92
Buffalo Gap National Grassland, 88
Bureaucracy and land management, 103–14, 123–24
Bureau of Land Management (BLM), 11–14, 16–17, 20–23, 98–99
  as a bureaucracy, 102–8, 123–24
  and disincentives to private investment, 153–54, 173–74
  and grazing permits, 125–32

Cadillac Desert, 175
Calef, Wesley, 125
Carrying capacity, 117–18, 127, 128, 129
Carson, Rachel, 185
Carson National Forest, 113
Carter, Sterling, 137–38, 154
Chaco Culture National Historic Park (Chaco Canyon), 189–90
Chaos: Making a New Science (Gleick), 218–19

Charles M. Russell National Wildlife
  Refuge, 4
Chase, Alston, 175, 189, 209
Chiloquin, Oreg., 215
Chisum, John S., 57
Circle Bar Ranch, 1–6, 9–10, 17, 24–
  25, 36–38, 55–56
"Civil Disobedience" (Thoreau), 28
Civilian Conservation Corps, 164
Clapp, Earle, 110–11
Clements, Frederic, 183, 184, 185,
  187, 188, 192, 195, 219, 220
Clepper, Henry, 108
CMAs. *See* Cooperative management
  agreements
Coconino National Forest, 154,
  193
Coggins, George, 62, 63, 72, 131,
  204, 231
Commons, western, 124–25, 139. *See
  also* Tragedy of the commons
Community allotments, 159–63
A Conflict of Visions (Sowell), 27
Conservation reform, 99–103, 114–20
Cooperative management agreements
  (CMAs), 116–17
Copeland Report, 109
Coppinger, Raymond, 221, 222
Council on Environmental Quality,
  104–05
Crèvecoeur, J. Hector St. John de, 32,
  33, 65
Custer National Forest, 3, 5–6, 9, 55,
  158, 161, 242

Deep ecology, 185–87, 202
Deep Ecology (Devall and Sessions),
  187, 202
Democracy in America (de Tocqueville), 25
de Tocqueville, Alexis de, 25–26
Devall, Bill, 187, 188–89, 202
De Voto, Bernard, 19, 180
Dickinson, T. Wright, 162–63, 171–
  72

Dunken-Pinon plains, 199–201
Dyson, Freeman, 227

The Earth as Modified by Human Action
  (Marsh), 14
Earth First!, 175
Eastman, Clyde, 157
Ecology, 38–39
  Clements's, 218–20
  deep, 185–86, 202
  of freedom, 247–48
  landscape, 220
  of visions, 44–50
Edwards Plateau, 127, 128
Egler, Frank, 220
Ehrenfield, David, 41
Enlarged Homestead Act of 1909, 84
Entropy, 45
ESPs. *See* Experimental stewardship
  programs
"Even the Bad Guys Wear White
  Hats" (Abbey), 19, 175
Experimental stewardship programs
  (ESPs), 168–70

Fallini, Joe, 121–23, 145
Fallini, Susan, 121–23, 145
Fauske, Ingebert, 87
Federal Land Policy and Management
  Act of 1976 (FLPMA), 106, 107,
  117, 119–20, 151
Ferguson, Denzel, 175
Ferguson, Nancy, 175
*Fire and Water: Scientific Heresy in the
  Forest Service* (Schiff), 50
Fire suppression, biological effects of,
  49–50
FLPMA. *See* Federal Land Policy and
  Management Act of 1976
Forsling, Clarence, 110
Fort Pierre National Grassland, 82–
  83, 88
Foss, Phillip, 13
"Four Changes" (Snyder), 202

Free Our Public Lands! (Jacobs), 19, 175
Frome, Michael, 15

GAO. *See* General Accounting Office
General Accounting Office (GAO), 17, 106, 107–8, 145–46, 147
General Land Office, 109. *See also* Bureau of Land Management
Gila National Forest, 130, 156, 158
Gleason, H. A., 218
Gleick, James, 218–19
Godwin, William, 28
Gould, Jim, 149, 153
Grace Commission, 133
Grass Mountain Allotment, 140–42, 145
Gray, James R., 157
Grazing lands, public, 10–14
    allotment management plans for, 143–50
    as ecosystem, 40–41
    management of, 1–6, 125–39, 155–63, 195–96, 204–5
    overgrazing of, 57–61
Grazing permits, 114, 115–16, 120, 125–32, 150–51
Grazing Service, 101. *See also* Bureau of Land Management
Great Plains. *See also* Western range
    land policies for, 84–93
    Nebraska sandhills, 93–96
The Great Plains (Webb), 67
Greenwood, Dale, 89
Grouse, sharp-tailed, 3–4
Gunnison National Forest, 171–73
Guthrie, Woody, 179

Hardin, Garrett, 61–62, 63, 70, 139, 160, 163
Harris, Joe, 168
Harrison, Benjamin, 56
Harrison, Russell B., 56–57
Heaton, Bard, 59, 97–99, 153

Hetch Hetchy Valley, 174–75
High Country News, 180
The Historical Roots of Our Ecological Crisis (White), 41
Homestead Act of 1862, 67, 68, 69
Hormay Grazing System, 144
Howes, Calvin, 24
Howes, Levi, 2, 9–10, 24–25, 36, 55–56, 58, 64, 243
Hudson, C. W., 151
Hyde, Dayton, 137, 138, 215–17, 238

I-Bar-X Ranch, 73–75
Infinite in All Directions (Dyson), 227
In Pursuit: Of Happiness and Good Government (Murray), 245
Institute of Range and the American Mustang (IRAM), 215
The Institutional Imperative (Kharasch), 103

Jacobs, Lynn, 175
Jefferson, Thomas, 30–31, 32–33, 34–35, 64–66, 68, 134, 181, 194
Junkin, Elizabeth, 179

Kaibab Plateau, 49
Kharasch, Robert, 103
Kinkaid Act of 1904, 84, 94

LaChapelle, Dolores, 185–86
"The Land Ethic" (Leopold), 18. *See also* Leopold, Aldo
Land reform, 66–69, 78–79, 232–41
Landscape ecology, 220
Landscape visions, 25–30. *See also* Western range
    agrarian, 64–66
    environmental, 176–81
    market of, 223–30
    progressive, 76–81, 86, 89
    utopian ideals of, 201–3
Lands of Brighter Destiny (Junkin), 179

Land utilization (LU) lands, 87–88, 89–91, 95
"The Law of Public Rangeland Management" (Coggins), 204
Leopold, A. Starker, 189
Leopold, Aldo, 185, 189, 205–6
    land ethic of, 18–19, 184, 187, 212–13, 214, 219, 230, 244–45
Letters from an American Farmer (Crèvecoeur), 65
Lincoln National Forest, 132, 147
Lincoln National Forest Plan, 73
Little Missouri National Grassland, 85, 89
Livestock farming. *See* Grazing lands, public
Locke, John, 31
Louisiana Purchase, 65
Lovelock, James, 40

McGinnis, Corby, 148–49
McGinnis, Miles, 148–49
Man's Responsibility for Nature (Passmore), 213
Margalef, Ramon, 206
Marsh, George, 14, 18, 182, 183
Marston, Ed, 180
Meeteetse, Wyo., 149, 193
Metzger, Herb, 154–55, 193–94
Miller, A. L., 87–88
Montana Game and Fish Department, 5
Montana Stockgrowers Association, 56
Mountains Without Handrails: Reflections on the National Parks (Sax), 181
Muir, John, 19–20, 28–29, 30, 174, 175, 179–80, 182–83, 187, 188, 195, 209, 221
Multiple use, 118–20, 132–39
Multiple Use–Sustained Yield Act of 1960 (MUSYA), 117, 119
Murray, Charles, 245

MUSYA. *See* Multiple Use–Sustained Yield Act of 1960

Naess, Arne, 185
Nash, Roderick, 181
National Environmental Policy Act of 1969, 80, 170, 173, 214
National Forest Management Act of 1976, 206
National grasslands, 82–93, 96
National Land Reform movement, 66–69
National parks, management of, 188–91
National Park Service, 188–91
National Wildlife Federation, 17
Natural Resources: Bureaucratic Myths and Environmental Management (Stroup and Baden), 207
Natural Resources Defense Council, 17, 179
Natural Resources Defense Council v. Interior Secretary Hodel, 115
Natural Resources Defense Council v. Morton, 152
Nature's Economy (Worster), 184
Nebraska sandhills, 93–96
Nelson, Robert, 146
New Deal, land policies of, 86–89
New resource economics (NRE), 21–23, 224
Niobrara Cattle Company, 58
Northwest Ordinance, 65
Nozick, Robert, 226
NRE. *See* New resource economics

Odum, Eugene, 220
Odum, Howard, 220
"On Divestiture and the Creation of Property Rights in Public Lands" (Smith), 232
Operation Stronghold, 92

O'Toole, Randal, 175, 231
Otter Creek, 37–38, 44–48, 242–48
"Our Ailing Public Rangelands," 17

Passmore, John, 213
People for the West, 136
Perspectives in Ecological Theory (Margalef), 206
Pinchot, Gifford, 22, 68, 77–79, 102, 118, 119, 156, 174–75, 181, 195, 201, 209
Plant Succession: An Analysis of the Development of Vegetation (Clements), 183
Playing God in Yellowstone (Chase), 175, 189
Popper, Deborah E., 191–92
Popper, Frank J., 191–92
Potter, Albert F., 60, 61
Powell, John Wesley, 10, 57, 68, 157
Prescott National Forest, 159
PRIA. *See* Public Rangelands Improvement Act of 1978
Public Grazing Lands (Voigt), 19, 175
Public Land Law Review Commission, 89–90, 153
Public Rangelands Improvement Act of 1978 (PRIA), 106, 107, 168

The Question of the Commons (Anderson), 71

Redwood National Park, 189
Reforming the Forest Service (O'Toole), 175
Reisner, Marc, 175
Religious freedom, 30–31
Report on the Lands of the Arid Region of the United States (Powell), 10, 68
Resettlement Administration, 87
Rocky Mountain National Park, 190

Roosevelt, Franklin D., 86
Roosevelt, Theodore, 78
Roszak, Theodore, 41
Rowley, William, 151

Sacred Cows at the Public Trough (Ferguson and Ferguson), 19, 175
Sandoz, Marie, 94
Santa Fe National Forest, 135, 156–57, 159
Sax, Joseph, 181, 187
Schadler, Jean, 169
Schaffer, William, 219
Schiff, Ashley, 50
SCS. *See* Soil Conservation Service
Second Treatise of Government (Locke), 31
Sessions, George, 187, 188–89, 202
Shanks, Bernard, 15, 180
Sheldon National Wildlife Refuge, 42–43
Sierra Club, 123, 174
Skinner, Bob, 167
Slaathaug, Donna, 83–84
Slaathaug, Dwayne, 83, 92
Smith, Adam, 28, 224
Smith, Charles, 221, 222
Smith, Henry Nash, 32
Smith, Vernon L., 232
Snyder, Gary, 202
Soil Conservation Service (SCS), 87–89, 90, 101
Sorenson, Lloyd, 60
Sowell, Thomas, 27–28
Spann, Ken, 171–73
Spark, Charlie, 162
Stephenson, Bill, 73–75
Stephenson, Kelley, 73–75
Stevens, Bill, 1
Stevens, Marc, 1–6, 9, 36–38, 158, 161–62, 242, 243
Stroup, Richard, 21, 207
Sustained yield, 117–18, 120, 128–30

Taylor, Edward T., 59
Taylor Grazing Act of 1934, 59, 76,
  105, 110, 153, 155, 168
This Land Is Your Land (Shanks), 180
Thoreau, Henry David, 26, 28, 29
Tragedy of the commons, 61–64, 69–
  72
Twin Springs Ranch, 121–24

Udall, Stewart, 189
U.S. Fish and Wildlife Service, 4, 43
U.S. Forest Service
  as a bureaucracy, 102–3, 108–14
  and disincentives to private in-
    vestment, 154–55
  fire suppression policy of, 49–50,
    191
  grazing policies of, 1–6, 11–13,
    16–17, 20–23, 37–38, 125–29,
    173–74
  mission of, 77–78
  and national grasslands, 89–93
  progressive vision of, 78–81
  wilderness management of, 191

Vale Rangeland Rehabilitation Pro-
  gram, 166–68
Vigil, Elizardo, 140–42, 145
Virgin Land (Smith), 32
Voigt, William, Jr., 19, 175

Watson, Paul, 183
Webb, Walter Prescott, 67
Welfare ranchers, 163–70
Wells, Phillip, 155–56
Western range. *See also* Grazing lands,
  public; Great Plains

commons of, 61–64
democratization of, 231–41
destruction of, 14–18
diversity of, 221–23
early visions of, 25–35
as ecosystem, 38–44
environmental vision of, 176–88
and environmental welfare state,
  201–6, 212
impact of various visions on, 50–
  51, 142–43, 173–76, 210–11,
  217–21
management approaches to, 206–
  10, 213–14
natural management of, 188–94
overgrazing of, 21–22, 57–61,
  75–76
progressive vision of, 78–81
responsibility for, 18–23
Where the Wasteland Ends (Roszak), 41
White, Lynn, 41
Whittaker, Robert, 218
Wilderness and the American Mind
  (Nash), 181
Wild Horses and Burros Protection
  Act of 1971, 122
Williamson, Robert, 112
Winema National Forest, 217
Winthrop, John, 25
Wood, Harold W., Jr., 186
Worster, Donald, 184
Wyant, William, 14–15

Yellowstone National Park, 189
Yosemite National Park, 174

Zion National Park, 99

ABOUT THE AUTHOR

Karl Hess, Jr., is a writer and analyst on western environmental issues. He holds a Ph.D. in range ecology and degrees in economics and history. After spending two years overseas in the north African nation of Tunisia working on a rangeland rehabilitation project, Hess settled in New Mexico. From 1985 through 1989 he worked as a range resource specialist at the New Mexico Department of Agriculture and taught a graduate course in public land policy at the School of Agriculture, New Mexico State University.

Since 1989, Hess has concentrated on research and writing. In particular, he has focused on the laws and policies that guide the Forest Service and the Bureau of Land Management, exploring how those laws and policies might be changed to encourage greater stewardship among land users. He has written extensively on this topic, emphasizing the importance of incentives and free market forces in attaining the well-being of western lands. Hess is also a senior associate with the Foundation for Research on Economics and the Environment. At this time, he is working with FREE on a comprehensive study of the National Park System.